Wonder Child

**REDISCOVERING THE MAGICAL
WORLD OF INNOCENCE
AND JOY WITHIN OURSELVES
AND OUR CHILDREN**

PETER LORIE

CONSULTANT EDITORS:
FREDERICK LEBOYER
JOSEPH CHILTON PEARCE
GEORGE MEREDITH M.D.

A FIRESIDE BOOK
Published by Simon & Schuster Inc.
New York London Toronto Sydney Tokyo

Fireside
Simon & Schuster Building
Rockefeller Center
1230 Avenue of the Americas
New York New York 10020

FIRESIDE and colophon are
registered trademarks of Simon & Schuster Inc.

Designed by Padma Morgan

WONDER CHILD was produced by
Labyrinth Publishing S.A., Switzerland
Printed in Hong Kong by C & C Offset Printing Co., Ltd.
Color separation by Fotolito Toscana, Florence, Italy.
Typesetting by Parole Immagini S.A.S., Florence, Italy.

10 9 8 7 6 5 4 3 2 1

Library of Congress in Publication Data

Lorie, Peter.
    Wonder child : rediscovering the magical world of innocence and
joy within ourselves and our children / Peter Lorie ; consulting
editors, Frederick Leboyer, Joseph Chilton Pearce, George Meredith.
      p.   cm.
    "A Fireside book."
    ISBN 0-671-67799-3
    1. Children--Miscellanea. 2. Parent and child. 3. Creative
activities. 4. Experiential learning. I Leboyer, Frederick
II. Pearce, Joseph Chilton. III. Meredith, George, 1944- .
    IV. Title.
HQ781.L67 1989
306.8'74--dc19   89-5886
                                                 CIP

CONTENTS

"And a woman who held a babe against her bosom said,
Speak to us of Children.
And he said:
Your children are not your children,
They are the sons and daughters of Life's longing for itself.
They come through you but not from you,
And though they are with you, yet they belong not to you.
You may give them your love but not your thoughts.
For they have their own thoughts.
You may house their bodies but not their souls,
For their souls dwell in the house of tomorrow,
which you cannot visit, not even in your dreams.
You may strive to be like them, but seek not
to make them like you.
For life goes not backward nor tarries with yesterday.
You are the bows from which your children
as living arrows are sent forth.
The archer sees the mark upon the path of the infinite,
and He bends you with His might
that His arrows may go swift and far.
Let your bending in the archer's hand be for gladness;
For even as he loves the arrow that flies,
so He loves the bow that is stable."

***The Prophet* — Khalil Gibran**

THIS BOOK IS DEDICATED TO BENJAMIN AND LILY.

"Yesterday a child came out to wonder
Caught a dragon fly inside a jar.
Fearful when the sky was full of thunder
and tearful at the falling of a star.
And the seasons, they go round and round
And the painted ponies go up and down.
We are captive on the carousel of time.
We can't return, we can only look
behind from where we came and
go round and round and round in the circle game.
Sixteen springs and sixteen summers gone now.
Cart wheels turned to car wheels through the
town.
And they tell him take your time it won't be
long now,
Till you drag your feet to slow the circles
down.
And the seasons, they go round and round
and the painted ponies go up and down."

Joni Mitchell

PREPARING FOR THIS BOOK

"The highest to which man can attain is wonder; and if the prime phenomenon makes him wonder, let him be content; nothing higher can it give him, and nothing further should he seek for behind it; here is the limit." ALAN WATTS

Wonder Child is not a book to instruct us in how to care for children. It's purpose is not primarily to give practical or detailed guidance, for there are many volumes available which set out to do this.

Wonder Child is a book of discovery, a search for magic within ourselves, within children and the environment which surrounds us all. The purpose inherent within the words and pictures, is to induce a response in the reader which will *result* in practical and detailed guidance, coming from within the individual, and this response will occur because of a feeling that hopefully will be gained by "getting into" the book, not because of any teacher-pupil relationship between author and reader.

In other words, it is not intended that the reader should follow the contents word for word as one might a recipe book, but allow the material to be absorbed and then note the changes that occur. When it works, it is a little like magic.

The process may come as a bit of a surprise to some, for it is not always the way that we adults have operated in the past, being so much involved in following the instruction and advice of others. As an author, however, I have found it more useful to express ideas and attitudes in the form that follows for in my experience with parents and children it rarely works to "tell" people what they "should"

do — after all is said and done, how would I know what you should do!?

As a father I might be singularly ill-equipped to write this book, for fathers can sometimes suffer a poor reputation in terms of knowing about children — they do not *have* children after all, at least not in the biological sense.

From the scientific viewpoint I am also not the ideal exponent for, even though several highly qualified individuals have helped me compile and verify the information contained herein, I cannot claim to be intimately involved in that particular area of life's investigation. As will be seen in the coming pages, however, science is taking some extraordinary strides away from the old reductionist and divisive views of the past.

From the position of intelligence and the inner realms of consciousness I can only stand alone and look around at the wealth of material that is available for any reader and experiencer of life. But as one who can remember childhood I claim to know a great deal and as one who has been a father, has studied science closely and has spent many years in the company of Masters of the Eastern philosophies I can apply all this to those memories of childhood and make something of it all that would seem worthwhile. I can also say, with my "hand on my heart", that having gone through the processes of growing down and then growing up, reaching the ego and the mind's form of awareness during the latter years of my adult life, I am very happy that the child in me is still present, for without him life could be a very serious and distressing occupation.

And the most interesting and absorbing aspect of this "childish" viewpoint is that when I look at the world as a child I see a very different picture from when I look at the world as an adult. The adult world, it seems to me, knows very often very little about children. Adults are grown up, they are mature, analytical and thoughtful, older, taller, bigger, wiser and more serious than any child and in the main they have forgotten everything they ever knew when they were children. Adults are involved in the mind, in the world as they see it, in a kind of domination of this planet and all the natural things that happen upon it. The intellectual education that they give to children is not only overrated, it is, in its solitary preoccupation, often dangerous to the well-being of mankind in general. All mind and no spirit, no heart, makes man a very dull person indeed.

Adults are essentially separated from life. Since the Greeks first demanded that there should be a life vs a death, a good vs a bad, a right vs a wrong, mankind has lived according to a dualism that disconnects him from the very oneness of existence and this simple and extraordinary form of behavior alone separates the adult also from children. Because children are not dualist, they are not separated from existence and they are not *in* the mind. Put very simply, adults are largely separate from everything, including children and in this state of aloneness there is no conceivable way in which they can view the state of existence clearly, because they believe themselves to be outside it.

Children, on the other hand, *are* existence.

We will be looking closely at this throughout the coming pages but briefly we can mention here that it is not a matter of children somehow being *inside* existence for this too is a dualistic approach — if we are inside something we can therefore, it follows, also be outside it. Children *are* existence insofar as their very nature and formation is the whole and everything, they contain the inside and the outside. It is not a matter of objectivity or subjectivity for a child, those words and their meaning don't exist.

For the adult, father, scientist, philosopher, thinker, this is an extremely hard concept to digest, for if we consider it using the brain/mind as the tool, we have already failed. The mind's state is a separate state.

A question was once asked by a disciple of his Master — "I am constantly in a state of doubt about my life, about the way I am, the way things are around me and what I should be doing each moment within myself. This doubt does not exist on a day-to-day level — I have no difficulty with normal decisions and the life-support systems which keep me comfortable — it is on a much deeper and more subtle level — a profound internal doubt which I believe is common nowadays to many people. How can I overcome this state and bring my life into greater certainty?"

The answer was very simple — "Drop doubt, drop certainty, you do not need either of these things — simply *be*, out of love."

This is the non-dualist view. Doubt and certainty are opposites. The individual who asked the question was striving, in the normal Western, ambitious style, to "overcome" doubt so that he could "become" certain. He imagined himself somehow to be a strange, tangled creature — a walking doubt — and preferred the idea of being an upright, proud and sparkling creature — a walking certainty — instead. It did not perhaps occur to him, until the answer was given, that he could let go of both these things and simply *be* without any ideas of what shape he was in.

And we adults live permanently in this state of one thing or another. We either love or we hate, we either live or we die, we either make love or war — we do everything "either/or" and think about it all the time.

We have reduced our feelings into war against themselves — we feel good or bad, happy or sad, jealous or secure, proud or weak and very often we even deny those feelings as though they were bad — wrong to feel bad, wrong to feel that we are wrong to feel bad etc. etc., ad infinitum.

With this all-pervading method of life, there is essentially no way that we can feel childhood. With all the practical home-help, parenting, child psychology manuals and books, articles, studies and tests that are in publication today, few of them are much use in feeling how it is to be a child. And if we do not feel how it is to be a child how can we relate to children?

Actually, what we need to do is play.

Having said all this, it should be pointed out that within the pages of this book there *is* science, philosophy, the father and the mother. There *is* much of the adult, for in order to get through to adult playfulness we must take the route of the mind first and the mind feels insecure unless it has the "facts" of modern science to look at.

In any event science is a wonderful toy — a map of reality that can give us pointers. Philosophy is also a great game to play, for it sneaks around the corners of life and pops up with wonderful perspectives that we hadn't thought of. And best of all, the words of the Masters bring an insight which can be the most exciting game of all — that of enlightenment and innocence. And occasionally there are very special individual adults who manage to combine more than one state — scientist, philosopher and Master. An example is perhaps Erwin Schrodinger — founder of Quantum Physics — who said it all far better than most of

us could: "Inconceivable as it seems to ordinary reason, you — and all other conscious beings as such — are all in all. Hence this life of yours which you are living is not merely a piece of the entire existence, but is in a certain sense the *whole*... Thus you can throw yourself flat on the ground, stretched out upon Mother Earth, with the certain conviction that you are one with her and she with you. You are as firmly established, as invulnerable as she is, indeed a thousand times firmer and more invulnerable. As surely as she will engulf you to-morrow, so surely will she bring you forth anew to new striving and suffering. And not merely "some day".

Now, today, every day she is bringing you forth, not *once* but thousands upon thousands of times, just as every day she engulfs you a thousand times over."

And even in this gifted man's language there is evidence of his separation for he uses the word "you" in preference to us, thus separating his understanding from ours and he states that "this life of yours...is in a certain sense the whole..." — not in a complete sense, not that this life of "ours" *is* the whole. By the very nature of the language *he* is separate from *us* who are in turn separate from *each other*. This is the very nature of all language.

But it is not the nature of children — children are not only not separate from the world but they are also not separate from us or from one another — and what's more they do not need to know it — they simply *are*, without question and without answer.

This is ultimately the purpose of this book — to give us adults the chance to play with children so that we no longer need to think of them as *our* children that need *our* protection, for children need no protection, they have it bound up inside them from the moment of their birth and before, and it is the adults who take that natural protection away from them by making them adults who have forgotten how to be children.

Predominantly, this is a book about children, but you cannot have a book about children which is not also about adults. And in this simple, initial statement we have already separated the two — children are one thing and adults another. Is this really so?

Think back. Remember, if you can, a single event in your childhood — perhaps it is the day that you began school or the moment when your father picked you up and bounced you on his knee! It might be a happy event or an unhappy event — for our present purposes it does not matter which. Remember how it was on that day. Was the sun shining? How were the surroundings of the room you were in? What did your mother or father look like then?

Perhaps you might dig out the old and dusty family album or the battered box of photographs that resides in the attic, buried under a pile of worn-out boots and bicycle parts. Take them out and refresh your memory and you will find the recollections come flooding back — times you have put away in the attic of your brain under equally dusty thoughts.

Remembering childhood events is a strange process. Probably you will recall unconnected moments which may be separated by years of forgetfulness. You have a memory of something that happened when you were nine — a single moment that may be surrounded by considerable detail but the whole period of the rest of that year is gone. At six or five you can dredge up the odd snippet here and there — the friend who used to live next door, the old cooking pot that mother would cook potatoes in or the park where you used to play after kindergarten.

Going back still further, to five and four years old the detail becomes still more distorted and vague — you are not quite sure whether you lived in the house that "rings a bell" or whether this is a place that your mother told you about. The memory may not be your own but a second-hand one — a memory of someone else's memory. There may be only a very small part of the memory trace left but this is enough. What we are looking for is not the accuracy of the memory but the feeling it produces in you. Consider this. Does the memory bring happiness or sadness, security or insecurity, pleasure, pain, anxiety, delight?

Remembering the feelings of childhood is the very beginning of understanding children — of bringing the adult closer to children for it reminds us that we were once children ourselves. This is the fundamental theme of this book.

Having begun the process of remembering the distant past we can then go one step further — a step which may be a little more difficult to swallow. And that is that not only *were* we children *once* but we still *are* children *now*. We are still quite capable of attaining a state of childhood even after the years of accretion that have buried our more evident childish ways.

So much emphasis is placed by our surroundings — our culture, our laws, our parents, our teachers — on the *important* business of growing up, that we largely lose touch with what still remains — a very young and very child-like part which has been effectively tucked away into that same attic of dusty memories.

But why would we want to become children again? That is exactly the point of this book, for it is the understanding of the author that un-learning adulthood is the way to learn childhood and the way to be with children.

Those of us who now have a frightening picture in mind — a picture of hundreds and thousands of fully grown adults running around playing childhood games, climbing trees in the park, pulling people's hair and generally behaving like "Dennis the Menace" have got it wrong — the proposal is not that adults should *be* children or behave in an insane manner in order to appreciate childhood. It is that adults can learn to appreciate the child-like nature they have residing within them and that this appreciation will bring a lasting and intimate communication with children which will work for the benefit of both, for childhood is naturally a kaleidoscope of fabulous events and experiences which most of us too readily forget after the age of ten if not sooner. *Wonder Child* is therefore not only a book for the better appreciation of children by adults — it is also a book for the better appreciation of adulthood with childlikeness in mind.

A more scientific encouragement towards the re-adoption of child-like ways can be found in the first chapter of the book under the heading "Inheritance."

In the meantime the following simple exercises may provide a practical technique.

A. Just for fun, one day, on your way to work, or at the office, out shopping or doing whatever you normally do — make a special point of observing the people around you. Make a big deal out of it for yourself — but don't let them know about it — don't make a spectacle of yourself.

Just watch them discretely. Notice the simplest things they do: their expressions, their mannerisms, their walk. As you watch them, consciously compare their ways with those of children. Imagine that each of these individuals you are watching is not an adult at all, but a child!

To begin with, it may not be easy — it is an "art"; something you can only acquire by doing it. At first you may not see any likeness, but concentrate — see how the guy in the office makes faces, when he is self-conscious or shy, that liken him to a child. See how the bus driver hardens his expression when in difficult traffic, or when someone gives him the wrong fare — making him look like an angry child, a little boy who cannot get his own way. See the serious expression on your boss's face and remember how small children make this same face when they are trying to prove to mom that she must not laugh.

Watch people in the streets; people just walking by, crossing the roads, getting on and off public transport, buying things in stores — watch the ways they express themselves in each action and watch also how like children they are.

After a while you will have difficulty preventing yourself from giggling or even laughing openly — it is something very beautiful and very endearing to see how much we adults have not changed since childhood.

You will only, of course, see these likenesses as long as you remain friends with the image. The moment you begin to feel superior or angry or cynical about those around you, at that precise moment the ability to liken adults with children will vanish — a bit like some of the more popular fairy tales! The "art" is only granted through the pleasure of it.

B. The second game is more demanding but equally rewarding. It needs a partner who is sufficiently intimate with you to accept what you ask.

Take a large number of cushions or pillows and gather them around you on the floor of your warmest room. Curl up in the curve of the cushions and invite your partner to sit close to you so that you can tuck your body into his or her lap. You are now surrounded by warm, comforting things.

Put your thumb in your mouth and suck it. At the same time put the other hand between your partner's legs into the warmest place. Close your eyes and remain in this position for at least five minutes, breathing gently.

You can, if your partner agrees, be sung a lullaby and if this makes you feel like sleeping, try to stay awake and simply enjoy the sensation of security. Equally if you feel like crying, just keep it gentle and don't become cathartic — remember, you are not a baby really — you're simply doing something to remind you of what it was like to be two, three or four years old.

After the allotted time has passed sit up and remove your thumb from your mouth. If you feel shy or stupid let this continue, don't try to cover it up — even exaggerate it. Pretend that you are four years old.

When you've finished feeling like a child take up a mirror and look at your face - especially your eyes - notice the differences.

These two simple exercises will have begun something in you. The more fun they were for you, the more you will have found in them. If you got nothing at all out of them or didn't even bother to do them because they seem silly then you are the loser. But not to worry, there's more to come and in any case you may be a "slow starter."

Perhaps you remember how parents and teachers love to call children slow or late starters, even applying the term to their own children if it is likely to have some impact. Conversely, if you did find something in the game or you are now pretending that you did, you may remember the times, as a child, that you were congratulated — what a good boy/girl you were.

Adults concern themselves with children, largely, in a time-honored way — a way that is very much associated with the belief that adults and children are somehow from different worlds.

Often, if we observe adults talking to children it looks a little ridiculous; as though the adult is talking to a complete moron. The language is totally different, consisting of shortened word-forms, strange non-existent words and various alien sounds that the adult imagines the child understands!

Children are as much individuals as adults. Because they lack, very often, the same ideas, the same social consciousness and because they do "embarrassing" and unexpected things, adults often imagine that they must somehow be treated as inferiors, talked down to and kept under control. Fundamentally this idea about children is faulty and accounts for much of the deficiency and unhappiness that results, years later, in the grown-up version of that child.

C. **As a third exercise try the following before embarking on the body of this book:**

For one entire week seek out the company of children. If you have young people or small children at home then you're in luck, you can play this game just once and you will be surprised just how it will renew the flavor of your relationship with the children. Speak and behave with the child or children as though you were with an adult.

Make a conscious effort throughout the week to follow the exercise ALL the time and in ALL things.

Because this game often requires a major readjustment of adult behavior and therefore a major adjustment in the child's responses, a few direct hints are herewith provided — follow them as diligently as possible and the result will be more worthwhile.

1. There is no need to change any of the practical arrangements that you have with your children. If there is school there is still school — adults go to school too. There is no reason why any practical arrangements need change.

2. What does change, however, is the entire way in which you approach the situations:

"Mom — I don't want to go to school..."

SOME OLD RESPONSES

"You go to school or you don't get to go out this week-end."

"Don't be silly dear, how are you ever going to be clever and get a good job if you don't go to school?"

"I was talking to your teacher the other day — she said you were the brightest in the class — surely you don't want that story to change — do you love?"

These are false answers and very few adults would speak to other adults in this way.

NEW RESPONSE

"Why?"

The old answers are typical of parental response to children. They are all ready made and highly sophisticated lies. They contain perfectly formed and un-original judgments about the child, the teacher and the society that supports the lie as well as the parent who is uttering it.

Many adult statements to children and of course to other adults, contain what we can call *Box Judgments.*

A *Box Judgment* is a ready made, pre-patterned, TV dinner-type judgment. It contains not one ounce of originality and was derived from at least one whole generation of false thinking. Box judgments are passed on by word of mouth, largely, not through any direct malice because most people are not malicious by nature, but through straight-forward habit or laziness.

It is easier to utter a box judgment than to reply with some authenticity. Box judgments are borrowed from people who borrowed them from others who borrowed them from others who borrowed...a thousand times removed.

It is especially convenient also, to use a box judgment instead of listening. The old answers above provide the adult with the opportunity not to have to listen to the child at all. After all, children can be judged as not worth listening to. They say, very often, things that adults do not wish to hear because listening to a child might involve a change of attitude and this takes energy and open-mindedness, something that we often do not have.

The new response opens a door — it throws back the response mode to the child. "Why don't you want to go to school?" The answer may bring something new and unexpected which could change the whole relationship and actually improve the conditions for the child and maybe also for the adult.

It is also the response that any intelligent adult, out of respect, would apply to another adult.

One thing that may be noticed during and at the end of this week of adult communication — you, the primary adult, may find yourself utterly exhausted because this game has forced you to re-appraise your own life as well as your view of the child. Exhaustion is a sure sign of fulfillment.

The second feature that you may notice is the attitude of the child toward you, in your new incarnation to him/her. The reaction will range from complete astonishment and disbelief to re-newed love and admiration. Depending on how automatic your responses have been previous to this week, in relation to children, the response of the subject will be, at the very least, worthy of note.

You never know, perhaps you and the child may enjoy the whole experiment very much. If so, continue with it and if you manage it permanently, you no longer need this book.

Simply speaking, the whole purpose of this book is to show that there is no basic difference between children and adults — we are both the same in our potential; we are come from the same species, the same planet and the same neighborhood. Children are only regarded as inferior because adults created them that way and adults are only regarded as superior because they have big egos!

Look into the mirror and what do you see? Sometimes a child and sometimes an adult. Look at your child in the mirror and what do you see — sometimes a child and sometimes an adult and sometimes a reflection of yourself — who are you then, at that moment? Are you adult, child or copy?

CHAPTER ONE
WHAT IS A CHILD?

"...it is here that I have begun to feel wonder again, like when I was a kid and this makes me deeply happy." NEVER CRY WOLF

"...I am sure the movement has begun...How long it will take to arrive at a concrete, visible and organized reality? I don't know. Something has begun. It seems it's going to be the onrush of the new species, the new creation, or at any rate a new creation. A reorganization of the earth and a new creation... but even today, the overwhelming majority of people and intellectuals are perfectly content with taking care of themselves and their little rounds of progress. They don't even want anything else! Which means that the advent of the next being may well go unnoticed, or be misunderstood. It's hard to tell since there is no precedent to compare it with; but more than likely, if one of the great apes ever ran into the first man, it must simply have felt that that being was a little... strange. That's all. Men are used to thinking that anything higher than they has to be...divine beings — that is, without a body — who appear in a burst of light. In other words, all the gods as they are conceived — but it isn't like that at all. It is almost as if a new mind is being formed. And the body is learning its lesson — all bodies, all bodies."

The Mother — The Mind of the Cells, Satprem.

19

This book is designed to show that
we are living in the presence of a new kind of child.
A child that lives in a state of wonder, which is
our natural state, and which we are still capable of
recognizing if we know where to look.
For we have only forgotten it,
lost along the way somewhere.

Our lives are so circumspect, so constantly involved and busy with affairs of the mind that we cannot normally find the space to see what is available to us — in all patterns of our lives —

and for the purposes of this book, especially those that involve children.

If this sounds a little daunting, as though somehow we are talking about some God-like

20

creature instead of the small humans that we are accustomed to relating with, then this is accurate. We *are* talking about God-like creatures, though there is no need to be daunted, for the methods set out in the following pages are designed to illustrate that this God-likeness is entirely normal and not something to be in awe of. For we all have it within us to understand and recollect what is being suggested, even in a way which will sound strangely familiar, as though we knew it all along.

Essentially, we have largely been looking in the wrong direction when observing children. We have been looking through the eyes of our fathers and mothers who have presented us with a perspective which perhaps once worked for them, but which should have died many generations ago. The present generation has the opportunity to cut the umbilical cord of the past.

There is so much magic and excitement in the changes that are already happening in the world that we cannot lose by bringing them to children and to ourselves. The new wonder child is immensely sensitive and beautiful and hopefully in the following pages we can together recollect some of the qualities of magic and begin to see them and apply them to the children around us, perhaps even recognizing them in ourselves also, for truly we are all still children.

CHILD

The old stories of swaddling bands wrapped around children from birth are well known. It was commonly believed that a child should not have the opportunity to use his hands in case this led to damage of the eyes or face. Swaddling bands were also used to prevent a child from touching his genitals as this was considered bad practice at

any age, especially a few weeks!

There were many excuses provided for such behavior — for example, that the warmth of the urine would be retained by the swaddling and therefore cut down the possibility of diaper rash! But actually, the prime, if often unconscious, purpose was to break the child's spirit. For some children this might produce more strength in the rebellion against it, but whether this would generally be the case is unlikely, and in any event, one might question what other attendant factors come with that rebellion which might not be so happy.

So, adults began the life of a child in the manner that they intended to continue — by prevention. The strangest aspect of this was the premise that the hands were put on the child in order to do damage! This is a little like saying a flower grows leaves in order to strangle itself.

Foot binding in China was another well-known torture of small girls, performed on the pretext of improving beauty. We don't do these things to our children today, at least not in the Western hemisphere, but we do other things instead, things which may not be obvious torture but which are equally effective in closing children's availability to the magical world around them.

So, the picture drawn is of children as they are under our control, for we do control children, because this is what we feel we have to do.

When a child is first born, and for the first four to seven years of his life, at this one time in life there *is* a difference between the way he works and the way that he will work for the rest of his life, given the normal indoctrination. The difference, though, is not in any inferiority of the child to adults for children have something extraordinary to offer to adults while still in their natural state, and today, at the end of this millennium, there is a new generation of children who are still more different, still more special.

Our first look, then, at this wonder child, will give us an outline of a general theory which can then perhaps be put into practice. At the same time we can examine the ways we currently see children and perhaps look at a new way — a different angle.

INHERITANCE

Animals have in their central nervous systems innate structures that are somehow in harmony with the natural or proper environment of the particular species. The Gestalt psychologist Wolfgang Kohler named these structures "isomorphs." With these inbuilt devices, the animal is immediately in touch and on good terms with its natural surroundings. In other words, a lion cub, born into the wilds of Africa, will know immediately how to live there, what to eat, how to avoid the heat, what the various sounds and smells indicate. The process requires no learning and is instant upon birth. It is almost as though the pup walks straight into a ready-made story, knowing the plot-line perfectly from the start. It follows also that if the animal is born into a strange environment, confusion results and the animal quickly becomes prey to predators through disorientation. These isomorphs are chemically oriented biological devices within the body which hook into everything around the animal which is natural to its existence. The lion cub, therefore, is capable of speaking to life. In fact we could say that the cub *is* life.

These isomorphs, otherwise known as "innate releasing mechanisms" (IRMs), are closed, i.e. there is no choice in the matter for the animal. It is either in harmony with the environment or it dies. The animals cannot say "I don't want to be in harmony with my environment!"

In addition to these closed mechanisms there are also other IRMs that depend for their functioning on particular experiences. These mechanisms are open i.e. waiting for something to happen. They are susceptible to impression. And, what is most significant is the fact that once impressed — the first time — the imprint becomes definite, requires less than a minute for the internal reaction to take place and is thereafter irreversible.

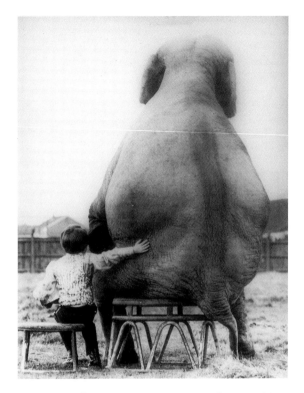

(N.B. there are experiments with animal behavior which may indicate methods of behavior modification but it is not clear yet whether this is merely the imposition of further responses or whether the old responses are cleared and replaced).

In other words, once the animal has experienced the event and the impression is made within the body, that response remains an unbreakable habit. It is rather like a protected computer instruction — imprinted on the animal's unconscious memory system and from then on fixed for the whole of its life. A typical example might be territorial rights — where an animal learns through the IRM not to stray into the territory of another group of animals of the same species. Many such responses are based on the threat of death.

We humans have the use of both these mechanisms, though on a different basis and scale, and the difference is related to the way in which we are born into the world.

THE PREMATURE HUMAN

Animals are born able to deal with life almost instantly. There is very little training needed by the parent before the puppy can survive the world and cope pretty well within it. On the other hand, the human child is helpless for the first years of life, relying totally on adult supervision and conditioning — for his or her existence.

Every experience, every event that the child confronts in those early years sets up the patterns, throughout the innate mechanisms, for the later life responses.

And because the child is so much more vulnerable than the animal, the time scale and the degree of effect are both far greater. Parents have around twelve years to impress the IRMs of the child — that's a whole lot of responses, though it must be admitted that these responses, once laid down, are not as fixed as they are in animals.

One of the concerns of science and medicine, in looking at the differences between animals and humans at birth, has been to ask why the human appears to be so much at a disadvantage. Is it simply because of the upright posture? Perhaps this unnatural stance has created a problem for nature which she has not yet resolved. Or is it that the human head is disproportionately large for the mother's pelvis and therefore birth needs to take place earlier than would be the case if we did not have such large brains. The job of maturing the human child is perhaps therefore unfinished at birth and left smartly in the hands of the parents. That is, if any of this is really a disadvantage at all.

The size of a child's head doubles in the first year of life — as though nature has left that part of human development until after birth simply to save the human female from an embarrassing physical appearance during pregnancy.

So we are born helpless — and clearly with major differences from the animal world. Animals walk on all four legs, they are covered in hair, they do not speak, make poetry or art, have no reasoning power and they cease to be child-like after the puppy-ways have passed and the "responsibilities" of avoiding death surround them. It is at this very point, in fact, that the puppy learns to seal off the experiential IRMs — when the parent introduces it to the dangers of predators. Adulthood occurs rather suddenly and the romping and playing of childhood ceases at that very moment.

The hairless human, on the other hand, is greatly more sensitive than his hairy counterparts. The sensory nerves that run within the spine, for example, are hugely more numerous than in animals

and the very fact of our nakedness creates a far greater range of responses and stimuli than if we were still completely covered in a carpet! The face, for example, has such an astonishing range of expression and effect, not only because it is totally visible but also because of a greater arrangement of muscular and nerve systems which permit such mobility.

These enhanced facilities available only to human beings and there perhaps *because* of our premature birth, permit us to enjoy a more open reflexive response to events and experiences that come our way.

But perhaps the most notable difference between animal and human, resulting from this higher intelligence, or greater capability, is the immaturity itself. One of the most evocative descriptions of the human condition in this respect has been made by the animal psychologist Konrad Lorenz:

"Every study undertaken by man was the genuine outcome of curiosity, a kind of game. All the data of natural science, which are responsible for Man's domination of the world, originated in activities that were indulged in exclusively for the sake of amusement. When Benjamin Franklin drew sparks from the tail of his kite he was thinking as

little of the lightning conductor as Hertz when he investigated electrical waves, was thinking of radio transmission. Anyone who has experienced in his own person how easily the inquisitiveness of a child at play can grow into the life work of a naturalist will never doubt the fundamental similarity of games and study. The inquisitive child disappears entirely from the wholly animal nature of the mature chimpanzee. But the child is far from being buried in the man, as Nietzsche thinks. On the contrary, it rules him absolutely."

So, the child is born too soon with greatly more response mechanisms available and far greater sensitivity than an animal. The child needs caring for, for much longer than an animal but the child also contains innate releasing mechanisms — the environmental patterns — and the open, experiential patterns. A child needs to fit into her environment and takes up the patterns of that harmonious tendency, becoming disoriented if suddenly placed in a wild jungle in the middle of the Amazon or more relevant perhaps to our way of life in the West, even the next village from the familiar habitat. In fact, a human child becomes displaced and disturbed if simply deprived of her mother. No doubt most of us are familiar with the panic on a child's face when she suddenly discovers in a crowded supermarket that mom has disappeared.

The environmental patterns, though, can also be adapted so that a child does not spend the rest of her life terrified of moving from one place to another.

And the experiential response mechanisms also have a chance, either to be fixed by the lack of awareness or variability, or flexible , should the parents provide ample and intelligent wisdom to give the child the necessary room in early life.

What we have then, in our tiny newborn child, according to modern scientific understanding, is a blank slate with certain very ancient and primitive mechanisms that are simply lying there ready to take up an imprint of the world. This, we will see later, however, may be an over-simplification of the true potential of a child, for, from a more un-reasonable and as yet non-scientific viewpoint, the child is far from being a blank slate.

THE DUCTLESS GLANDS AND THE COSMIC THOUGHT FIELD

In very recent research into the functioning of the immune system, scientists have found great variety in the systems controlled by endocrine glands — parts of the body which were hitherto largely a mystery. The other name for these glands is the ductless or thalami glands and they include the thalamus, the hypothalamus, the pituitary and the pineal glands, each nestling deep in the between brain region of the forebrain, between the brainstem and the cerebral hemispheres. The word thalami means deep chambers.

The task of these glands appears to be to convey and expand information flowing into the brain, before it reaches the cerebral cortex — supposedly the memory and higher thinking center. All sensory signals, whatever their nature, pass through these glands — rather like a central telephone exchange for the brain. The pituitary gland orchestrates the delivery of hormones (the name hormone is derived from the Greek word meaning to set in motion) throughout the body affecting such functions as sexual maturity, food conversion and general physical growth. Under the control of these glands then is both the reception system for information flowing into the body, and the most powerful courier system for messages communicating with the rest of the body — two extremely important tasks, both apparently performed by the one set of biological organs.

But the most enigmatic of the ductless glands, for the medical scientist, is the cone-shaped pineal, once considered to be the vestigial third eye perhaps because of its susceptibility to light.

Both Eastern philosophy and Western science have taken these mysterious glands very seriously and their dual tasks of receiving information and controlling the hormones is of particular interest to our study of the wonder child.

One of the most interesting explanations for these tiny glands is that they are the radio station receiver system for the human body and that a great many of the received "radio waves" do not originate in places that we can necessarily immediately be conscious of. From outer space, for example, from other people too far away to be visible or audible, from the past and the future, from the dead, from animals, plants, birds, insects — in fact from everything around us, then and now.

It may be, and it is suggested here, that the ductless glands resonate with a complete thought field.

Much research is presently in process by scientists, such as, for example, Gazzaniga and Eddelman, into this particular area of discussion and this concept of a "cosmic thought field" resonance device in the ductless glands, can only be presented as a hypothesis, but it is one nevertheless worthy of discussion.

If we consider that the innate releasing mechanisms which each child contains in the earliest years are open to anything coming in, and that we, the adults, effectively close certain of them in order to protect the child from danger, it may become clear what could be happening inside the system. The glands, receivers of stimuli, have learned to accept certain input from this thought field and to refuse other input so that a great deal of the stimulation available from the cosmos is simply cut off at source.

"There are occasions when this vision of the world takes us by surprise, the mind having slipped unconsciously into a receptive attitude. It is like the oft-recurring tale of coming upon an unexpected door in a familiar wall, a door that leads into an enchanted garden, or a cleft in a rock that gives entrance to a cavern of jewels. Yet when one comes back to the place again, looking for the entrance, it is no longer to be found. It was in just this way that late one afternoon my own garden became suddenly transfigured — for about half an hour, just at the beginning of twilight. The sky was in some way transparent, its blue quiet and clear, but more inwardly luminous than ever at high noon. The leaves of the trees and shrubs assumed qualities of green that were incandescent, and their clusterings were no longer shapeless daubs, but arabesques of marvelous complexity and clarity. The interlacing of branches against the sky suggested filigree or tracery, not in the sense of artificiality, but of distinctness and rhythm. Flowers — I remember especially fuchsias — were suddenly the lightest carvings of ivory and coral."

Alan Watts.

It is as though our thinking processes as adults work so rapidly that the very input from the surroundings, the cosmic thought field, is blurred and shadowed by their rapid movement — that the extraordinary and harmonious clarity of our surroundings does not evidence itself through the complex lattice-work of "mature" consideration.

For, lying alongside any brief realization of the true nature of the world, such as that evidenced by Alan Watts in the above quote, is invariably the sense that everything is right — not in the sense of being correct by some greater judgment, but in total harmony and without need for any form of critical judgment. In effect, the glimpses

given to a few fortunate people *always* create a logically nonsensical sense that there is no need to think, investigate or discover anything for everything is just as it should be.

The suggestion is that children exist permanently in this state without being at all aware of it — or aware that there is anything else to be aware of that is different. The process of this innocent state then slowly and sometimes recognizably fades into adulthood and is rarely if ever recovered just because of the shadow and the fog of our intense socially imposed thinking structures.

CHILDHOOD'S LIGHT

"It was a morning in early summer. A silver haze shimmered and trembled over the lime trees. The air was laden with their fragrance. The temperature was like a caress. I remember — I need not recall — that I climbed up a tree and felt suddenly immersed in "Itness." I did not call it by that name. I had no need for words. It and I were one."

Alan Watts quotes Bernard Berenson.

I can remember, when I was about four or five years old, I was in this state of open innocence and connection with reality. I would wake up in the morning and instantly there was a complete glow of light and happiness about me. The outside world shone into my room with such intensity that I would barely be able to remain still, such was the excitement and pleasure within me.

The immediate awakeness that I experienced was so glorious and lively that I would be up and doing at once and my sense of joy and appreciation of life was so great that I hardly even stopped for a second to remind myself of any negative quality in my surroundings. Basically I didn't care about anything, and I cared about everything.

I also knew, at that tender age, that this state would not last; that at some time in the future I would cease to feel this way and the glow of my existence would pass away into some kind of shadow — which I did not conceive consciously, nor care to consider, but I knew that it would come and that I might never return to this happy and "enlightened" state.

Sure enough, at around the age of 7 years, roughly at the same time as I began to suffer from allergic asthma, the innocence drifted away into less and less frequent occurrences until it was gone altogether, leaving a faint memory trace that is still with me today.

If we consider that many children have been in this state at some time in their early lives, it becomes clear that we may have to adjust our ideas about children altogether and that our determination to socialize them may be the exact system which takes them away from their natural state.

" All that you do makes it impossible for what already is there to express itself."
U. G. KRISHNAMURTI

This state of innocence for an adult is what might be termed a real big deal. For a "grown-up" to go into a condition of this kind, appreciating and sampling his surroundings with such quintessence, is really something.

It is not suggested here that children are in a permanent state of enlightenment in the same way

as those such as J.Krishnamurti or Buddha discovered, for this is a particular state far beyond all
other states. But it is suggested that the state of
innocence in childhood samples a comparable
connection with reality, which, if retained through
into adulthood, can bring astonishing beauty and
joy. Many children feel this light-filled and natural

form of existence everyday and not only think
nothing of it (!) but would not begin to consider
writing reams of descriptive matter on it. The
greatest tragedy of this profound situation is that
adults are unable to understand the innocence of
childhood in its full form *at all* — simply because
the natural state does not exist to be understood

— it is not a matter of the intellect. This results in us being unable to appreciate the condition of children. *Child-likeness* is one of the many envied and glorious states of existence, one that, if permitted to flourish through adult appreciation of it, can bring both the child and parent closer together. But because the adult has forgotten it, consciously, he/she does not wish to complement it, very often out of simple misunderstanding.

As a young boy of four years old I would climb trees everyday and feel the Itness of existence — a oneness with my blessed environment. Why would I not feel this way? Life was perfect, exactly so, and I had not a worry in the world. All my feelings, determinations, desires, were instantaneous and passing. Nothing prevailed upon me for I lived each moment to the full, totally spellbound and involved in my life and everything that touched it. Fundamentally there was one major difference between me and the adults around me — they were afraid of everything and I of nothing. I was in love with life and everything in it — its freedom and its lack of restrictions — my own innocence was the reason for my spellbound condition.

Imagine an adult up a tree and you will see fear, quite naturally — "What if I fall?", "What a fool people will think I am — a grown man up a tree." The parent more often than not will hand on that fear and pride to the child — "No you can't climb trees — you might fall and break every bone in your body and then what would we do with you in hospital for months — you wouldn't be able to play with your friends and besides you might damage yourself so badly that you might never walk again or you might even die..."
End of world.

We pass on our fears to our children — step by step, as we move through their lives beside them — protecting them — and in so doing we manage also to wipe clean their joy, their freedom and their innocence.

This fear and the resultant attitudes of adults towards children is not only evident in major acts like climbing trees — it is evident in the tiniest most infinitesimal acts that are performed by the adults towards the children — in effect in everything they do, for fear is like a disease that permeates the entire life of many human adults. It is also to be remembered quite clearly that children take in every little thing through those tiny ductless glands and the innate releasing mechanisms and learn from our adult responses exactly what they can and cannot do in life.

"THEY FUCK YOU UP,
YOUR MUM AND DAD.
THEY MAY NOT MEAN TO
BUT THEY DO.
THEY FILL YOU WITH THE FAULTS
THEY HAD
AND ADD SOME EXTRA JUST FOR YOU.
BUT THEY WERE FUCKED UP
IN THEIR TURN
BY FOOLS IN OLD-STYLE HATS AND
COATS,
WHO HALF THE TIME WERE
SLOPPY-STERN
AND HALF AT ONE ANOTHER'S THROATS.
MAN HANDS MISERY TO MAN.
IT DEEPENS LIKE A COASTAL SHELF.
GET OUT AS EARLY AS YOU CAN,
AND DON'T HAVE ANY KIDS
YOURSELF." PHILIP LARKIN

So, what we have in our midst is a creature awaiting the stimulation of our world — of the world into which we have invited the child — like a welcome guest — or an unwelcome guest! And, although we do not know it, that child is already *the world* when he or she is born. It is not that he is part of the world but that he *is* it. He contains the capacity for the greatest magic available to anyone alive and unlimited receiving mechanisms willing to accept literally everything from the outside.

Additionally, the input from these resonating glands are also perhaps remembered. There is a particular memory system which, as we shall see, science is just now beginning to expose, that perhaps operates both inside and outside the body; within the cells and around the body in an aura — a kind of God-mind, or foundational memory, rather like a hologram, which connects the body structure to the universe by means of a resonance with life. This memory may have no filter, no censorship and may absorb all things.

The conclusion of such a theory is of course, that we, the adults, who have unconsciously operated this memory from childhood, still have access to it now.

But more of this later in the book. For the time being, in this initial chapter, we will concern ourselves with the other aspects of early childhood which will later influence the human adult's happiness.

"As a baby I remember crawling around inquisitively with an incredible sense of joy, light, and freedom in the middle of my head that was bathed in energies moving freely down from above, up, around and down through my body and my heart. It was an expanding sphere of joy from the heart. And I was a radiant form, a source of energy, bliss and light. And I was the power of Reality, a direct enjoyment and communication. I was the Heart, who lightens the mind and all things. I was the same as everyone and everything, except it became clear that others were unaware of the thing itself."

Da Free John.

34

THE EARTHING OF CHILD

During the period of the child's life when he or she is most dependent upon adults/parents, i.e. babyhood and perhaps the first few years, the child is creating an awareness of the shape and form of the body which has been brought into the world. Not until he is around seven or eight years old does he become earthed through his own knowledge of himself, now sufficiently confirmed and substantial enough for him to let go of that unwavering need for attention from the outside which he needed to fix the form of his body. The concept of earthing may be thought of in the same way as electrical earthing in which the current of electrical power is always directed to the earth. Children undergo this same process as they become accostomed' to the ways of the world in all their forms — the child becomes literally earthed to the planet. It is not unlike what we call "grounding," such as when we say that we are grounded in a particular subject

once we have learned it. The only difference is that it has nothing much to do with the mind — it is not really that the child "learns" through mental intake, but that his or her whole being is absorbed into a connection with Earth herself.

This is, in effect, the equivalent of the animal's innate response mechanism to harmonize with the direct environment.

In the first years of any child's life there is a continuous need to be attached to the parents and much of the child's understanding of him or herself derives from the contact made through this need. The need to fix himself relates both to people and the Earth itself — it is a kind of hunger of perceptive understanding which in many cases is mistaken for a hunger for knowledge — an entirely different thing. The parent, in terms of both human relations and Earth relations, is like a mirror in which the child sees him or herself and formulates

the way the body and mind will be and act at each moment. In effect the child is looking for things to experience and therefore understand or simulate. In most family arrangements it is the parents who *tell the child how life should* be — i.e. how it is for them, and this way the child will get only a vicarious experience and not a direct one. "No Johnny, you don't eat your food like a monkey, you use a spoon and please don't drop all the food over the front of your sweat shirt." It is this sort of learning that gives parents the opportunity to coo and cluck over the fact that their child is "so like me" or "so like his dad."!

Naturally, as the child is in such close and intimate proximity with the parents he will make himself more similar in appearance than he may already be. If the child were in a multi-parent environment, for example, such as a communal social

structure, his resemblance to the natural parents might not be so great, and indeed less noticed. Soon enough, perhaps around six to eight years old, the child is finished with "childishness" and begins to connect now with the predominant social structure into which he has been placed by his parents. He has, in effect, taken up the reflection of the mirror into which he was previously only looking. Depending on the degree to which he is forced to ape his parents, he has become, more or less an image of someone else.

The time of childhood before the earthing has taken place is probably the purest time — a time, as we have seen, of innocence, and it almost invariably happens that we ignore and spoil this precious period because we are so much in a hurry to educate and socialize children so that they quickly grow up to be like us.

TIME WISDOM

"Beginningless time and the present moment are the same... You have only to understand that time has no real existence." HUANG PO

Perhaps one of the most fascinating areas in which we tend not to understand our children is that of time. Before the age of about seven years a child has no perception of time. The child does not in anyway envisage or pictorialize existence as having past present and future, for the child's brain and body exist in a total present. This is an extremely hard concept for an adult to understand, for the adult exists largely *in time*, involved with it to such an extent that there is rarely any existential awareness available.

It is worth making just a passing reference to the way in which the human adult perceives time, for the constant presence of the clock has caused the subject to be taken for granted somewhat in our everyday lives.

When we think about the past or the future we cease to be in an existential present — i.e. we are so intent on figuring out what happened before and what might happen after, we forget and miss what is happening now. This is one of the most powerful messages from the Eastern mystics — that the path to enlightenment requires an awareness of the present.

But truly, the mind can only be in the present — it cannot be anywhere else. If we have a memory of seeing someone yesterday, that memory is not in the past, it is in the now, the present. If we have an expectation of receiving something in the future — tomorrow — that expectation is in the now, the present, for both these things are occurring in our heads right at *this* moment, not at any other moment.

We have this tendency to confuse present memory with past knowledge or future chance and with this confusion we have created time — literally a vast illusion.

> *"Mind is always* now. *There is really no before and after for mind. There is only a* now *that includes memories and expectations."*
>
> **Erwin Schrodinger.**

So that, in effect, the adult mind is exactly in the same state as it always was from childhood, in a perpetual present. The only real difference is that we have jammed it full of so much information and we have become so afraid of that information that we have converted our present state into a

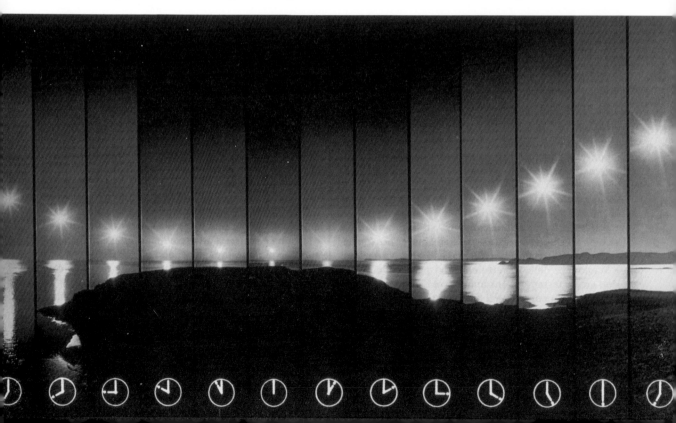

plethora of memories and expectations which clutter the present moment. We call this state time.

The child does not seem to reach an awareness of time until he or she reaches a point where there is a balance of opposites — i.e. a sense of dilemma, in effect a paranoia leads the human child into a state of time-ness. It is not necessarily an entirely natural thing, at least not in the strictness that it is imposed upon children, as we have seen we adult humans invented the clock. Nature's form of time-ness may be entirely different, as we will see.

At about seven years or sometimes older, the left hemisphere of the child's brain develops a serial, clock-like awareness of time passing. This portion of the brain then begins to reduce all events of arrival, departure, succession, duration, order, speed, direction into sharper and sharper units of time. The brain, can of course, do anything that it is instructed to do and time is a perfect example of its available precision.

The right hemisphere, however, takes a dif-ferent view of time — that of a spatial awareness — past and future or front and back. The left hemisphere projects a defined awareness of movement and the appreciation of units, while the right hemisphere gives the other part of the human dialogue, the space-time of that movement — past through present into future. It can, incidentally, be appreciated here, that the social time travel of the growing child shifts from a constant present into a constant lack of present. With this new understanding of past and future and no present, so the child loses touch with his or her innocence.

It is securely at this point that we see our departure from childhood into adulthood. The child's development into time-wisdom (or time-madness) also illustrates the constant dialogue that occurs between the two halves of the brain — like two completely different molecules in a chemical reaction, joining to become something different again. The simplest way to illustrate such a state of being is by trying it for ourselves.

GAME - TIMELESSNESS

The ideal span of time for this exercise would be a whole week-end, though it is understood that this may not be practical. A day or even half a day will suffice. The exercise can be undertaken by both adults and children. Children below the age of five or six will find it easier than adults or older children.

Go around the house and remove or hide all clocks and watches. No one in the house is permitted to have any sort of timepiece. They should be locked away somewhere and the key hidden by someone who is not taking part in the game.

Televisions and radios should be unplugged

and no newspaper should remain in sight. All this should be prepared on the night before the exercise begins. For both the Saturday and the Sunday (or if this is not possible then just one of these days) no appointments should be made with anyone outside the house and anyone wishing to visit should be discouraged. Tell the neighbors that there is someone in the house with a contagious infection!

For the duration of this experiment there are no fixed meal times — you will eat when you are hungry, however often that is or however seldom. You will sleep when you are tired, get up when you wake, do exactly what you feel like doing, whatever it is, whenever it is, however absurd the desire might be. The randomness of meal times, sleeping and waking will initially create a little chaos but the purpose is to separate the players from their normal way of living — to provide a disjointed condition which will upset the mind's continuity and provide an opportunity to forget the time of day. If you should find yourself awake in the middle of the night — say around 3.00 a.m., get up and do something that you would not normally do at that hour. Make a full sized meal or play football in the garden. Bake a cake or play charades with your family.

Equally, should you feel like a nap during the middle of the day, create the conditions of the night — close all the curtains, light a candle, have a bath and take off your make-up — go to bed for the night in the middle of the day.

During the day, especially, undertake a mini-game — the exercise requires cooperation from another member of your family. At any moment, whatever you are doing, whether it be cooking a meal, washing the dishes or just moving from one part of the house to another — STOP — and re-main still for a minute or two. It is best if you are told to stop by someone else so that it is unex-pected, though it is also fine if you tell yourself to stop.

There is no need to freeze like a stone statue — only that you cease the action you have been doing and remain still in that one spot long enough to look at exactly what you are doing. Observe your position, your action, what you are carrying, the facial expression if there is a handy mirror and observe anything else about your feelings at that moment.

You will find this part of the method partic-ularly useful for an awareness of a lack of time because it disorients and surprises the mind.

Most important in this exercise of timelessness is to cut you and your family off from the world around you. The very best place to be would be the deep countryside where there is no one around. But if all you can manage is an apartment in the center of the city, it simply requires a little more diligence — take the phone off the hook, lock the door, consciously cut out your social surroundings.

By the end of the exercise you should be thoroughly disoriented to time. With luck you will not even wish to put your watch back on and on Monday morning you will not wake up for work! So take the day off for once, let the children miss school and continue the exercise until that evening. The result will be even more dramatic because by then you will begin to appreciate what it is like to be a small child.

This game is especially good for parents who expect a new child.

If you have no awareness of time the world feels and looks very different. And this may well be the very quintessence of childhood. If you are not surrounded by thought, constantly in a state of worry and anxiety, if you do not spend ninety-nine point nine, nine, nine percent of your time thinking about what you are going to do *next*, then perhaps you might just see what is happening *now* at this very moment. And it is the suspicion, even the direct experience, at least of the author, that this is very pleasant indeed! Most of us, though, have known this state during the times when con-centration is at its highest — perhaps an absorbing book, or a fascinating new hobby, a sport or pas-time which completely demands the body to be in the present. The pleasure derived from such activities is related directly to their results. We feel better, more relaxed, more fulfilled, if we oc-cupy ourselves with such activities. The reason is simple — for those times we have been out of time, out of the mind and the results to the body and to the mind are incalculably beneficial.

It is not suggested, however, that a child should be encouraged to remain a helpless, thoughtless creature for the duration of life, for the human being, unless confined to a single room without light, without love and without stimulation of any kind, will inevitably start to think. And therefore to worry and become anxious. The purpose is much more to accept the childhood response of time-lessness and allow it to remain available as a game or practice which will later develop into a natural meditative state, living alongside the other, perhaps less happy responses.

THE CHILD WITHIN US

able to correspond more happily and easily with the children in our lives.

May it be said then, at this early point in the book, that this state, our natural state, is available to all of us and needs only a small act of remembrance and focused attention, and the more often we sample it the greater the habit becomes and therefore the more easily recalled.

On recounting the innocent state that I enjoyed as a child I feel a thrill of pleasure and recognition which is powerful and central enough to put it in a state almost equivalent to that remembered, and the more often I recall or experience such states, either directly through my own memories or vicariously through the memories or recountings of others, the more easy it becomes to enjoy it again.

The wonder child that is being born today has particular access to this state and carries within her frame the most delicate mechanisms to allow such a state to remain into adulthood.

Having taken this brief first look at the new wonder child, we can now move our attention to the current adult — the human that has learned to be the way he or she is by benefit or otherwise of that mirror which has been held up by past generations of mothers and fathers.

How much the above explanation, or painting, of the wonder child coincides with the reader's view is purely a matter of personal ideas, but one thing presumably can be supposed — that the majority of us would not object to being that way — even if only for a while and even if only to be

WHAT IS AN ADULT?

One of the first and most fundamental differences between adults and children in our current social condition is the adult capacity to think all the time and the child's incapacity to think a lot of the time. Very young children do not have a continuity of thought. They have a brain that will provide them with the information they need in order to function, but it has not yet taken up the continuous process of thinking and will not do so until the social requirements and the body provide this necessity.

So — adults think.

The item required to do this thinking is the brain — not, as many people imagine, the mind. The mind is a strange and nebulous ghost-system which somehow, somewhere resides within the body and occupies mankind in a disproportionate amount of consideration, both on its own behalf and on behalf of its objective view of the rest of the knowable universe. Another word for mind is time. The mind might be considered as a continuity machine (machine may be an inaccurate title as the mind has no mass and cannot be measured for it does not exist except as a device created to support the concept of continuity) and as such operates to give a continuous sense of existing. Mind creates continuity in order to be mind in order to create continuity. It has also other purposes, of course, and if it were possible for us to set the mind aside for use only when necessary, like many of the organs of the body, for example, then the continuity aspect of mind would not be needed. The mind/brain would then act for us instead of us acting for it.

Take a typical example: you receive a rude letter from your bank manager telling you that you are overdrawn on your bank account and you must put money into the account (which you don't happen to have!) within a week or the bank will take action against you. The contents of the letter enter your brain as information and should, in an ideal world, produce an answer. This answer might be to pay your next pay check into the account and not spend so much next month so that the overdraft does not re-occur, but this may not be the immediate result. Most of us will more likely allow the information to enter also into our minds and the mind will worry over the situation for all the intervening time until the pay check arrives and the brain has the opportunity to deal with the problem. The mind therefore acts as a continuity machine between the letter's contents and the brain's actions. In short, the mind worries over the event and indeed repeats it during a whole period of time after it has already entered the brain and in effect been answered. You know that your pay check will deal with the problem — the brain has provided this answer to your dilemma but the mind goes on fretting about it until the actual reality of the check has appeared.

There is a classic Eastern story which also helps to crystallize the way the mind works.

There were two monks who had been sworn to celibacy and were not permitted to have any contact with women in any way. During a journey through the countryside around their monastery they encountered a young woman by the side of a river. The woman could not swim and yet needed to cross the river so that one of the monks took her on his shoulders and carried her across to the other side leaving her happily on the bank. The other monk began to complain to the first monk that he should not have done such a thing and continued to complain the whole way to the market, an hour away.

Eventually the monk who had carried the girl stopped his friend and said:

"I carried the girl on my shoulders from one bank to the other and then left her — you have continued to carry her in your head ever since — you are the greater sinner."

This is an adult habit — small children do not do this for they have no minds as continuity machines. They have instead mind/brains which work when required to.

Looking at it another way, the human being operates within time only when he or she is thinking. Stop thinking and time goes away. The mind needs time in order to create a scale and a territory about itself. Space is not enough — or rather space is too much, for space is both nebulous and boundless whereas time is easily bordered; past, present and future with a particular emphasis on the first and last of these three. The moment the mind enters the present — even for one split second, that split second ceases to exist and so does the mind. The mind of a human cannot survive in the present.

Very young children are in the present while older children and adults, except for a very few very exceptional people, exist largely out of the present — in the past or the future.

So — adults know time.

Third on our lengthening list of adult classifications is the quality of fear. We have discussed this a little in the beginning of the book but it is such an important part of the make-up of the human adult that we cannot leave it out of the cake. It is also part of the mind. The body is not afraid. It may be aware of danger but it does not dwell upon fear or develop fear — it simply responds to danger. The spirit is not afraid. In fact the spirit, or as some would call it, the heart, is exactly the opposite of afraid. Through innocence and the inability to know fear the spirit/instinct/heart will take any risk that comes along — if, that is, the mind will permit it.

The mind is the only part of the human function that understands fear and of course this is a very necessary function because without it we would soon get eaten by lions or run over by buses! But this function has become a dis-function for fear has spread from being a simple and useful operation to being an all-pervading dis-ease that brings the human individual down and traps him inside his own regurgitated and often agonized fears until he becomes accustomed to this state and does not even notice it himself.

Children are not afraid — they can get into the most terrible trouble because they are not afraid! They are not afraid because they have not been taught to be so. Their minds don't have a store of useful precautionary information to begin with and therefore they rely upon their instincts and their hearts and thus take risks that terrify adults into a state of horror.

So — adults are afraid.

The fourth one may sound obvious, or at least more obvious than the others, but in fact it encompasses all the others in one item. Adults are

older than children. To become older and grow into an adult is easy. To become older and remain somewhat of a child is tremendously difficult. If adults were more able to remain children as they grew older, other adults would soon be much happier and so would children!

The fact of adults' elderness is meaningless on its own. You get old, so what. It is what goes with the aging process that is the difference. Adults: 1. think about their age, 2. consider the time involved in their aging and 3. are afraid of getting old. It all fits!

So these four items will be the basis of our character study of the adult as opposed to the child. A child is none of these four things, an adult is all of them.

It is only after the first seven or eight years when the reflection process of earthing has completed that the child takes up the image of the adult and becomes involved in these four processes.

Rituals of politeness mask whatever may truly be felt and whoever might have once truly been inside the image. Spontaneity largely disappears. (Incidentally, the Greek meaning of the word "person" is "mask.")

The adult mind is in a constant state of organizing what it imagines is going to be the future, rehearsing everything that is expected to come. The fact that almost invariably the expectation of the mind is not fulfilled is constantly forgotten — so that there is little sense of having wasted the vast stores of energy that lie within the body for use in preparation for non-existent futures.

Take a typical example of a likely event. Perhaps someone has insulted you. It could be almost anything, even the simplest situation like a good friend who passes you in the street one morning and does not say hello. The event upsets you so much that you spend the rest of the day rehearsing what you are going to say to that person the next morning — reprimanding her for not being polite or friendly. The following morning she stops you and immediately tells you that she has had a terrible experience in which her aunt has died in an accident and yesterday morning she was totally preoccupied with the problem and did not see you.

Your anger and the energy that went into rehearsing the reprimand for the following day was all totally wasted because it didn't occur to you that it might have nothing to do with you, but could be some event of hers that had created the lack of communication. Always for the adult the universe spins around our heads!

Then of course, the mistake will be forgotten and the experience conveniently tucked away somewhere so that next time that exact same situation occurs, the same reaction will take place — over and over and over again.

The adult mind is not in the present for it is always rushing ahead to the next time or the next place. We are largely trying, also, to be like the rest of the people around us — still looking for mirrors to re-reflect ourselves in — trying to acquire the approval of others, not perhaps realizing that their approval is worth little and in any event they are doing the same to us so hard that they don't even notice us anyway!

This need for approval criss-crossing between all adults re-enforces the need for ritual conduct — we live for other people's opinions of us and so act out our required role in life in order to get that approval.

The final result of all this light bouncing off all these blind mirrors is people who have no originality and who exist without any knowledge of who they are. They know only that which others tell them. Because of that intrinsic habit that formulated in childhood — that period of unearthedness which was permitted to direct itself constantly at others and rarely encouraged to be in-

dividualistic — the adult is simply a grown up child who has temporarily lost sight of himself *and* his innocence. He has lost most of the good bits and gained largely the bad! Much of the contact with his own resources is also lost, as well as, in most cases, the sense of child-likeness which would so much help the anxious human condition to balance itself. This presence would then also provide the children around us with an opportunity to be NOT like us but simply *themselves*.

Finally, before we close this initial chapter, the following idea and the game that goes with it is designed to define one of the most delicate and sensitive methods by which a parent or adult may communicate with a child. It also leads conveniently to the next chapter — which occupies us with the wonder of child communication.

GAME - The Heat Experiment

As we have seen, a very small child is in some respects a little like an open, empty book or a blank slate. A more advanced simile might be that a child is like an unexposed holographic plate, or more precisely is an unexposed area of a vast holographic plate. Each section of a holographic plate is coated in a sensitive layer of silver oxide, specially treated to accept images and information which is recorded all over the plate.

The process is not the same as a light-sensitive film. A strip of film, once exposed, takes up the picture in a series of dots so that the whole piece of the film is needed in order to reproduce the picture. If you cut the film in half you will get only half the original picture and there is no way that you can get the other half without the missing piece. With holographic exposures the whole picture is recorded *everywhere* on the plate so that if you take only a small part of the plate and destroy the rest, you can still see the whole picture, although perhaps slightly less well defined, from the reproduction of that small piece.

Recent research by scientists such as Pribram and Ashley, suggests that we humans may not in fact contain our memories within the cells themselves, i.e. all over the body, similar to holographic plates. But for sure, if we look at David Bohm's concept of the universe, it is a legitimate point to consider that we are part of a "wholeness" which is universal and therefore operates in some way similarly to holographic systems. This is a very new area of scientific interest and cannot therefore be predicated upon in this book. However the concept of a thought field that we looked at earlier describes the general condition of humanity to be in a state of "one-ness" with existence — the body receiving or "joining with" the rest of the "cosmic thought field" to thereby complete the "exposure" of the holographic plate.

Experience gathered by a child, in that case, literally explodes into an awareness all over his body. This gathering of information and experience can either be of the quality of light or that of darkness, and it is we adults who possess the power to bring that light or darkness.

The following game is an exercise designed to enable an adult to appreciate first what it is for a child to gather the light and second to help bring that light to the child in his or her life.

Take a summer or spring morning. As early as possible, preferably just before the sun rises, when there are few or no clouds in the sky. Open the windows of your bedroom and pull back all hindrance to the sunlight's arrival. If the sun rises on another side of the house, choose that room instead and lie down with your head to the window so that when the sun comes up you will feel it and see it over the top of your head.

Lie down and wait for the sunrise. Close your eyes and wait. As soon as you feel the sun hit the top of your head take a deep, slow breath in. Inhale the light and warmth of the sun into your body and as you do so imagine that the rays of the sun are moving through your body — right through and down, all the way down to the tips of your toes and out the other end. Feel the sun's rays pass through your whole body and consider that those rays are a deep golden beam of light and heat that is passing through you. Consider the sun's rays to be a solid beam of light and imagine that it passes out of the tips of your toes and into the room like a continuous flow. You are, in effect, a channel for the rays of the sun and it moves through you without missing a single cell of your body.

At the top of your breath, making sure that your body is still fully relaxed, allow the air to release from your mouth in a slow long outward breath and with that breath the sun's rays are drawn back through your toes and still coming from the inlet at the top of your head these same untouched rays merge through your mouth and are released into the air of your room. Keep the image of the continuous flow of light in mind and see it in your mind's eye as its golden hue passes into the room.

Repeat this act as many times as you like for as long as you like and at least for a few minutes.

What you are doing is bringing the energy of the sun into your body and allowing it to enter all your cells, filling up the cells and expanding them and then taking their essence and blowing it out into the environment around you. The sun and you are now co-existent, both within your body and the room in which you lie.

When you have inhaled enough of the morning sun go to your child's room and take him or her in your arms. It is likely that at this hour your child will already be awake and under normal family life will be waiting either patiently or noisily for you to wake up. Children learn early that parents sleep after the sun has risen. This morning and perhaps others, if you enjoy the experiment, your child will get a treat. Speak to him or her, cuddle or stroke him or her and generally make a fuss!

What you have done is educate the child with the rays of the sun. Such an education may not impinge upon your conscious understanding at that moment — it may not cause the child suddenly to fling his or her arms about you in joyous exultation — in fact the child may still complain or demand or kick or shout. He/she may giggle, smile, laugh out loud and kiss you, but either way throughout your life and that of the child you will have filled his or her cells with the sun and your own essence and this will not be forgotten.

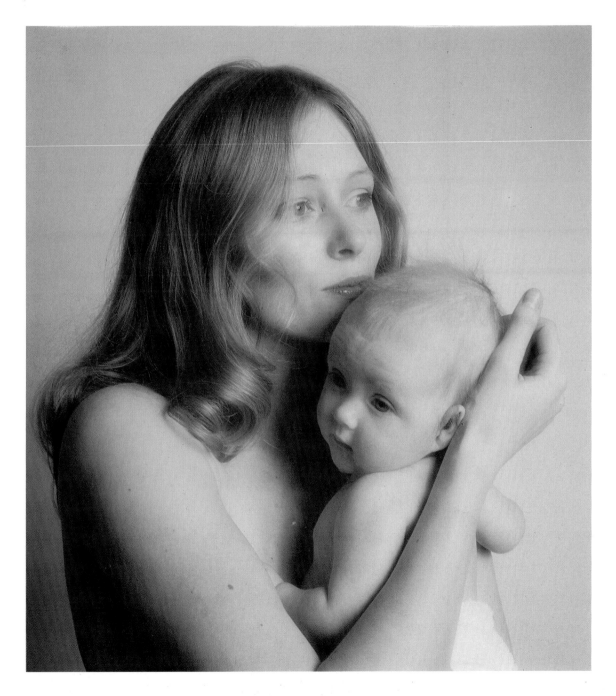

CHAPTER TWO — CHILD TALK

The communication that can occur between children and adults must be the most essential part of the relationship. We cannot find childhood unless we get in touch with it and communication forms the bridge across the river which divides the grown-ups from the un-grown. This chapter then sets out to show that communication does not only take place by talk as the adult knows it. There are other kinds of talk. In effect the child "speaks" a different language from the adult and by learning their language the adult can find a magic that is unsurpassed by any other form of learning for such "talk" comes from the child's heart to the environment on a subtle level and manifests through the eyes, the natural landscape, the touch of both the child's body and the effect that body has on that landscape. Think of landscape, though, in the broadest fashion — the landscape of life, for this contains the child, the adult and the whole of everything. In short, children talk to us with everything they have and if we can learn to talk to them with the same inherent skill we will change the relationship into something intensely magical.

50

"It happened one November afternoon. After we finished school we walked to Claudia's house, which was more than an hour away on foot. I remember that the last lesson was swimming and we still had wet hair; we had not had time to dry it, because we had to be home by a certain time and there still was so much to do.

We walked through the park that surrounded the school around the lake. The water at that time was very dark and the shadows of the trees reflecting on it could just be made out. The only thing I clearly remember of that moment was the sound of our boots on the wet autumn leaves that covered the pathway. We had both bought the same boots and we used to wear them with leather trousers and bright colored woolen pullovers. Claudia was particularly fond of a black leather coat that had belonged to a great uncle of hers whose job had been to drive the postal carriages across the Alps. She liked the smell of the coat, we both found it very manly. In order to keep it smelling that way she hung the coat on a hook in the stable every night so that the smell of cows and horses would impregnate the leather. I had a long cape made of green heavy material that I wore with an old cashmere scarf my mother used to put cataplasmas on.

I know people were crossing the park at that time of day, but we felt as if we were the only two human beings alive in the whole town. The traffic, the buses and the people waiting for them, the tiredness of the day on their faces — we seemed to ignore these things completely, as if they were lifeless ghosts around us, not worthy of any attention whatsoever.

The road that led up to Claudia's house was very steep — I remember laughing until tears ran because we kept slipping on the wet leaves and falling on the ground making a dreadful mess of our expensive leather trousers — the muck on them would make us look even more interesting, because we would tell we had been exploring in some wood.

The biggest thrill was to make an adventure of everything that came along — everything, absolutely everything was transformed into a game. In the few occasions in which our parents or some other adult broke into the picture about bad school reports and late homecoming and if they took the usual stand of grounding us, we would dramatize it: we would stop eating, talking; we would surround ourselves with an impenetrable cloud of self-chastisement and we would pass each other written messages on how we only had eaten three bread crumbs for lunch and only spoken one word in the whole morning. Teachers and parents thought we were mad, that we had taken the grounding far too seriously; what they did not understand was that we were playing.

Once we arrived at Claudia's house we would lock ourselves in her room, sit on the bed and talk and talk for hours. We would also draw, especially women, write poems and she would play the piano and I would dance with the dog.

We had bought a big book with blank parchment pages, which we had shared the cost of because our monthly allowance was barely enough for the bus and a drink here and there. In this book we recorded everything that we did — musical notes in preparation of the symphony that one day Claudia would write; our studies of the world of fairies and drawings of them — we were convinced that they existed; knitting patterns, hair plating techniques, poems, quotes from the innumerable books we read.

The sense was that there was nothing and nobody outside ourselves; that we understood far more than adults did about life; we called adults the clock-work machines; we did not hate anybody; in fact there was a great fascination with the essence of people, we totally overlooked the details. And most predominant of all was the great sense of adventure that the world offered.

Sometimes we would sit in the barn above the stables; the roof had a hole and the rain would fall inside a bucket we had placed under it. A worker was sent to mend it and we tried in every possible way to prevent him. Without the hole in the roof the barn would have lost the intimacy that comes when nature is allowed in the space of man."

Manuela — 15 years.

THE DOOR IN THE WALL

It is as though a child is standing at a door and beyond the door there is a magic that responds to the child's wonder, that answers it and gives back more than the child needs, rather like those doors that appear in C.S. Lewis children's novels. They are hidden and only a few, usually innocent children can ever find them.

But we adults are so much into protecting children that we cover up the doors and make them invisible with all our fears of danger and

53

abuse; all this madness that surrounds *us* the adults, especially in America for example, where madness is at its highest rate yet. And this protection means that the child's innocence and wonder is shadowed and fails to find the door, let alone the opening of it. So, how can we understand what it is like to be child-like — we are not just preventing the opening of the door, we are a hundred steps away from the one who can open it, holding her rein.

Someone once said it so clearly: "man stands in his own shadow and then wonders why it is so dark."!

This chapter then is about child communication, but from a different viewpoint, one that might not at first seem entirely obvious for it is not an angle we are familiar with — but perhaps this will lead us to the whereabouts of the magic doors and how to allow children to find them without our protection. We begin with the eyes.

EYE TALK

In Taoist understanding the eyes are of great significance for they represent much more than the simple seeing of the world around them. They also represent the male and female aspects of the individual. Modern science has established, for the moment, that the brain is divided into two hemispheres, the left and the right brain and these two sides of our selves may be called male — the left side, and female — the right side. For the Taoists, once the two sides come together in harmony this is called "Heaven".

Just as a simple experiment invite your partner or anyone close to you in the adult world and look into their eyes. Put your hand over the left eye of the other and look into the right and then cover the right eye and look into the left. You will see a distinct difference between the two if you look closely enough and drop any mind ideas about the person involved. What you will see when you look into the female, left eye is the *receiving* aspect of the person. That eye is open and accepting

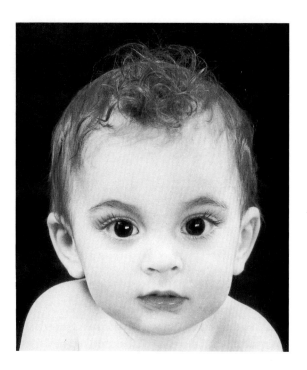

and in fact is the eye which welcomes and receives the world without much protection against it — very female. And when you look into the right eye you will see the male, projecting aspect of the individual — the putting out. This eye will show more fear for it has to deal with the separation and opposition to the world that we all believe to be necessary. In some people the difference is so great that you will be shocked by seeing the eyes in this light and in future you will begin to recognize people's fear of the world simply by looking into their right eyes (man or woman) and incidentally this is a good way of changing your own fear of people — by seeing their fear of you!

The Taoist alchemy involves the understanding that the presence of real light comes only to those who have found the male and female together within themselves and even our old friend Jesus had something to say about it: "When your two eyes become one there will be light."

In our own past history, in the western civilized world, the physicians believed originally not that

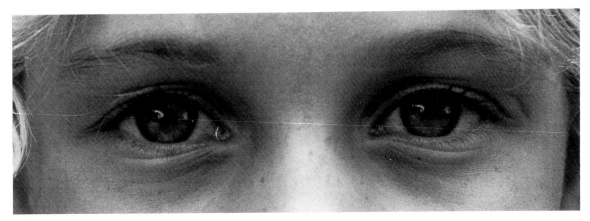

the eyes received light and thereby saw what was happening in the world, but that the eyes shone beams of light *out* from the head onto what was seen and this way found sight (see especially William Blake). It was as though there was a shining light inside the head which beamed onto the world. In some ways this is a very beautiful and spiritual understanding of how we operate for although it has been disproved by science (though interestingly very recent eye research may be moving back towards this concept), it actually gives a much more precise image of our connection with existence.

Our own deeply spiritual and self-oriented presence in existence is one of giving out from our hearts, through our eyes — the male projecting and the female receiving to focus at a point on life around us, not the other way about.

In fact, of course, it works both ways; life gives us and we give back — a continual toing and froing of light and darkness but the more "illogical" approach is perhaps the more revealing.

Also, as a side issue, you might notice in future which eye you look into when you speak to someone and which method of looking you employ according to how you feel about that person. For example, in simple conversation we almost invariably look into the left eye of the other because this is the receiving eye whereas if we are angry with the other we tend to move from one eye to the other quickly, back and forth, because we are trying, sub-consciously, to assess the potential danger — the degree that the other person is receiving or attacking us.

But now look at a small child's eyes. Gaze

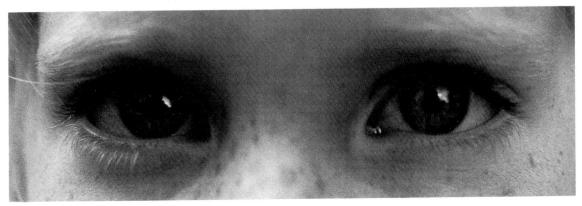

into a child's eyes, both of them, and you will see two left eyes! Both eyes are totally open and receiving. There is no projection, no male side yet for the child is completely available to all existence as a receiving unit without protection and without reserve. And this is the un-scientific child-talk that we all miss. A child talks to us through the eyes, through a willingness to receive us and *anything* we put into the child. Here then is another reason why we should learn honesty.

DISNEYLAND-UN-MAGIC

And speaking of honesty, or rather dishonesty, one of the best examples of how we manage to protect children from magic, how we manage to block their communication with us is Disneyland. At first glance, this might seem like a contradiction in terms — Disneyland — Fantasy-land, magical.

But whose magic is Disneyland made of?

There is nothing in Disneyland that has anything much to do with magic. It has to do with plastic, foam, sugar, tiny loudspeakers inside fake bird's heads, papier-mache copy elephants, tigers, pirates, strips of silvered paper being flapped in artificial blasts of air to imitate fire and an extraordinary number of immensely fat people who look as though they have been fed all their lives on the junk food that is available in Disneyland! Everything there is an imitation, a fake — "home of the bogus" — especially the food. It is as though we have had to do this because we cannot do the real thing. We do not see the way real birds fly because we rarely have time to look — we are too busy going to Disneylands. We cannot force ancient pirates to re-appear to order and not hurt us into the bargain. We cannot resuscitate Swiss Family Robinson on their island and, more to the point, we cannot truly appreciate these real life-forms in their natural habitat, so we build a fake version.

But it is not so much the fact of the fakeness of Disneyland — it is that we deliberately made it that way — and we like it that way. Effectively, the adult world has created a child's world especially for children which has nothing whatever to do with life, or children for that matter. It has been built in that bogus manner because this is what we adults imagine children want — what we fondly believe they should enjoy — what is good for them. In fact, Disneyland is a prime prototype for the world into which we intend to place most children — padded, plasticated, protected, shielded from all those nasty beasts out there who will do unto them what they did unto us.

And here is the final remedy for securing the lock on the doors of true magic — that we adults have been so blinded and deafened to the world that we have created a castle in the sky right here on Earth, all around us and our children, which is nothing more than an extruded Disneyland. It may be that this business of creating a false en-

CHILD LABOR

vironment for children all started some time around the beginning of the Industrial Revolution, or at least when it became necessary to protect the young from slave labor in the mines and industry. Effectively, the parents of that time decided to extend child-life as long as possible in order to delay the time when the child would have to enter work — that dread process which signifies anxiety and stress for us all. "Work as pain," rather than work as pleasure. Perhaps from this time on we developed the idea that we must protect all children and in so doing we also cut off their most subtle forms of communication with us.

It is not that children are somehow simply small adults wanting to take part in the adult world as quickly as possible, and to learn by doing. It is that children wish to learn by doing in a magical world which adults hide from them by creating a bogus world around them instead. Adults believe this will somehow delay the inevitable moment when adulthood arrives with all its trappings of discomfort and dis-ease. Given enough indoctrination the children, of course, eventually believe in this bogus world as well, for they forget the magical one.

In this closed childish social structure, the child learns by pretending, not by doing because the doing is shadowed within that strange and somewhat sinister Disneylandesque environment. With a combination of copy-toys and silly talk the child is beguiled and seduced out of life and into a land behind a door made of frosted icing. The kind of play that is encouraged around a child is one which is designed to postpone work. It is not that the adult teaches the child that work is play — that all of life can be one long and joyous game — because we adults do not believe this, or rather we have been so inculcated by our own parents and their parents before them, to believe (unconsciously) in work as pain, that we can no longer remember how it might be to have a good time

without plastic toys and idiot talk. So we pretend that Santa Claus will always come down the chimney every Christmas Day carrying a sack of goodies and that there is some heavenly place somewhere on the Arctic Circle where he lives surrounded by gnomes and elves making plastic trains and cars, teddy bears and guns that don't work. The fact that such a horrific habitat would kill Santa Claus in one season is neither here nor there! For that matter none of it is either here or there.

So, what we have is a kind of insane postponement of growth because the growth that the adult envisages is so miserable and troubled that no one would ever want a sweet innocent child to grow that way. We cannot imagine how it could be any other way as an adult, so what choice do we have but to hand the children in the world this sack of plasticated junk.

Another important reason for this state of

affairs is that toys and all the attendant paraphernalia of childhood keep the children out of our hair. With the frantic style and pace of a life containing domestic duties, school, stressed and unhappy husbands, the mother needs something to keep the little brats busy or the balance would soon be tipped and all families would end up in the divorce or child-beating courts.

It is doubtful that children really like this arrangement at all and perhaps the ready attitude is... "well, tough — but what else can I do". But the surprising thing about it all is that it is not necessary to operate a family this way even from the start. For there are some remarkable characteristics in children, which with the right approach can actually reduce the amount of stress and unhappiness within family relationships. The whole change of affairs could be summed up in one sentence. Children are not inferior beings that need to be isolated and protected — they are magical beings, all born with silver spoons in their mouths.

The ultimate device or toy that is today used by adults to divert, protect, get-rid-of children is, of course, the TV, that appalling and now for granted mush-spreader which people have even stopped complaining about! Loaded up, especially in the United States, with murder, mayhem and cutie-pie syrup, TV is a little like the TV dinners that we eat without conscious pleasure while watching TV. We shovel it down, already largely digested and vaguely wonder why our stomachs and heads hurt all the time. We take no power from television.

How many times have you sat in front of the television for an evening, gone to bed and then realized that you do not remember a single thing that was on the box that evening. It goes in, already digested, and disappears into nothingness.

Mush to mush.

But all this is very critical of the adult world — and none of us much like to be criticized so perhaps better to look at a practical alternative to the TV dinner/Disneyland mentality before exploring further.

The emphasis, however, is that we should begin

at the very beginning of a child's life aware that she or he is extremely unusual and extremely sensitive to our input and that this input is what makes the child the adult of the future.

We do not need to talk to children through cotton-candy when we can involve them in a different world which we may get something out of also.

The following game is about as simple and about as difficult as any game could be, but it does a lot to illustrate the precise opposite of Disneyland.

61

KITCHEN-ISM

One evening take a child in your life into the kitchen, before dinner time, boy or girl it does not matter. Ask her if this evening she would like to prepare dinner and not you. That you will help by being there but she will do everything.

If very young, perhaps you might have to take a hand in the procedure, but the main thing to remember is somehow to remove that element that we all have of expecting things to be done wrong by children — always somehow teetering on the edge of caution — "hey, be careful" or "no-no, not like that" even before the child has had time to mop up the mess herself.

Remove yourself from the authority of the job. Even if she messes the whole thing up, it's OK — so dinner will be late, so what. Maybe that way you won't have to spend so much of the evening in front of the box and when you do even-

tually get there, the programs will have a new flavor for the child will have found something new.

Mentally tape up your mouth and only give approval or answers when asked to. Children have this way of turning their heads towards adults when they want a response. Wait for the turn — and above all DON'T INTERFERE.

If the child finds the whole process engrossing and exciting, let it happen regularly and encourage her with recipe books and new ideas. No need to provide anything extra in the way of miniature dishes or pots — let her use what's there, what you use.

As a lesser form of this game, perhaps for very small children — always bring them into the kitchen when food is being prepared. The kitchen is a place of alchemy, of magic. When you make dinner you transform raw foods (hopefully) into combinations of new things which are designed (also hopefully) to benefit the body, the mind and the spirit. It's a cliche but it still very much applies — we are what we eat. Encourage the small child to talk or somehow get involved in the preparation of food. It need not be anything more than idle gossip but it happens at a time when the witch is brewing at her cauldron, making life go forward with her works. And it is in these moments that the child may be allowed to see that work is not pain but joy and play.

TV will remain off soon enough.

And as a last part of this game, extend it to the following:

FOOD LOVE

Make the next meal you have a religion! Imagine that you and your family are at a very important and powerful ceremony like a big wedding or royal feast in medieval times. You must prepare only the very best food, with the purest ingredients. You are making this meal for God himself.

Dispose of all plastic from the kitchen, throw it or put it away in the attic. Not even the smell of plastic should be permitted on this occasion. Wood, stone, marble, metal are fine.

Every step of the cooking should be a ritual, done slowly and with absolute meditation and purity of process. Sample and touch everything, caress the food and the utensils as though they were religious relics in the midst of an awe-inspiring rite.

And draw the child into the game also, explaining what is happening. You will find her totally happy and easily able to do all this.

The kitchen should smell incredible by the end of the game.

And then the eating of the food must be done in the same form. The dishes should be many and small, varied and well displayed. The eating should be so slow that you feel like you are in a slow-motion movie. Allow this play-acting to take you over but keep an essence within it for the purpose is to really taste the food. The best way to get the maximum effect from this game is to eat little or nothing for the whole day before the meal for then the taste buds and the rest of the appetite systems in the body are really ready to relish the food and this is what you are after. There is no need for the child to eat nothing prior to the meal for children have not lost their taste sense.

The end of the meal should be spent either in conversation or simply silently at the table for a few moments, in reverence for the food.

SWEET-TALK VULNERABILITY

Beginning at the earliest age of a child, adults have extreme problems with the child's vulnerability, the sweet-talk of a child's life.

The story goes that society — that which the parent intends the child to grow up in — is a rough environment where nasty people do nasty things to one another. The child needs to be tough therefore, or at least aware of the tricks that will be played upon him/her. A vulnerable child is therefore in danger of... what? Being cheated? Being conned? Being physically harmed? Being emotionally harmed? So many dangers available for the vulnerable child.

So — the plan goes that the parent must educate the child as early as possible NOT to be vulnerable, make the child tough. Leather is tough,

thickening the skin is the only way to survive the dangers of social structures, the social structures that incidentally the same adults are building.

The problem with all this is not that the skin becomes thick, because of course it doesn't. Perhaps you can remember the game that was suggested at the beginning of the book, in which we looked at the bus driver as a child, the female boss as a child, and we quickly saw the same propensities and characteristics that we see in our children. So people who profess to be tough or thick-skinned are not really. Actually they are relying upon one simple factor in human development — people's inability to see just how sensitive other people are.

Because we are generally so busy with our own problems we do not have time or space to see just how sad, lonely, vulnerable other people are. All we see are the gruff and serious looks that people plaster onto their faces in order to give the impression of being thick-skinned.

So — de-sensitizing children doesn't work. What it actually does is make them very unhappy when they are young and also when they get older because their heads are full of nonsense about distrust and caution — about watching out for the other guy who "will cheat me or harm me if I let him."

And more important — thickening the skin causes communication to retreat. If a child believes that he is going to be damaged or blocked by the communication he wishes to project, he simply stops talking and this retreating of verbal emphasis becomes a physiological problem and eventually the child can no longer communicate at all.

And the problem is not even, mostly, as extreme as this, for most children have a natural facility for communicating on a very subtle level which may simply be missed by adults. And this, "gentle autism" is equally as harmful to healthy growth as the more obvious version.

metal is tough — human beings are not tough. It is by imposing this toughening ritual upon a child that the parent curtails the vulnerability at an even earlier stage than these nasty people who are later going to cheat, con, harm the child. This way the adult imagines that the child is prepared for the damage that is going to be inflicted because the damage has already been inflicted before by the parent!

This system is a little like emotional inoculation — preparing the emotional center by embattling it. The method may work for infectious diseases (though this too is still uncertain) but it certainly does not work for the emotional center.

The other word for vulnerable is sensitive. The meaning of sensitive is to be aware, not blind. Desensitized people or tough cookies are therefore, by definition, blind. Actually they may also be deaf and dumb too, depending on how thorough the early parental conditioning was. Another word for this condition is "thick-skinned." There are still many people alive today who believe that

AFFECTION

"The body is affected by everything that is happening around you; it is not separate from what is happening around you. Whatever is happening there, is also happening here — there is only the physical response. This is affection."

U.G.Krishnamurti

We don't normally think of affection in this way. Affection to the adult world is something to do with care and love of someone else or care for ourselves. But the real meaning of affection is *being connected with*.

If we consider the presence of ourselves in our world, our environment, as something completely connected — i.e. that we are part of existence, then we are affected by everything. It is only the strength of the mind and our determination to be separate that disconnects us — we are therefore not affectionate about our environment, for if we were there would not be any pollution or war or any of the other crazy things that mankind has done to his planet for we would feel about our environment the same way as we feel about our children.

Just a passing thought — children are affectionate towards everything around them — they concentrate upon every single item because they love every single item in the purest sense of the word — they are affected and therefore affectionate. This is their deepest form of communication.

HIDDEN NATURE GAME – FEELING THE WEATHER

If you are caught out in a storm without an umbrella or raincoat, you feel the weather — you get soaked and you feel wet and cold — this is what we might normally call "feeling the weather." If you lie on the beach in the summer and allow your body to be burned by the sun then you feel the weather as you lie in bed groaning that night.

Again, this is how we normally interpret the concept of contact with our climate — i.e. we are here and the sun and rain are there — somewhere above us, descending on us.

But this is not the way we mean "feeling the weather" in this game.

It is also not relevant to the game that we look upon weather as separate items such as rainy, wet, dull, sunny, snowy or mild — in the way that the weather men tell us on TV. We know one thing for sure — the weather men always get it wrong anyway! So what do they know about our climate?

Climate is like emotions, in fact climate is the emotions of the planet, constantly flowing and changing through all kinds of combinations and feelings. The weather may be dull but within that dullness there is something astonishingly beautiful that we miss because we are so involved in the

depression of it. Here is Mother Earth dark and mysterious, frowning down upon her body from the roof, like a traveler on the astral plain viewing herself as a ghostly presence.

For the purposes of this game any kind of weather will do. Make sure that there is a child in the house when you begin the first sample of feeling the weather because a child will guide you more easily than another adult. If you take the game outside, as will be suggested, go with a child and the playfulness will come more easily.

THE RAINBOW

Perhaps the rarest type of weather, the rainbow,
is a perfect start for it does not exist without you
being there

If you see a rainbow from your window or while outside driving, leave the house or car and walk towards the rainbow. If you can, while walking, change your position in relation to the rainbow — walk to the west or east, north or south in relation to the rainbow and keep going towards it but keep moving from one side to the other and always with your eyes on the rainbow. Notice what effect this has on your viewpoint. Does the rainbow change its position? No, it does not, it remains in exactly the same spot, coming from the other side of a hill or from the horizon or from a cloud, curving across and down to the same spot, regardless of how far you go one way or the other and regardless of how close or far you are from it. In effect, your position, your observation point is not relevant to the rainbow — it doesn't care where you are and even if there are fifty other people in fifty different locations around the rainbow it will still look as though it is in the exact same spot. There are, of course, very simple reasons for this — that the rainbow is made from tiny drops of water that reflect the sun's light rays and therefore they form the same image from all angles — there is actually no rainbow there at all, only water and light which reflects through the observer's vision and forms a shape in the brain. Without you, there would not be a rainbow!!

It follows then that we can begin to feel the rainbow because it is actually inside our heads!

Watch the rainbow together with a child and both or all of you keep your eyes open without blinking for as long a time as you can until they begin to water a little — then close them and remember the appearance of the rainbow — its colors, its shape, the feeling that it evokes inside you.

Hold the rainbow inside you, not only in your head but throughout your whole body — feel its presence inside you for you are making the rainbow — it is *your* rainbow alone. Make it your own and feel what it is to you.

Become the rainbow.

THE STORM

Storms are perhaps the most dramatic forms of weather, for they encompass many emotions and changes in nature, therefore in us.

The storm is rain, wind, cold, heat, power, fear, anger, light and darkness and thus provides a great chance to feel the weather.

When next there is a storm around your house turn off all the lights inside the house and open some windows, allow the storm to enter your home as though it were a welcome guest.

Sit with a child or children somewhere in one of the darkened or daylight rooms. You are going to sample the storm with each of your senses in turn, starting with your hearing. With your eyes

creates ripples and movements. Use your sense of sight to its maximum without paying attention to the other senses.

Keep in tune, during this game, with the child also, doing the same things as she or he.

The most dramatic part of this game involves you and your family getting into a bit of a mess! In order to feel the storm fully, with all your senses together and in order to get in touch with the feelings that the storm invokes in you, you need to go out there and get thoroughly stormed!

Of course, if you live in an apartment in the middle of town this may seem a bit difficult, not to say embarrassing, but really it is nothing more than if you were to get caught in a storm on your way home from work.

Go outside without an umbrella and without a raincoat. For once don't worry about how wet you are going to get, about how much of a cold you will suffer from or how you will "catch your death" as my grandmother use to say. These are all tricks of the mind to keep you separated from your surroundings and out of touch with reality. Take a risk — even if you do catch a cold it will have been worth it.

Find a space somewhere where you can dance or jump up and down to keep warm and to stop yourself from feeling a fool just standing there in the storm. Follow the child with you — children love dancing and shouting in the wind and rain. It is a great experience and immediately gives a sense of freedom because by rejoicing in the storm you become part of it. Watch the children and do like they do, completely and without reserve. No matter if people look — they are probably feeling envious anyway because they are too serious and adult to have fun in the rain. If there is strong forked lightning stay away from the trees as they do not welcome human contact during storms, there is already too much going on for them!

Once you have had enough, go home, back into the house and close the windows and doors. Take off all your wet clothes, shower or bath and rub yourself and the children vigorously with a thick dry towel. The storm is still inside you and you will feel great energy and pleasure.

closed listen to the sounds of the storm. Listen to the wind blowing and listen to the leaves rustling and the trees moving. Listen to the sounds of the windows banging or the distant sounds of the wind. Then, after separating each sound in turn, allow all the sounds to merge into one sound — the sound of "storm."

Now, keeping your eyes still shut, forget about the sounds and concentrate on the smells. Smell the rain and the wind as it moves outside and inside. Realize that the storm is entering you through your nostrils, coming into your body and filling you up with smells. Feel the smells.

Next, open your eyes and look at the storm. Notice the way the rain falls and how it moves in the gusts of the wind. See how the trees are affected and the grass. See how the rain on the ground

SNOW

Snow is one kind of weather we are all quite familiar with the feeling of. We associate Christmas and staying at home and gifts with the snow and we readily enjoy the frolicking of children in the snow and the good feelings that gives us. But still, as serious and mature adults we tend to imagine that we cannot follow the child's example. We do not throw snowballs unless we get caught in a game by chance. We do not generally build snowmen (perhaps I should say snow-persons) because — "there is no time," or "it's too cold" or some other excuse.

But actually, if we allow it and learn by our children's example, there is more to snow than we might realize.

The cold of snowfall weather is a very sharp cold and produces energy in the body that does not come from other kinds of cold weather.

This cold is a crystallized cold and one that makes the body jump with energy. Children feel this immediately which is why they become excited when the snow begins to fall. They want to get out there and play around. Adults forget this feeling because they have become so much bound up in caution that the pleasure of the body's reaction to snow disappears.

In addition snowfalls bring more positive ions to the air — make the air sharper and cleaner, somehow more pleasant to breathe so that snow is like something to clean the air. If you live in Switzerland as I do, you notice the difference in the air from the air in other countries. Switzerland has a lot of snow all the time on the mountains and so this crystallized air is always present. It may be one reason why the Swiss are so ordered and efficient, because the air is ordered and efficient and healthy there!

So, to feel the snowy weather, all you have to do is get into the snow with children — play with the snow until your hands have had a chance to warm up and you don't feel the cold any more. Build a snow-person, in the shape you like — perhaps a sexy woman or a handsome man — make your own sculpture and follow the children's games. Play them yourself.

There is another aspect of snow also — the indoor aspect. Snow makes home more comforting, more secure. Staying indoors is great when it has snowed deeply. You even have the excuse that you cannot go anywhere because the snow has made it too difficult to travel. We are constantly looking for excuses not to do the things we have to do and snow is one of the best excuses. So feel the weather by staying indoors doing simple ordinary things like baking bread or cakes with the children in the house.

CLOUDY WEATHER

There are two kinds of cloudy weather – there is white cloud and there is dark cloud, but in essence they are the same, for our purposes because it is the clouds themselves that we are interested in.

Choose a cloudy day and take the kids in the car out of town into the country. Find a hill, for in this part of the weather game we are going to follow a Tibetan meditation.

Go to the top of the hill and sit down in a meditation position. It does not need to be strict, just comfortable with the legs crossed loosely. Now watch the clouds as they pass by. Watch them with your full concentration and consider the followings questions:

Where do clouds come from?

Where do they go?

How do they evolve?

And how do they dissolve?

These are not geographical questions, or meteorological questions. You do not need to go into the details of condensed rain and all that scientific stuff. Those are reasons, they are not feelings and for this game we are only interested in the feelings of the clouds.

Clouds are a complete mystery — they are mysterious things for they have no purpose, no direction except where the wind takes them. They are not concerned about aim or arrival, they simply drift and as such form a perfect opposite of us adult humans. We always have an aim, a direction and a reason for everything.

So today, become a cloud and simply drift. If you allow this to happen for a period of time each day or at weekends you will find that you merge with the cloud and lose your separation from life. And as you become un-separate so a new door opens and the mundane, everyday world disappears: the world of division and dualism, of question and answer. And the new door opens onto a world of mystery and oneness where there are no boundaries. Try it, you will be surprised at the change in you. You can also use this game/meditation as a method of combating the depression which sometimes results from dark cloudy days.

A NATURAL CONSPIRACY

Before Alexander Fleming stumbled on penicillin there were no cures for many sicknesses and diseases. The discovery supposedly happened purely by chance — or did it?

Remember times when you have lost something, something very precious, and you have a feeling that it is somewhere, somewhere you did not think of, in other words, your brain did not search through memories to find the item, but somehow and seemingly from nowhere, the feeling came that you knew where it was. You go there and it is waiting for you to find it.

How about if this was the way that penicillin was discovered? That Fleming felt unconsciously that a cure was badly needed for sicknesses that were causing great sadness and suffering and it was time that these sicknesses were banished. How about if he felt the presence of penicillin in the bowl of algae, even though he was not consciously aware of it? How about if nature was conspiring, equally unconsciously, with him to make this finding? And together they found it lying there waiting for them.

Penicillin could be like the rainbow. Without moisture, the sun and an observer there is no rainbow. Without a culture, a particular mold and a discoverer there was no penicillin. It did not exist until a conspiracy was made between Fleming and his surroundings so that it could emerge into that existence.

Hidden Nature consists of all the things we have not yet invited into our existence — into our usable presence. Hidden nature contains all the things that we have not yet observed: in other words these things do not yet exist in relation to us.

If we look closely at the word exist we soon realize that it is a word used to imply those things that are: those things that have our attention in the surrounding universe. We need to know about them before we agree that they should be in our exist-ence. But hidden nature has a thousand and one other things — minus things that we have not conspired with her to observe and therefore bring alongside the rainbow and the penicillin. These minus things are somehow waiting there in some minus dimension for us to stumble upon them and we will not stumble upon them until exactly the moment that we most need them.

If we try to find them they will simply refuse to be seen. If we desperately force ourselves to be the way we think they wish us to be in order for us to find them, they will disappear to minus minus. So how can we make this partnership agreement with Hidden Nature in order that she will reveal a cure for cancer or for AIDS or give us an enlightened view of the world around us or simply allow us to communicate on a more subtle level, as do children?

It is not that we should keep away from Hidden Nature, not that we should consciously avoid investigation, it is more that we need to learn how to work in harmony with the form or field that gives us the things we need.

And it is in childhood that this ability is inherent.

OUTSIDE AND IN

Here we must get into imagining again! Consider that you are a cave man! — Just for a few moments imagine that instead of going to the supermarket or the local store to buy the foods you will prepare for the day, you actually have to go out and kill it! There are quite a few people in the rural areas of many countries who still do this but the majority of us don't have to anymore. But for now, just imagine that everyday you or your husband/wife had to tramp out into the wilderness or the forest around your home and kill dinner. This would be survival. We don't have to survive like we used to. Or do we? What about the traffic in the main high street. What about the robbers and muggers down town? What about the job, the stresses, the problems of paying the mortgage, the school bullies, the nasty games people play in everyday life? We have to survive all this. So we still have the instinct to survive but we are using it in a totally different way — a much more stressful way.

The man or woman who went out and killed a deer for food knew the land, knew the places deer moved in, knew the sounds of the animals in the forest, the way of the weather and the way the land would respond to it. The rush of adrenalin through the body was connected with the hunt, a basic, primeval urge that had been planted in man from the very first, through necessity.

That same urge is there today. When a child is born she already contains all the basic primeval urges, the urge to walk, the ability to swim, the power to express. Sure she needs protecting for there may be predators in the area — hyenas, eagles, unfeeling doctors! But fundamentally she is fully equipped with absolutely everything she needs to survive. If allowed to grow in a completely wild environment with parents that are in touch with the land, with their sister nature, this child would find her own way and live to adulthood happily.

But in our modern social environment the same instincts, powers, the same adrenalin and energy are put to use in a different way — a way that has nothing to do with nature, with hunting;

The outer world is what we give one another and our children — with plenty of games, training and exercises to teach the child that this is what it is all about out there — but not very much in the way of training, games or exercises on what it is like inside.

We do not give our children any balance.

It is a bit like sitting a small child with only short legs on a see-saw — plonking him at one end with no one on the other and saying, "go ahead, see-saw." The child is forced to push the see-saw up and down continuously without the pleasure or relaxation of being balanced by someone else his own size and shape who can take a partnership in the game, his inside partner. It's all push and no pull.

"All work and no play makes Jack a dull boy." The original meaning of this proverb was not applied to work as we see it today. The work in question was the process of dealing with the world, the idea that we *have* to live; and that that *having* to is the work while the play is the other part — the part·in which we recover. The silent stillness which brings back what has been taken out.

"Going inside" does not need teaching, does not take any time and has nothing whatever to do with meditation classes — exactly the opposite in fact. The golden light of a child will not shine unless it is allowed to break through. And it is not that anything needs to be done, it is that we must find ways of allowing the child to be herself, to discover the inner light that she has, a light which is her own and no one else's.

And it is this inner light which when allowed to shine through becomes the outer sensuality and contact with the world which we discourage in our prejudices and fears of, for example sexual understanding, for sexuality is one of nature's most powerful forms of communication with existence.

nothing to do with being in touch with anything. The adrenalin pumps maybe every ten minutes or more when we are in a street environment — the cars, the police, the people — life is one big running tyrannosaurus rex rushing at us all day long.

The result is that we become exhausted, drained, overpowered, without remedy and without understanding because we are relating to a foreign world all the time using intimate capabilities that were not designed for such outside activities. We haven't adapted to the new world we have so happily and unwittingly created around us.

BODY TALK

Sexuality is also perhaps the most delicate of all the areas of child communication and there are two anomalies to start us off:

1. **That a child matures into areas of life that are normally considered to be the exclusive realms of adulthood, much earlier than has hitherto been suggested and**

2. **That a child remains a child in other ways for far longer than we normally consider to be the case.**

These two factors are what might be called interconnecting anomalies and their existence in duality is still more interesting than their separate existence.

It is suggested that puberty, an area of childhood which troubles and fascinates adults, begins very much earlier than we adults have ever considered it should, from around the age of eight years. For adults this is a gritty problem because when a child enters puberty in the form seen by adults, he/she enters sexual awareness (in the form that we adults imagine it to be) and therefore:

1. **The child needs to be taught how it all works and**

2. **May start doing things that embarrass adults or**

3. **...things that cause pregnancy....!**

If adults were perhaps more aware of the child's true state of sexual understanding — that in fact the child has been in a state of sexual presence since he or she was a few weeks old — the whole situation might be different. Puberty would not contain the same amount of power because the subject of sexuality would be familiar by the puberty age. Additionally, relating to a child of three in terms of sexual feelings is altogether different from relating to a child of ten or more. Sexuality is nothing more, for a child, than a method of communicating with the world and with those in the child's environment. It is we adults who convert it and them into something frightening and awesome, and we do it in the strangest ways, effectively bastardizing something extraordinarily magical into a nightmare of trappings, cautions and pornography. And this protective instinct which is not at all an instinct but a perversion, manifests itself not only in the direction of sexual growth but all areas of growth.

The greater part of teen-age and adolescent problems occur, not because of the perpetual reactions of parents during these difficult times but because of the perpetual reactions of parents throughout the child's life, and especially in the earliest years.

What we are trying to explore is a new way of looking at the child/parent relationship from square one — the beginning of the child's life. And through this new way of living, the problems which we otherwise encounter during adolescence can literally disappear.

If we look closely at child sexuality without our normal prejudices we may begin to see how extraordinary and beautiful an aspect of childhood it is. We may also see what it entails for the child and what it means for the adult. The most important aspect of the subject is that knowledge of the way life really is in this realm can bring the child and adult together in the most intimate, happy and lasting way.

Love energy is provided by nature so that people can be close to one another. The relationship may be between lovers, in which case the energy takes a certain form and results in sexual inter-course. Or the relationship may be between parent and child or brother and sister, in which case the energy is much softer and results in care, love and intimacy, but it is the same energy and it comes from the same people. Nature provides her multi-dimensional devices for many different reasons. Our dependence on and conditioning by social attitudes brings us to the false conclusion that sexual energy is somehow to be avoided or repressed, whereas it is the most natural form of contact available in all relationships. This first aspect of childishness is perhaps the most important one.

Before getting into the practical examples of a child's sensual awareness, perhaps we may first look at some of the scientific information available today.

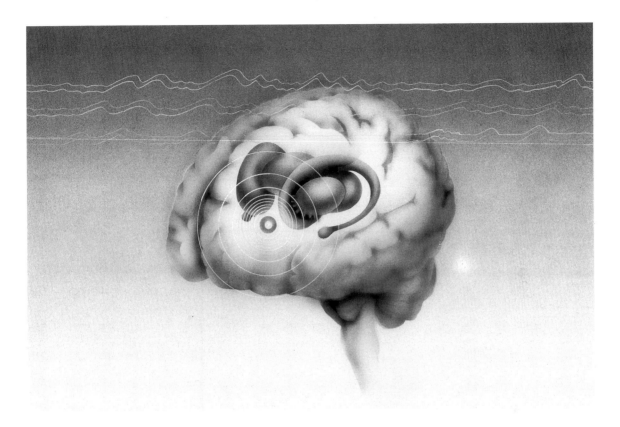

SOFT FACTS

The human brain is intimately involved with sexual emotions and with sexuality itself. Sexual activity occurs due to events which touch the sense organs or the hypothalamus, the tiny "ductless gland" found in the between-brain region.

If we remember the discussion regarding the ductless glands in Chapter One, these glands receive information from the outside world (or universe) and act as a radio station, interpreting the signals and then ordering the response through hormonal activity. Such responses are genetically programmed and exist in all humans naturally. In other words, they do not need, initially, to be told what to do — they know already, from birth. Effectively, and at a primary level, this means that the newborn

child "knows" that he is a boy or that she is a girl. Certain hormonal stimuli during very early life will dictate the sexual behavior of the child throughout the rest of his or her life. For example, an excess amount of female hormones, if introduced into a male child, will adapt that child into greater female behavior than normal for the balance of his life.

And there is more to it than this. Certain hormones have direct responsibilities. For example female hormones have the ability to reduce the level in the brain of chemicals named "monoamine oxidase inhibitors." People with low levels of these substances are highly arousable. This is said to explain why women are held to be more easily frightened, stressed or otherwise aroused than men. This also apparently accounts for the fact that shortly before menstruation a woman is more susceptible to emotional upset, because a greater amount of hormonal activity is hitting the brain.

But adult studies of "sex" in the human child generally seem to stop short at the difference between male and female-ness.

The hormonal activity in the body is responsible for defining the sex of the child — male or female. This is clear.

But these same hormones, directed by the incoming stimulation into the ductless glands, fix the behavior of the small child for life, not only in terms of whether he or she is going to be more macho or more womanly, but also on a much subtler level — indeed in the levels which relate to the combination of sexuality and love. We are not concerned here so much with the major ways in which a child can be damaged, for example, that a male child can become prone to homosexual behavior through the early stimulation of excessive female hormones, or that a female child will become manly in behavior later in life because of too little female hormonal activity. These matters have been covered by various scientific and medical studies.

But what is less clear in modern published works is the presence of an awareness of child sexuality in relation to love.

As adults we are prone to separate sex and love. We tend to think in terms of passing sexual behavior having little or nothing to do with love and love being something that develops later in life through a bonding relationship with lasting sexual partnering.

If sexual behavior in men or women is *always* accompanied with love, the energy exchanged and accepted is going to create a far greater satisfaction and happiness than if love is not present in the exchange. And love in this context, indeed in all contexts, is not some soupy, soppy, syrupy, goo-goo thing. It is not the absence of anger, hate and all the other attendant emotions. It is much more wondrous than that.

Love is two things — perhaps the two most extraordinary and difficult things in life — allowing and honesty.

Allowing indicates a willingness to provide the space for an individual to be what she or he is and not to spend an ounce of energy on trying to make that person something that she is not. This trick is very hard because the first, normal and human reaction is to try to figure out what the person is so that we can allow her to be that! But in allowing others to grow through their own way we don't need to know what they are, for knowing what they are is impossible. We cannot know what another person is, we can only know how we see that person, and we see her through our own eyes which are already so filtered and conditioned by our own life and background that in effect all we see is a mirror of ourselves. The method derived from this mirroring is to try to manipulate the faults of the other that most irritate us. This, in fact, is a manipulation of our own faults projected on the other.

And honesty, the other part of our definition of loving, is not not-lying. It is something much deeper. Lying is not a big deal. All children lie much of the time, usually because they are so invaded by the parents and other adults that lying is the only way the child can find some peace and privacy. Many parents are totally freaked-out by a child's lying because it makes the parent feel insecure — out of control. How can you control a child if you don't know what he is doing — thinking?

This process can be seen in extremes, for example when children go somewhere and sit alone silently doing nothing. The parent becomes paranoid at the silence and the absence of the child and will call the child and push her constantly to be doing something so that the sense of uncertainty disappears. It is no wonder children often wish to leave home young — simply to get away from the constant interference in their peace and quiet.

The new child — our wonder child — is for sure far more silent and meditative than our generation was ever allowed to be and this silence is part of the greatest wonder the child can ever enjoy.

So dis-honesty in its true sense is not the protection of lying, it is an awareness of emotional feelings and the manifest output of those feelings.

Let's take a practical example. Babies cry a lot sometimes and this sound can often cause discomfort to the mother or father. Parents often feel guilty about their true responses to the noise of a baby crying and therefore approach the child completely dis-honestly, perhaps taking up the child with all kinds of gurgles and reassurances while feeling angry with the child for having been woken up in the middle of the night. The eyes of the parent will therefore show one response while the actions another. In this situation the parent's eyes lie.

The tiniest of children are aware of this lying. They feel the mother's response of anger, literally in the vibrations of the body, in the heat of the hands, and especially in the eyes which always give away everything. It is not that the child thinks — "Ooh she's angry with me" for he has far more subtle responses inside that will trigger the knowledge of the anger.

Now there is nothing whatever wrong with anger but there is something ridiculous and damaging about the suppression of it. The mother's "oochie-coo" words accompanied by the anger in her eyes will cause a confusion in the child which will lay down a response mechanism for all time. The child will thus learn the same trick and pass it on to her child, as has been the case from time immemorial, and in the meantime, during her whole life, she will operate everything from this dishonest position. Many of the later-life emotional responses will derive from this early confusion, but the adult who has learned them will have forgotten why they were learnt and will therefore have little chance of changing the automatic response.

There is no need to lie to children — a good honest yell of anger may produce an alarmed reaction, but the child will know always that he is getting the real thing and that he too can do the real thing. So, allowing and honesty.

This ability combined with sexual responses produces such beauty and such fulfillment that if a parent or parents can provide it there is almost nothing more to be done in the up-bringing of a child. Where love is present all children become wonder children.

CHILD SEXUALITY

The following is a quote from T.G.R. Bower's "A Primer of Infant Development" — it is somewhat typical of the modern attitude towards child sexuality. It refers to pleasure-seeking activities in very small babies. "The adjective libidinal comes from the noun libido, which has a complex technical meaning. (Erik) Erikson defines it as pleasure-seeking urges, which are not sexual at this stage."

The statement passes without obvious importance in the book but if we look more closely it epitomizes the adult and especially expert attitude towards child sexuality. The word libido is very simple, it means "psychic drive or energy, especially that associated with sexual energy" — but the author passes it off rather like an embarrassed father faced by awkward questions from a child, as something technical and complex. And the latter part of the statement simply denies that a young baby could have pleasure-seeking urges that are sexual. How can physical pleasure-seeking urges *not* be sexual?

The problem lies in the fact that we adults associate sexuality with the sexual act and of course babies don't make love!

In the 20th century we do not literally put our children in swaddling bands, not literally, but metaphorically and emotionally we still do.

At around the age of four or five most children begin to display sexual awareness, that is, adults become aware of it. Actually sexual awareness, or more precisely, sexual energy, is flowing within a child's body from birth, though at that time in life it is less apparent and, as far as adult awareness of it, it will take the form of genital touching only. In the text books on child upbringing and even in the more sophisticated publications barely any mention is made of this subject. Adults find it very hard to understand that sexual energy exists in very young children because this produces so many conflicting feelings and questions so many accepted values that they prefer simply to leave the subject somewhere well out of reach. The awareness within a child of sexual energy can take many forms. The slightly older child may enjoy displaying his stomach or backside or genitals to visitors or friends or other children. The child may spend time rubbing the naked stomach on the cool tiled floor, perhaps with a slightly embarrassed or doubtful smile on the face!

Very often parents find this whole experience extremely difficult to handle, as it touches upon their own sexual inadequacies and doubts which may have been hidden for years or which may happen to coincide with sexual problems they are having within their own relationship. It is an unerring truth that with close and intimate family units the various members of the group are in close touch with one another's feelings and/or problems. Some parents, of course, do not see the matter as a problem — they simply sweep it under the carpet as quickly as possible, not even wishing to look at it at all. The result will be the same — the gradual relegation of the child's freedom of sensual expression to a similar dusty location.

The problem is, of course, made worse if other children, coming in from other families as friends, are involved in the child's sexual experiments. Very likely the parents of the other child will not be any more open to the situation than you are — perhaps much less so. This raises problems of talking neighbors or prejudicial attitudes which bring fears of rejection within a local group.

The method outlined in this section can be applied first to the needs of your own child who comes inevitably and rightly first in any situation, but secondly to a situation involving other children.

From a physiological/psychological viewpoint the process in children of body-interest is very easy to understand. First, the child is interested in his own body. As the process of fixing the bodily shape is happening so the feelings and sensations of that body become apparent. It is a natural pro-

gress, from all the parts of the body, toe to head. The genitals and their responses to touch are part of that new discovery. Once the child has begun to explore his or her own body, the next step will be the beginnings of interest in other bodies that are similar: boys in other boy's bodies and girls in other girl's bodies. It is like a mirror, looking to see whether the others of the same sex are actually the same and comparing the responses for confirmation that "I am normal." We adults do the same, both in sexual matters and in other things such as comparisons of emotional response and attitude. The whole business of gossip is based on this comparing activity.

After the child has grown through realization that others of the same sex are actually the same, then the next step will naturally be to explore the other sex — to look at the opposites. This entire process will occur from approximately the age of four to six years until the early teens when the child enters open sexual awareness.

It should be remembered first and foremost that in the case of a very young child there are no attitudes towards sexual or sensual behavior — a child only feels. There is no conceptualization behind or around the feelings, they are simply there. The child can therefore be made to feel bad about the feelings or good — the choice is very simple and almost totally in the hands of the adults in the child's life.

The resulting feeling of the child, good or bad, will inevitably influence the sexual behavior of that child for the rest of his or her life. This you can be sure of. Another matter which may affect the method to be adopted by a parent or both parents is the believed difference between the sexual attitude of a "social man" and that of a "social woman." Insofar as sexual behavior is concerned, men and women are believed to be different, and this idea of difference generally leads us into misapprehensions about ourselves.

So before embarking on the practical methods we can briefly look at adult sexuality.

GROWN-UP SEXUALITY

The social or cultural conditioning that we have imposed on our sexual behavior generally relates sexuality to the mind genitals. Or, in other words, grown-up sex is a very serious matter indeed; there is rarely any playtime in adult sex. The story begins in the earliest childhood years when mother sees the child displaying sexual or sensual behavior and says "don't do that dear, it's dirty."

Even before the child is old enough to understand verbal commands, he is playing with his or her genitals and finding an innocent pleasure in doing so which contains no element of guilt. The mother's insistent removal of the child's hands from that area of the body and the inevitable look in her eyes, will be picked up by the child and will represent a tacit order — a form of censorship — which will shock the child and produce fear connected with this simple and natural pleasure. At that very moment the child's receptive brain will encounter guilt. It is from this moment that the child begins his or her training in the ways of adult sexual behavior. In this respect the training is the same for a female or male child. In adulthood both men and women appreciate the same varieties of sexual response — both are capable of interest in pornography, casual relationships and all other responses that are derived from the entering of the mind into sexual activity. And it is these mental responses that also produce so much unhappiness in the adult world of relationships.

If parents wish to allow their children the freedom to maintain a flow of energy within and outside the body which will allow the heart to have dominance in sexual matters, then the time to begin is when the child is a few months old and shows sensual pleasure in the existence of his or her body.

At such a time it is possible, with sensitivity and the natural care that comes with parenthood, to provide the freedom needed by a child which can result in a much more glowing future than that normally given with sexual prejudice and anxiety.

Sex has been called the original sin — it is neither original nor sin! The tides and turns of social attitude towards sexuality are of no consequence to a child, but the imposition of these prejudices and ideas are of considerable consequence to the next generation.

METHOD

First thing — when you notice your child has become interested in his or her genitals and plays gently, allow it. There is no need to encourage, of course, no need to make a big deal out of it. Simply do not prevent the child from touching. Nothing terrible will happen — the child will not suddenly become voraciously interested in other babies!! Even if the child appears to have orgasmic pleasure from such stimulation this is not the same as adult orgasm and does not contain any of the perhaps alarming physical responses which occur in adult sexual behavior. The child's innocent pleasure will gently subside and is not likely in any way to become something unhappy if allowed to take its natural course.

In giving this very delicate and simple space to your child, presuming that you continue a similar attitude during the rest of the child's life, you have provided a greater reward for yourself in the child's later life than you can possibly imagine.

And this brings us back to the very beginning of this chapter — in which we spoke of the later life of the child and how this can be made happier if the earliest part of that life is allowed and communicated with honesty.

In adolescence the main problem for a child is confusion. The emotions are immensely strong and constantly changing. They are too strong to

be controlled and too many to be counted. And truthfully there is no need to count them, there is only a need for honesty and allowing the child to go through whatever he or she needs to experience in order to gain some perspective on their personal growth. If the adult has spent the early years practicing these love methods, there is no reason why he or she should not be pretty good at it by the time the child is in the most difficult emotional stage of life.

And also with the aspect of love and sexuality safely combined in the understanding and conditioning of the child, relationships will be a lot more fun.

GROWING SEXUALITY

And speaking of relationships, of course, the process of relating for the child will continue as an increasing and powerful influence in life. And the emphasis here is in the difference between "relationships" and "relating".

But here we enter potentially murky waters because when all is said and done, even if the child is given the maximum amount of loving and guided space to develop within, the mirrors that stand around him or her will inevitably influence the way the child believes the world can be.

We, the adults, display our own relationships to the child and the child takes them to be "the way it's done", so to speak. And, as we all know, very often adult relationships can be troubled and not necessarily the best examples of the ideal form of being together. But there is a way.

And it has to do with that very fundamental difference between relationships and relating.

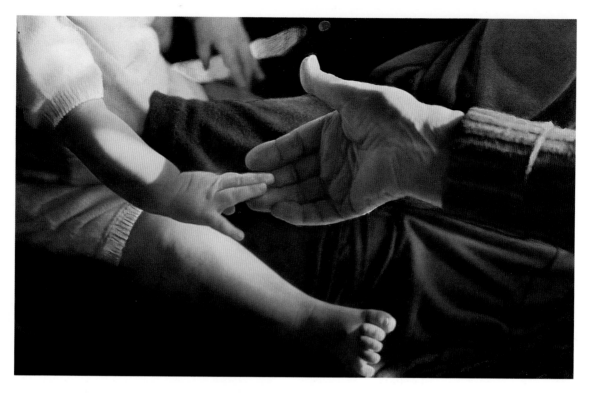

THE ART OF RELATING

We are all looking to be loved and to love someone. We seek a satisfactory relationship in our lives and hope always that it is the best we can find—true, fulfilling and lasting. This is the goal of almost everyone.

It is also the greatest source of happiness and the greatest source of pain, for very often it either does not come at all, or only fleetingly, leaving us with a deep sense of dissatisfaction, disappointment and bitterness.

We can often be so desperate to hold on to a relationship, even a bad relationship, that we will do anything in our power to stay within it, however boring, painful or unsatisfactory it may have proved to be, again and again. And the fundamental reason for this repeated and unhappy state is that we rarely learn how to relate to others, we only learn how to be in a relationship.

A relationship is something we make with one other person — exclusively — speaking now of course in terms of sexual behavior. We are taught by our parents and by society in general, that this form of sexual behavior is the best and perhaps the only reliable method of seeking happiness. And when we bump repeatedly against the blank wall of bad relationships, we wonder why, for we think that there is nothing else.

A good and happy relationship, of course, is not a problem, and those of us who have achieved such a thing need not trouble insofar as our relationships also with children will be as happy as our sexual relationship is with another adult. But where possessiveness, jealousy, domination, suspicion, doubt and exclusiveness have entered our sexual relationship, there will not be love but ugliness and this ugliness will teach our children likewise.

A bad relationship is like a concentration camp with two jailers and two prisoners, the same two. A good relationship contains friendship as well as love and passion and exclusivity. The friendship is the key to relating for friendship is probably one of the highest forms of love, alongside perhaps pure mother's love, but then mother's love also contains friendship if it is not to be possessive.

In learning, through childhood into adulthood, a growing sexuality needs to know also how to relate to people. This is not at all to say that children should be encouraged into multiple sexual relationships. With today's predominance of sexually transmitted diseases, the one-to-one relationship has grown to have greater significance and greater meaning. Relating to people is an art which, if learned by a child early in life, will provide that child with the wisdom to know when a relationship is good and lasting and when it is not. The art of relating will bring the child to an ability within a relationship which will provide so much more generosity of spirit, patience with the other, caring behavior and an allowance and honesty which will provide space for the other, that any relationship entered into will have the very best chance of success. But, equally important, the grown-up child will not be afraid to leave.

In our dealings with others, especially where sexuality is concerned, we carry a lot of fear with us — mostly in the form of insecurity. This insecurity carries through to the fear of death, in the form of the end of the relationship. We speak of the relationship being "forever" — "I will always love you, and never leave you." Such promises

turn sour and leave us bitter and unwilling to embark on a new relationship for fear that it will happen again.

There is a story, told by a woman who was unfortunate enough to be on board one of the very first aircraft to be hijacked in the 70s. The craft was Israeli and the hijackers were Arabs. The victim of this horror story was an American Jew. Not unnaturally she was terrified of what the hijackers might do to her and in that intense fear she was additionally afraid that the fear itself would cause her to go out of control and therefore make her still more vulnerable. She was afraid of being afraid.

Eventually she realized that to be afraid was completely OK — in fact wholly appropriate — so she simply allowed herself to be afraid and then the most amazing thing happened to her. Fear, at this level of human behavior can become so intense that a point is reached where the mind/body can no longer sustain it because the tension involved is simply too great. And this was the experience of our hijacked friend. She simply let the fear go and relaxed and in so doing probably increased her courage and common sense of her situation. She is still alive today to tell the story.

The action of letting go of fear is one of the most extraordinary human experiences for it creates a rush of freedom which can only be understood by doing it. There is no intellectual method of making it felt. Shortly, we will look at an experiential method, however.

In effect, letting go of fear is accepting death — accepting that, come what may, we are willing to surrender to life and this brings, even if only momentarily, the greatest joy. It can also remain with us as a lasting and life-time change. What can a hijacker do to someone who is completely surrendered?

This story may be excused as something extreme and therefore more easily achieved, but the same process applies to all life, even at its least obvious moments of fear.

During the years when E.S.T. was the fashion, a colleague of the author was in the midst of a week-end training course and after some time of undergoing the methods applied by the trainer suddenly woke up to the simplest, most fundamental truth — that everyone else in the room was more afraid of him than he was of them! Sounds a bit strange perhaps, but if we look at it closer it becomes significant.

We spend much of our lives believing that those people we connect with are going to hurt, hate, talk about, put us down.
It rarely occurs to us that they are thinking the same about us — indeed perhaps even more than we are.

"I remember lying there on the floor of the therapy room and suddenly there was this sort of flash of awareness that I did not need to be afraid of anyone, because they were all more afraid of me. In this sudden realization I knew that I could care for other people, knowing that I need not be afraid of them."

This is the same fear as the hijacked woman, just on a different level, and it is the fear that prevents us from relating with one another.

A child needs to learn how to relate to people, all people, and this means knowing how to deal with difficult people as well as easy people. The art consists of learning clarity of vision not judgment, for judgment is merely another form of fear. Adults have a habit of passing on those *Box Judgments* we spoke of at the beginning of the book — TV-lunch type statements about how stupid and bad and ignorant or beautiful and smart and good the rest of the world is. This is not clarity. Sometimes it can be fun but often it gets serious.

Children watch everything we do and given enough box judgments they will adopt them as gospel.

Try the following game:

THE END OF THE LINE

For one whole week — first thing each morning before breakfast, take a few minutes to follow this thought process.

First check out what the day has in store for you — make a quick noted list on a sheet of paper or in a diary. Write down *all* the items that you expect for the day, both good and bad. When the list is complete cross out the good things — delete them completely from the list and go back over the bad things. They might consist of having to face your boss for some mistake or having to go before the child's school teacher to hear a bad report or going to visit a relation you don't like — an examination, a bank manager — whatever. Now, out of the smaller (hopefully) list of bad things circle one that is the worst.

Now take that one event — let us say it is facing the bank manager because you have been hauled in for not reducing your overdraft — and extend it. What will happen in the bank when you get there? The worst thing that could happen? The bank manager is going to close your account. No, there has to be something worse than that — he is going to bring legal action against you immediately and you will have to go into bankruptcy. No, the bankruptcy will cause you to have to give up your home, your money, your job — everything. No, your wife will leave you totally alone. Worse — you will contract a disease because you will have to live on the streets without money or sustenance — worse — you are going to die!

Now how bad does it feel to be simply going to see the bank manager? Big fears swallow up little ones.

This method should be employed each day until it becomes a habit to do this with every fear and soon you will begin to see how easy it is to give up the small and constant fears of everyday life.

Now play the game with the child or children in your family — bring the game into relationships with people — sow the seeds of relating.

CHAPTER THREE
GROWING OUT

"I was six when I saw that everything was God, and my hair stood up, and all," Teddy said. "It was on a Sunday, I remember. My sister was only a tiny child then, and she was drinking her milk, and all of a sudden I saw that she was God and the milk was God. I mean, all she was doing was pouring God into God, if you know what I mean."

J.D. SALINGER – "TEDDY"

In the last chapter we looked at communication — the way in which children provide us adults with a chance to understand and learn from them and the way in which we adults fail to do so. The next, most natural aspect of childhood is that which gives power to communication — the emotions.

CHILD POWER AND THE HIDDEN EMOTIONS

According to most of us there are four primary emotions: fear, anger, joy and sadness. All other feelings arise from these four. If you are jealous it is because you are afraid, if you are resentful it is because you are angry, if you are depressed it is because you are both angry, afraid and maybe sad all at once. All these emotions arise from the same four primary emotions. Or so they tell us.

Important things seem to come in fours quite often — the four seasons, the four elements. Except that this begs the question — which came first, the elements or the fact that there are four of them? The emotions or the word four, summer, winter, spring and fall or the flow of the seasons which we then divided into four?

Certainly the language did not come first: the definition was created by mankind long after the world already existed for us to see, feel and otherwise experience. It was only after we decided there should be a boundary to everything that we set the words to work. And it was at that precise moment that we chopped out about ninety percent of the world from our perceptions.

To say that there are only three primary colors is to make nature into something little better than a "paint-by-numbers" game and to say that there are only four elements is to reduce the world to a compartmentalized package in which we miss nearly everything.

In this same fashion we name our and our children's emotions.

We say "I am angry," "I am jealous" and we believe that this definition somehow makes us this thing — a walking "angry."

How does a walking angry look? Is it a flaming red blob on legs? And how is a living fear? A cowering, broken patch of humanity on feet? Ridiculous of course... isn't it? But this is much the way we set up our lives — in divisions: neatly packaged parcels all tied up with string, analyzable, quantifiable, *REAL*.

But look at a small child. Just as part of this particular experiment with human nature, spend joy, to fear and rapidly back to joy again, all so fast that the words cannot even come through quickly enough to keep up with the changes. So don't try. Don't label those emotions, let them simply flow around him and around you and observe the way it feels inside you too.

You will also experience the different feelings, in and out, in and out and perhaps you might consider this — perhaps they are not different, perhaps in fact they are all one feeling which up

the next couple of days simply watching the child in your life in relation to her or his emotions. For that period of time try not to put names on the responses you observe. At first it will be hard as we are so conditioned in the way of pigeon-holing that we do it automatically. But for the moment just watch him — watch the way the expression of his emotions flows in and out: from frustration at not being able to make a toy do the thing he wants, to a quick burst of anger, to sadness, to

until now *you* have separated into convenient parcels so that you could say "Why do I feel this way" in the belief that this "why" will somehow solve the bad feelings and make them go away.

This why is the very basis of all emotional suffering. The fact that we compartmentalize our feelings and then ask why we have them is the root cause of all confusion because the mind is not equipped to answer the question why in relation to the feelings. The mind is not made to feel and the feelings are not made to think, so to try setting one up to answer the other is ridiculous — it causes, of course, a split. Questions from the mind do not produce answers, they simply produce more questions — those who need answers would do better sitting silently watching a child.

> Emotions are one continuous movement, ever changing and flowing through and around each of us and through and around the others that are close to us.

You know the feeling! A child sitting in her push pram is trying to persuade her mother to buy candy and mother is not giving — mother has her reasons — but the little girl is not interested in reasons. She *feels* really upset, she wants those candies, she doesn't think about bad teeth or sick stomach — what are candies for, if not to fill her mouth with delicious tastes and sensations? She cannot get her way though for her mummy is strongly determined that her daughter is not going to have the treatment *she* had when *she* was young when *her* mother fed her all kinds of rubbish and now look what *her* teeth are like, all falling out! So the little girl starts to scream — she's really enraged. The screaming reaches a peak of fury until mom finally can't stand it any more — all the people in this street are looking and thinking what a dreadful mother she is — easier to give in — hands over the candy bar. Wham — the child's face changes so fast that it is as though there never was a single cell in her tiny body that ever felt the slightest anger. She's happy — her face lights up with joy and her mouth is already covered in chocolate smudges.

But now mother is angry instead because her resolve to *make* that child do as she should did not work. Her determination not to have a daughter who has bad teeth and who also "gets her own way too much" has not panned out. She has failed as a mother once again. Now *she's* angry and the stroller gets shoved along so fast that the small child drops her candy bar. "Well, serves you right for being so spoiled." The candy bar is left lying in the road and little Dora is without.

The face changes again, tears well up in the eyes, the mouth turns down, the sound coming from the mouth is no longer sharp and shrieking but whining and clear. Dora looks like she is about to die of sadness. The thing she fought so hard to get has been denied her once again. The tears pour from her eyes, the sobs come so deeply and so strongly you would not believe the extent of her pain.

Mother feels bad — guilty — what a cruel woman she is, how could she do such a thing to her own daughter — what harm, after all, could a small candy bar do? She'll make it just one a day and this can be the one.

Back up — recover the bar, not too dirty on the road. Wipe it down, hand it to Dora — wham. All good again, but not quite so much joy this time. The whole operation has taken a lot out of Dora — she's tired now and within minutes she is lying in the stroller, her hand clutching the candy bar, her head on one side, a slightly lost expression on her face — seemingly far away. What is her feeling now? Joy? She does not seem to be laughing or smiling. Sadness? There are no more tears and her expression looks immensely tranquil. Fear? No way. Anger? Not a trace of it. So what is she feeling? No name feeling? Nothing?

She must be feeling something...or maybe not.
It is at this precise moment that Dora, in her state of exhaustion from the flow of multi-colored feelings that have passed through her body, is in a state of complete meditation. She is still, resting. All of a sudden the candy bar is of no interest. There are no thoughts in her head about what she wants or what she does not have or that she hates her mum. She is still. The flow of energy in her body has moved to her center because it is time for a break. Watch her, feel her and above all do not ask why.
It does not matter why.
But what are you feeling? Peace at last, now there is time to think about what to cook for lunch, what time the next appointment is, when it is necessary to get back to the office. So much to think about, no room for our own emotions.

But before getting into the practical side of living with children's emotions and our own emotional changes, perhaps we can start by looking at the so-called primary emotions. The best one to start with is the most powerful.

FEAR

Fear is a very hard thing to look upon. We are all so engulfed in it that we cannot stand outside it enough to make a clear examination. We also apply this to a child's fear, which reflects back on our own fear like a bouncing ball going between two surfaces. Our scientists, psychologists, sociologists all look in every available direction for the reasons why we are afraid. We analyze each of our feelings in turn as we would a dot on a map while forgetting all the time that the rest of the map contains valleys and mountains and terrains we have not seen for the microscope's lens is too narrow.

Fear is a non-existential faculty — it has no borders. You cannot fill a cup with fear — it is not containable and so cannot be examined. If we try to find out why we are afraid we end up emphasizing the fear, creating complications to the fear and having more fear — more of that nothingness that hurts us so much. We can give every reason why we feel afraid — because the car almost ran us down, because the night is dark, because our boyfriend doesn't love us any more. These answers may help for a few moments but we will still be afraid — the fear will come back almost immediately.

It is a little like spending our whole lives buying things — buying cars, fancy pens, beautiful houses, summer holidays, watches — buying buying in order to fill the hole that exists within us. It doesn't help. If anything, the more we buy, the bigger the hole gets.

We should not try to fight with non-existential things — the gulf is too big for us. Instead, in a state of fear, first: be afraid! There is absolutely nothing wrong with being afraid: we can let the knees shake, sweat, feel that cold condition — be as afraid as possible! If we take note of how children respond in frightening situations — even if it is merely a scary movie or someone going "boo" in the dark — we can see that the child goes for it totally, allowing the full energy of the fear to flood the body. The adult, on the other hand, will hide the response more readily than express it for fear of looking foolish.

Perhaps the greatest problem of living in our western civilized culture is not the emotions themselves, not the fear, the anger and the anxiety, but our denial of them. We have been taught constantly not to be angry, not to be afraid.. "Don't worry," "Don't be afraid," "Don't get angry" — always don't. Imagine how it would be if people were to encourage anger —
"Come on, get angry, be really angry" or

"Why don't you get reeally scared!"

In a state of fear, if we are conscious enough to allow the fear, to feel it, there comes a moment when the consciousness is sufficient for us to detect a place inside us which is not afraid. And the more we practice seeing our own fears, the more conscious we become of this place. Eventually, with this center where fear cannot touch slowly growing and becoming more available, all fear vanishes.

But we can't all be enlightened — there must be a simpler way!

And of course there is. Going back to the empty cup — that if our cup is empty what is the point in trying to figure out the nature of its contents — why not fill the cup instead with something we can experience.

Take a practical situation.

You are eighteen years old and you have found a man that you would like to marry or live with, but your father is very possessive of you. Whenever the subject of this man comes up, your father's face becomes hard and bitter and he speaks badly of the guy the whole time. He is jealous for he is afraid of losing the young woman whom he so much loves, who so much resembles his wife when she was young, who he knows will be taken away from him by this man.

It is like a jealous lover, although of course we do not dare admit this because this would be incest, so we hide the jealousy, we hide the strong sexual feelings the father has and we pretend that the husband-to-be is merely inadequate for our daughter. Here, in this scenario, a very common one, we have fear. What can the daughter do? The father is certainly of another generation and probably the gap between his way of thinking and his daughter's is large enough that discussion and argument are useless. There are two different languages being spoken — they will get nowhere by arguing.

The fear is there — the father fears the loss of his child, the daughter fears that the father will somehow prevent her from acquiring her new lover — fathers have this power, daughters think. So the non-existential state is entered and they argue, they fight, they get nowhere, they exhaust each other and the fear brings hate. The daughter leaves the house, the father hates the husband and maybe this condition continues for years.

The other way is simpler!

The daughter has the power in fact for she is free. She is leaving, whether the father wants it or not — there is nothing he can do for even the financial support is now in the hands of the new man. The father is trapped by his fear. All the daughter needs to do is love him. Take his hand in hers, kiss his cheek more often, bring him presents, make him meals, fuss over him as much as possible. This is the end after all, the last times she will get the chance to do such things — so they should be done more often. Fill up his cup with love and care and for sure the fear will vanish.

Ultimately, fear is just one thing. If we take all the emotions, all the fears and we make of them a funnel with a point — the point being the fount of all fears, then it is the fear that we are not — the fear that we do not exist. From this one huge, all- pervading fear, arise all other fears and all other non-existential emotions. Even joy, in a way, arises from this for we feel happiest when it is confirmed to us that we *do* exist, when our ego is reinforced we feel happy and this too arises from the fear that we are not.

Here is the reason why children are not afraid, apparently, of anything around them — they will plunge their hands into a fire, jump off a cliff and grab a sharp knife — they have very little more than a bodily caution, and sometimes not even that, because they do not have the fear of not being in existence. They *are* existence, why should they be afraid? It is we adults who instill the fear — our fear.

ANGER

Anger frightens people. Other people's anger and their own anger. It is socially unacceptable to be publicly angry and so we repress it more than almost anything else in our emotional lives. We are taught to repress it from the earliest times. Parents discourage their children from anger.

In a recent study being carried out at Birmingham University in England a Dr. Patti Mazelan undertook to analyze why people get angry: the

central emphasis within the research is how to *control* anger. Such an approach shows a complete lack of human understanding. The idea that we must *control*, stop ourselves from being angry, is somewhat ridiculous. It is the same as saying that we must control our impulse to live.

If we consider normal anger, i.e. that which arises for any number of reasons in today's busy and anxious social surroundings, we must consider it as a necessary outlet of emotion. The more we learn to analyze and say why to it, the more we will learn to repress it. This in turn will lead to greater anxiety in that same society because everyone will be employing all kinds of methods to stop themselves from being angry and this again will lead back to greater individual paranoia and therefore more anger and on and on.

The repression of any emotion is a vicious circle and ultimately destroys the controller. It is that simple.

In the last line of an interview that Dr. Patti Mazelan gave to The Times in 1988, after having discussed solely the concept of control, she says:

"It takes more energy to control anger than to give in to it." Here should be the essence of any research into the matter of emotional behavior — methods of allowing people to express, not control and it is hoped that the eventual purpose of the research will have been just this.

Take a typical situation — you are at work and your boss shouts at you because you have done something wrong. You dare not be angry because you will lose your job so you keep quiet and then you feel sad, depressed because you were inactive — you didn't do anything about it. But when you get home, any little event, any tiny act against you by your husband or wife will spark off that anger and you will shout at him/her, even though the initiator of the anger was someone else.

The saddest people are those who have no one to be angry at.

Avoiding or repressing anger is very difficult and harmful — it will come up again somewhere else like a boil on the surface of the skin. But it is possible to change the body which in effect changes the anger. The Tibetans say that if you are angry you should run. Running changes the breathing and the changed breathing alters the emotional state. Anger cannot survive if the body and the breathing change.

Actually there is no need to run — simply breathe rapidly and strongly and the anger will vanish just like that. There are many people in cities such as New York who take the Tibetans' advice very seriously. Though they might not know that it is the reason why they run so much, it would seem obvious. It may also be one of the major reasons why city workers spend so much time "bustling" about, with a seeming need always to be intensely active. City dwellers are surrounded constantly by things that make them angry so running or staying physically and mentally active is an excellent method of changing the anger into something easier to handle. Here again, watch a child when she is angry. She will grow red in the face, almost as though about to burst. She will stomp up and down on the floor and throw a fit with her anger, waving her arms in the air. Her natural facility for expressing anger will then be directed in one way or another by the parents. Either she will be encouraged to "stop it" or the parent will pander to the anger and "give her her own way" and then resent it. What a child needs is neither of these things. A child needs to understand only that it is fine for her to be angry, that it does not necessarily get her what she wants but it is wholly normal. Any fears that the parent has about the child "dumping" anger on others need not be serious as if anger is freely expressible but cannot be employed as a device with any effect, the child will soon understand its effect on others in the light of the effect, or lack of effect on the parent. This does not necessarily mean that the parent should ignore the outburst or respond dishonestly — one can still love and care for an angry child — perhaps even more so.

SADNESS

Notice that during times of sadness there is mostly a tendency to be silent. When we allow ourselves to be sad there is no great desire to speak or do things. It is largely an inactive state.

Sadness is also a very deep emotion. Happiness is on the surface, very quicksilver-like and superficial, whereas sadness produces a depth of feeling that is far more profound. Of course, like anger and fear, we have been taught to suppress sadness — "don't cry," "don't be sad!" — other people tell us this because they feel sad when they see us being sad. They also want to avoid this depth, this profundity, because to be deeply sad is to be deeply within oneself and this is scary. But look at your eyes after a good cry — how crystalline and clear they look, as though they have been washed. Crying from sadness is a cleansing, it brings a clarity of sight, not only of the eyes but also an inner clarity. It clears away misconceptions and gives a depth of insight into oneself and others. So, don't avoid sadness — children don't. When they are sad they cry like hell and then it is gone and they look so beautiful and clear-eyed.

The emotional force behind sadness in adults can be instrumental in making major changes within the psyche and if we stop and look closely at the background to sadness we will find hidden motivations for these feelings that we might not suspect. I can remember a period of my own life in which sadness was often present, when almost everyday I could have cried and often did, each time wondering why. We always ask why? It was only several weeks into this strange and compelling time that I began to see something of the foundation to my feelings, for the times of sadness were spent very much in a state of silence and aloneness. It became clear that I felt somehow that I should not be sad — that my sadness was so strong that I was shadowing the beautiful things in my life and that perhaps this depth of sadness was a regret somehow that I was no longer able to be free and happy as I had been as a child.

But the truth of it was more simple. I, like so many of us, regretted the regret — denying the single beauty of deep misery and somehow pretending through my mind that this misery was a bad thing.

But misery and sadness are as much part of the beauty and glory of life as their opposites, as the flowers and the trees, the animals and the birds, for sadness too is existence.

JOY

Looking separately at these four primary emotions makes one thing clear, hopefully: that the emotions are interlinked, they are not separate at all. Anger comes from sadness, joy brings sadness, fear arises out of anger which brings fear, sadness and joy etc. And all these obvious emotions are also intermixed with hidden feelings that are impossible to define and name. In fact, we have a lot more fun with our emotions if we do like small children and just feel them without trying to put categories onto them.

Thinking about feelings is ridiculous. It is like saying the rainbow is the moisture and the sun and the observer — the rainbow is none of these things, it is the mixture of them together which makes something else completely. If you take a rose and you say to a scientist — "Look at this rose, how lovely it is and how wonderful it smells" — the scientist will take the rose and cut it up, trying to find out where the smell and the beauty comes from. Once he has cut it up it is no longer a rose. Then he wonders why he can't any longer find the essence of "rose."

First there is your being, the core of your existence; then there are feelings surrounding that being, that core; and then finally there are the thoughts which surround the feelings. Thoughts don't change anything — they are just fantasies, castles in the sky — feelings do change things, they are essential and powerful. And then beyond those feelings comes the center, the being which can be reached through the feelings, not through the thoughts.

Concentrate on your feelings, change the emphasis — don't trust the thoughts — they are always of the past or the future. The feelings can always be trusted for they come from the heart. Learn this and the first major step towards being a child and understanding a child has been taken.

This is joy!

Game - BLIND MAN'S HUFF

In order to de-intellectualize these concepts there is need of an experience which will sink the idea into a feeling

Choose a day when there is nothing much to do — a Sunday! Ask your son or daughter to stay at home and join an experiment with you. It is a kind of blind-man's buff. For at least an hour one of the parents should be blindfolded and have to feel his or her way around the house and particularly around the child. The child might be encouraged to make expressions which indicate certain feelings and ideas — for example a desire for food or love or an expression of anger. The parent should deduce the emotion or request with the hands on the face.

The next hour should be spent without hearing. The ears should be completely blocked with cotton and then covered with ear muffs or headphones so that nothing can be heard. The child might then be encouraged to express things through sign language and eye contact. In this fashion (and with other exercises in this section) the parent will begin to appreciate the child in a new way — i.e. that he is not a chip off the old block, in fact that he is totally different. There will also be a reduction of the taking-for-granted aspect of the relationship.

Game - I'M ANGRY - YOU'RE TO BLAME

Make a deal with your nearest and dearest relation, whether this be husband or wife, son or daughter of older age or close friend. The partner in this case needs not to be a young child and should be in your company for an extended period — i.e. a member of your own family.
The deal is that during the day coming that person

is going to do the things which she or he knows upset you — deliberately and without warning!

The best is that your antagonizing partner does nothing for several hours so that you have forgotten the intention and then pounces the first event on you without warning.

These events can be quite simple: leaving used toothpaste tubes in the bathroom, bumping into you from behind, making a mess in the kitchen, allowing the cat to sleep in the car or whatever most irritates the partner.

The signs for the antagonizing partner to watch out for are: once the responses reach a point where your partner is beginning to say things like — "that's enough now — a joke's a joke — stop now". This means you are getting somewhere — keep it up!

Eventually the receiving partner will get angry — at *you*. Now the experiment can really begin.

You should note your response — what do you feel? After all, this whole method was proposed by a book and you can't get angry at a book with much effect. Perhaps you wish to tear up the book and throw it away — it is, after all, to *blame* for the fight you are now having with your wife/husband.

So now, stop and regardless of how angry or guilty or upset you may feel, sit down with your partner — she/he is still your partner, even if that partnership was a fighting partnership! Sit down and run over the whole story *backwards*. Take each event like a film running in reverse and look at what happened. The result will inevitably be laughter, even if at first there is some sulking about how you took the method too seriously or how you did it too effectively and what revenge you are having on her for the last fight you had, etc. etc. Laughter will come.

The anger has evaporated into laughter — both anger and laughter derive from the same place — *you*. And the reason why the anger has evaporated is because by running through the events backwards you displaced them from your ego and understood what happened. Anger cannot survive understanding.

MIXED EMOTIONS: THE SUBTLE ART OF JEALOUSY- Who hates who?

Jealousy is perhaps the most fascinating of all our personal emotional responses — for first it does not exist! Jealousy is a another name for insecurity, which is in turn another name for fear.

Jealousy is a very complex creation. It contains cowardice, egotism, possessiveness, competitiveness and inferiority — a basket load of negative conditions and it also hurts. It hurts both the one who feels jealous and the one against whom jealousy is directed. People always say that they enjoy it when their partners are jealous but this is only when the jealousy is more light-hearted. When jealousy becomes serious it is painful and constricting.

The Masters have often stated that of all the emotions to go beyond, on the pathway to enlightenment, jealousy is the last to drop. That is because jealousy has to do with sex and of course sex is the last to drop. Knowing what jealousy is can sometimes help with its presence in a situation. Jealousy towards children is a particularly stupid and unpleasant expression. And when we see jealousy in a child we are simply witnessing a form of question. A small child who has jealousy feelings for a new brother or sister is doing nothing more than asking for attention — without perhaps knowing him or herself that this is the specific nature of the question. The parental answer is even more simple — more love.

MAKE ME GUILTY-I'LL HATE YOU- Who suffers?

Possible scenario:
Mother to father: "He's never been a bad boy, he always eats his dinner up."
Son: "But I'm not a good boy now, I have no respect for myself."
Father: "But I respect you son — because I respect a man who respects himself."

This complex double-bind situation, reported in a child-psychology journal, is designed by the parents, who are quite innocent in their method, to tie the child up in a sense of guilt that will bring him into the "normal" social state — in this case, of doing what his mother wants whether *he* wants to or not!

The resulting guilt — i.e. that mum cooked the food with such care, that dad worked so hard to earn the money to buy the food, that sister eats all hers up etc. etc., will create such a complex anxiety in the child that he/she will always remember it.

The memory may not be of the event itself because probably such events are constantly present in one form or another, but the sense of guilt and anxiety will remain imprinted on the child for all his life. The result of such constant events in the life of a child will be, and this is guaranteed, hatred of the parents. This hatred will emerge at some point or another — probably shortly before his mid-teens as he works up his courage to leave the family home.

Creating guilt in children is the same and no less than committing physical violence against them.

DOUBT AND CERTAINTY

Did you ever see a child doubt — children don't care for doubt — they simply do. Adults have built much around the concept of doubt — they call it modesty, uncertainty, indecision — it can be either a good thing or a bad thing, depending on what is desired to be achieved from it. But you can be sure that it's a fake. It's a trip, a trick of the ego. There is no need for doubt.

Equally there is no need for certainty, for certainty is merely the opposite of the doubt — i.e. it can be confidence or arrogance depending on who is looking! Another ego trip.

We adults have a tremendously hard time with doubt and certainty — it is a constant hazard, particularly in the presence of children and it is one of the greatest reasons why we prevent children from doing the things that they would otherwise naturally do. All the way from stopping the child from touching himself in pleasure-seeking activities as babies, right up to the teen-age years when we continuously instruct the growing child not to come home too late from parties. All this arises out of our own views of how the world "should" be, having nothing whatever to do with allowing the child to form his own views.

Joseph Chilton Pearce, in his book *Magical Child* says:

"If the child's security with parents is un-questioned, then his concern over survival will never become an issue. The child is designed to enter into experience freely, without pre-judgment, and evaluate that experience after it takes place. Concern over survival, safety, or well-being immediately forces an evaluation of experience before the ex-perience can take place. Such concern immediately fires into effect some form of flight-fight arousal, which then screens all present and potential for its flight-fight value (its potential for the child's harm or well-being). This ties intelligence into a decision based on the value of the experience. There is then no unquestioned acceptance of the given, which is the hallmark of the whole child. Anxiety over survival causes a screening of information through the question: Am I safe? The bonded child does not formulate this question. The bonded child asks only, Where am I?, and moves to interact accordingly."

It is the phobia of the parent that directs the child away from experience and it is the adult doubting-ness that creates the vicarious attitude of the child. The experiential ability of the child becomes curtailed through training and the amount of potential life-experience, both "good" and "bad," available to the child is re-directed towards the avoidance of anxiety instead of the confronting of life.

Once again, the simplest method is to play: GAME — I TORT I TOR A PUDDY-CAT. The original cartoon story of the cat and the "tweedy-bird" had the lines in it — "I tort I tor a puddy-cat a-creepin up on me — I did I tor a puddy cat as mean as mean can be." The basis of this cartoon tale was death. The bird sat in his cage and the cat tried to kill the bird and presumably toss him about for half an hour before eating him bones and all. Anyone who has lived in the countryside and owned an outdoor cat will have shivered or screamed while such a real-life story was unfolding.

But in the cartoon story, of course, the "real-ity" of crunching bones and scattered feathers does not arise. The child sees a silly yellow pictured bird and a stupid cat quite unable to make the kill — constantly acting out the pre-death scenario and getting more smashed up than the bird, but always somehow coming back with a fresh glossy black coat.

The cartoon was created largely for children though adults get a kick out of it too.

For this game we play with death! We take a selection of experiences which could occur to our children and we make a cartoon charade out of them.

The purpose is to illustrate the difference in approach — the adult approach and the child approach. The game is OK for any age of child up to around eight years old. The available experiences around which each charade can be made are as follows — pick any one and do it in your living room with your family of friends:

1. Getting hit by a car.
2. Sticking your hand in a fire and getting burned.
3. Falling out of a tall tree.
4. Being in the hospital.
5. Dying of a fatal wound.
6. Being arrested and thrown in jail.
7. Failing an important exam and ending up a tramp in the Bowery of New York City.

8. Make up any of your own.

The bottom line of all doubts and fears is death. We are scared to death that our children will die before we do.

Allow the child to express the whole of the resulting feelings within the game and allow talk and perhaps questions to follow — the basic charade will form a guessing sequence which will perhaps then result in some searching inquiry into one of the most fundamental fears of humanity.

The adult may watch how he/she handles the charade and then how the child handles it. The child will also be watching — first how the adult handles these "real-life" experiences in the living room and second what he, the child, feels in such make-believe situations.

They should be played to the full with as much drama and determination as possible. They should also be played as fun. The purpose is not to replace the real things, for ninety-nine percent of children's lives will not confront such experiences. The purpose is to share and show the fears that the adults have and give them a chance to watch how the child is concerned only in the game itself — that the child knows how to deal with any experience that comes along — or how to avoid it.

DIS-EASY

Probably the single greatest fear of all adults concerned with the care and up-bringing of children is that the child will die or be seriously disabled by a disease. The scenario of this fear is that the disease will strike unexpectedly and over a short, or worse still, long time, the child will die a painful death, a horrible death, any kind of death. During the 1930s through to the 1950s there was a plethora of movies produced largely in America, that took advantage of this extreme fear and the sentimentality with which it can be expressed on the big screen. Any normal adult is struck hard by any suggestion that a child — any child — and especially hers or his, is dying.

There are a number of very fundamental issues involved in the examination of disease.

1. The word "disease" originates in the concept of discomfort with an additional element of psychological discomfort — the word "ease" relates both to the body and the mind. Man sees his physical malfunction as something disturbing — the body, the person, the mind is being tampered with by some outside force over which he has no control. Further, this sense of dis-ease arises, quite naturally, from the fear of death. We do not wish to die and an illness severe enough to kill us is awarded the title disease. Looking down through the history of illness we can see how diseases were allocated this title until they became curable by medicine. Small pox, consumption, gout, syphilis — all were given the title disease and then relegated to "sickness" or "malady" or simply illness, after the discovery of the cure.

2. Nature, on the other hand, *does* wish us to die. And here once more we approach the same story as in every other part of life — it's us against them — we are alone and nature is out there separate from us — somehow our enemy because SHE wishes us to die and if we somehow misbehave ourselves she will exact a terrible revenge on us by bringing a disease which will kill us or our children. There are, of course, religious connotations in this — there are still people who believe that somehow, some remote God sits in judgment over us and if we don't pray regularly or we commit adultery or some other such terrible sin, He will strike us down. As we have seen in other sections this kind of idea, which we usually strike off as primitive, is actually more of an excuse for not facing the truth of the matter — if we know that God does it all, we can shift all responsibility etc.

3. The other problem with disease relates to the availability of cure. If there is a cure in existence then the extent of fear diminishes rapidly — the disease will be cured — everything will be OK. If the disease is such as cancer or AIDS or some other incurable ailment, the fear is in direct proportion to two factors:

1. The incurability of the disease and
2. The publicity surrounding the disease.

Cancer is a horrific and unhappy disease which causes the sufferer extreme discomfort (especially if some of the modern cures are applied) and almost invariably results in death. Everyone is afraid of getting cancer and somewhat in awe of those who have it. There is no reason to hate people with cancer because they cannot pass the disease itself on to us and so there is no social disgrace or discredit attached to the disease, unless of course it is related to selfish adulthood when childbirth is permitted where a proclivity to the disease is passed on. The fear is therefore largely related to the incurability of the disease itself.

In relation to AIDS on the other hand, the factors involved which raise the level on the fear barometer also include a sexual element which simply increases the power behind the disease.

So why are these diseases seemingly so predominant in our lives? Is it:

1. Because we hate ourselves?
2. Because there are too many people on the planet and we need to reduce the numbers?
3. Because we like to punish ourselves?
4. Because we don't know any better?

1. Anger 2. Evolutionary overview 3. Revenge/Anger 4. Ignorance

Which of the above four motives would you choose? Which one signifies the greatest intelligence? Number 1 or 3? Anger and revenge are always there but to use them on such a grand scale surely indicates a racial madness which would by now have resulted in complete extinction — we are not that mad with ourselves. How about 4?

If we consider our present stage of develop-

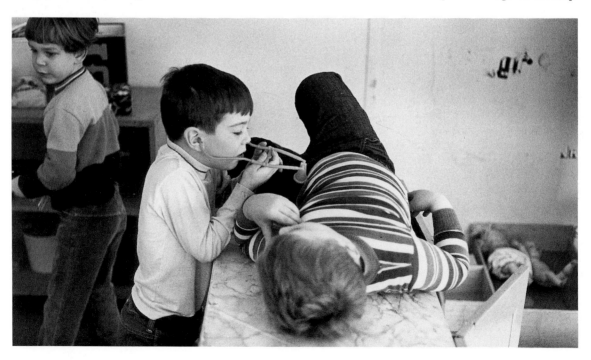

118

ment as one of very early learning in the whole course of mankind's growth, then perhaps we still simply haven't got it together yet. In this frame of thinking we may be considered to be an ignorant species. But if we are as ignorant as this then how come we have managed to do all the other reasonably intelligent things that keep this planet at least habitable?

So that leaves 2 — evolutionary overview. Perhaps we deliberately create diseases in order to keep our population growth at an optimum level for the conditions of the planet at that particular moment.

But why keep making new diseases? Why not fail to cure the old ones, then the job could be done in the same old way all the time! But that wouldn't be man, would it? Man likes things to change, he enjoys challenge, drama, fear, excitement and a good new disease, worse than the last one, keeps him on his toes and advancing forward — better science, better cures, etc. etc.

And what if we/nature conspire together to cure the disease at just the right moment: just when the population situation has turned better again, the conditions have improved, the numbers reduced, the cure is found. Sigh of relief- period of calm- start all over again!

It becomes, from this viewpoint, an involuntary contribution to mankind's existence — his partnership with nature in survival.

This is, of course, only a hypothesis — not something that could easily be proven! But whether proven or not it provides us with a more positive view of something which during the era of major diseases like AIDS is not otherwise happy.

So how does all this go with our child? If we are in conspiracy with nature and therefore ready to die for the sake of the rest of the world, it's a little like war except that the enemy and the friend are one and the same! The care of child in relation

to disease is a balance between a special kind of concern during the early years of life and a realization passed on to the child that death is not an enemy. That you/the child and nature/existence are both friend and foe — that life is death and not fear of death.

If you, the adult, can make friends with your greatest fear then you will have the greatest gift to give to your child that anyone can give. Put simply, give your child death and you will provide the greatest cure for dis-ease.

SHOULD

If there was ever an original sin it was the word "Should". The English language would be better off without it. The very moment a child begins to use and follow the word should she has entered the realms of division, condemnation and appreciation. A simple but very hard game to play is that the parents have to pay the children one dollar for every time they use the word should. Very soon the child will be wealthy and the parent poor.

Game - DRAWING THE EMOTIONS

The idea of this game is to allow the adult to see something of the view that a child has of emotions in others. It achieves two results — one that you can understand better the child's point of view when you are angry, sad, frightened or happy. The other aspect is that the child can see by being offered the game, that it is OK for him to witness your anger etc., there is nothing hidden and you are not ashamed of the feelings. This will give him or her a direct experience of the mirror of emotions and make him realize that it is also OK for him or her to be angry also.

Simply take pen and paper, colors etc., and both you and the child draw anger. Firstly it should simply be the idea of anger. Second, and this may work out to be the same which is fine, draw what the child sees when mother and then father are angry. Draw the face or the body or anything else which represents mother and then father angry. Ask her, the child, what this makes her feel. Then repeat the game for fear, sadness and joy. If there is more energy try jealousy, guilt, resentment etc. These last drawings may go better with children over seven years old.

CHAPTER FOUR- CONSCIOUSNESS

*We have come a long way already. Through
communication, the art of the child to teach the
parent, to emotions, the power behind the teaching.
So now, what's behind the emotions?
Before we get into consciousness, a little lead up is
needed, especially as in this age of consciousness the
subject is so surrounded by mystique and
uncertainty, the reader may have heard only garbled
accounts.*

LOOK AT IT THIS WAY

*Have you ever been told that you are the sort of
person who leaps before he looks, or someone who
speaks without thinking? Are you the type of person
who responds to something instantly and inevitably
gets into trouble for spouting some incautious
words in a situation which may seem to others to
have required some tact?
If you are this impetuous person then you may
realize that it is perfectly possible to speak without
using your mind — without summoning a library of
thoughts before uttering a sentence. Think about it!
Had it ever occurred to you that the brain can
bypass the conscious mind to the speech center and
push out verbal constructions instinctively, that is
words without consideration?*

Most people have the idea that the mind is
responsible for everything that happens in the way
of speech and expression. That only the emotions
are somehow separated from the mind and only
they require no thought initially. Some will even
say that if they had a choice between believing
their thoughts and believing their feelings they
would choose the former every time. This is like
saying you trust the past more than the present.

But if you can speak on occasion without
thought, maybe you can do it at any time you wish.
There are some who can. They fall roughly into
three groups.

1. POETS — we call them poets in the broadest
possible sense. These people are capable of frequent
inspiration: they have learned the habit of relating
to their hearts/emotions more than to their minds
and so, under given conditions such as writing or
painting or composing, they can summon up a
direct line to the feelings which is not interfered
with by the logical and often dull repetitions of
the mind.

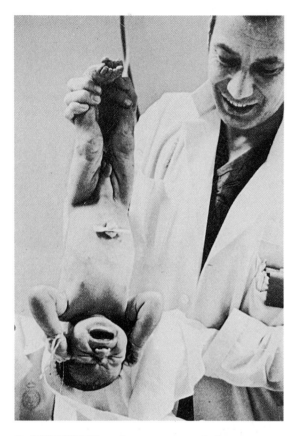

have no mind, since they don't need it. They need the instincts and so these, whatever they may be, work very well. Their words come directly from the heart. Hence the phrase — "Out of the mouths of babes."

Consciousness then, does not only have to do with thinking. A small child does not have language to communicate with, all he has is expression and the expression, as we have already shown, comes from emotional power. And it is this emotional power which derives from the child's consciousness and perhaps the consciousness of the world around her.

Picture a tiny baby. Directly after a bad birth experience (see section on natural birth), look at her face in your mind's eye. The expression of pain, the eyes screwed up and frightened, the mouth wide open and screaming, the hands and arms stretched out and then pulled back in an expression of despair, the legs kicking and the whole body crying out.

The problem is not that the child is unable to communicate, that she is not aware, but that we, the attendant adults are not listening because we think that she is somehow not capable of communicating with us.

Here is a living person, as much an individual as we are, with as much potential awareness and a profound consciousness within life. But we don't recognize it.

Just because a child cannot speak to us, cannot tell us what he feels, does not mean that that child is somehow under-developed.

The main problem with our relationship with small children is a lack of willingness to observe the true situations simply because we apply our own experiences to them. Because we abhor suffering and are afraid of anger or other forms of human behavior, we look away, avoid the truth and the result is a child crying in the emptiness of our environment, an environment that we have created very often out of false ideas.

So, in this chapter we will look at mind, memory, perception and consciousness and come to some conclusions about how the child perceives the universe.

2. GENIUSES — this category includes scientists, philosophers, world leaders (only very few nowadays), in fact genius can exist in almost any area of life. But one thing they will all admit to is that most of their genius does not derive from thinking.

Many of the better known scientists, such as Albert Einstein, openly declared that the end product of their discoveries was found in a flash of inspiration which did not arise from mental activity. The answer to their query appeared as if from nowhere and then all they had to do was apply the mind to the answer, working backwards to meet the initial question.

3. CHILDREN — young children especially do very little thinking and have a direct line to the emotions, bypassing the mind for, in effect, they

KEEPING IT IN MIND

"You can't imagine the extent to which, as you are now, thought pervades and interferes with the functioning of every cell in your body."
U.G. KRISHNAMURTI

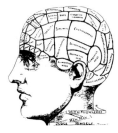

We take the mind very much for granted. Reading any of the most recent medical or child-care works, mind as a subject is always there — either in the form of information about mental growth and development or in some way connected with education or with problematic behavior. Every book, including this one, comes out of or goes into our minds — but because we are *so* much inside the mind, it is very hard for us to step out and look at it from another angle.

This chapter is going to attempt to do just that!

It may not occur to many of us that it is necessary to step outside the mind at all. In fact, the strange thing about mind discussion is that it is not until we suggest that there is another way than thinking that we ever conceive that there might be! Such is the power of our minds.

So first, let us look at some of the medical views of mind.

First it is admitted that thought is a tricky subject to think about. It's a little like the cartoon drawing of the vacuum cleaner suctioning itself into oblivion!

"If the brain were so simple that we could understand it, we would be so simple that we wouldn't!"
EMERSON PUGH

The simplest overall definition of thinking is that it is "active uncertainty". In other words the thoughts are always happening and fired constantly by an uncertainty of whether they are right or wrong. A scientist named Gordon Rattray Taylor suggests that thinking involves eight stages:

1. the recognition of a problem
2. an immediate restraint that prevents us from reacting in a habitual manner
3. a sort of detective's investigation around the brain to see what might be done to solve the problem
4. the selection of the results and consideration of all the available alternatives
5. the formulation of a plan based on what has been selected
6. the selection then of possible actions to implement the plan
7. an assessment of the likely results, and finally
8. storing away the answers in the library of solutions for future use.

Presumably at some time during this operation the mind/brain also directs the body to do what it believes is the best for the problem that resulted in the first place.

It is of some interest to consider that the mind is a problem solving machine but the problems are created by the mind in the first place so that

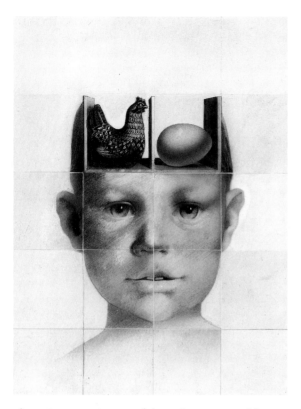

So we split our minds at least into two and perhaps more parts. Because the environment that we live in is so full of events, the greater majority of which can easily be identified as problems, we have, most of us, fallen into a trap. Our minds work all the time, except perhaps during deep sleep and because they enjoy this problem solving business, they get into a habit of always thinking. Much of this thinking can be defined as worry.

When thinking becomes worry is difficult to assess. Much thinking is fun. For example, fantasizing about a pretty girl, dealing with an intellectual problem, planning a vacation or day-dreaming about the next car we are going to buy. What happens in practice is that we have a fantasy about the new car and then the mind conveniently provides THE PROBLEM — can't afford the new car. The mind that dreams up the problems also dreams up the pleasures. It is the judgmental mind that makes the trouble — the restrainer!

After all, who says you can't afford the new car? This is not to say, of course, that the judgmental mind is not also useful — if it wasn't we would not function safely in everyday events. Unfortunately, however, the worrying side of the judgments can get on top of us.

But all this intense activity must need some rest.

Some of us get that rest during deep sleep when there is no dreaming and even the chatter of the mind has probably ceased. Some of us are so crazy with thinking that we do not manage to sleep. Insomniacs think sometimes twenty-four

there is a certain roundalay of constant self-consideration going on in the mind. Events occur each day that need to be dealt with, though it is doubtful whether they *begin* as problems, for the same event may seem a problem to one person and not to another. The mind is constantly needed to shuffle about in those corridors of the brain for the answer that was recorded to the last problem of a similar nature — and then to add a little extra piece of information which has been through the process and lastly to motivate the body and the mind to fix the problem.

So the mind thinks about its thoughts too. And here is the split: first the problem is thought up, then the reaction is stopped and the thought-up-problem is thought *about*. We are now in two minds about the problem.

The mind then investigates what is needed to solve the problem that it is in two minds about.

hours a day. Some of us meditate during the day and manage at least to quieten the mind. And lastly, some of us are children and have not yet become caught up in this constant mental activity. For constant mental work is not our natural state. It is something that has become increasingly imposed upon us by the environment that was originally created by our minds.

We made it all originally in order to organize our lives and then it outgrew us and now it very often dominates us.

There are plenty of people, however, who love to be constantly in the mind — many people enjoy the activities of intellectual study. At a certain stage in life, around the early teens to the mid-twenties, the need to talk is very important. But in the lives of many of us the time comes when too much thought becomes a burden and by that time it is seemingly too late to do anything about it. We have forgotten how it is to be still and silent.

Children do not operate through the mind as a continuity machine until they are forced to by social standards, by example, by rules and by mirrors which show them this way of living. They then forget the other ways. And what is perhaps more significant is that the methods and signs that are given to children to enable them to use their minds as continuity machines are not always the best ones.

So, those that live in the mind and teach their children to do likewise, operate through it exclusively for they cannot do otherwise unless they learn to employ the mental capabilities they have to a wider effect such as through meditation and the interests of the heart. Those that have stood outside the mind and seen just how much else there is in the world, can operate through the heart, through a space which adapts thought to a more constructive and directed result without the why and wherefore of doubts and complexities. But — perhaps you say — how does a child learn all the things that must be learned in order to live a normal life. "I would love my child to be calm and peaceful when she becomes adult but would she be able to operate in a world that relies so heavily on thought and reason?" The answer has to do with water!

THE RIVER AND THE TREE

A river flows continuously along between its banks. It moves in a natural and smooth manner unless there is something which is placed in its track. If it comes across a tree the water changes its movement and begins to flow around and around the tree continuously so that the pattern of flowing is stuck around the tree. This is how the child's mind works. He will operate completely on a flow of energy — his pattern completely happy and smooth and working according to natural laws that he knows nothing about. And then someone, probably a parent, will plant a tree in the middle of his flow and the river's water will start to wrap around that tree continuously, working around it, on it, over it, trying to re-establish the flow at first but eventually giving up and becoming accustomed to the tree — forever moving around and around the tree. And then another tree will be planted and another and another and another, until eventually there is only the tiniest amount of space between the trees for the river to flow smoothly. For the most part it will be wrapped around the many trees and soon enough it will stop flowing altogether and become stagnant. Plenty of trees will grow naturally in the river of a child's thought capabilities — there is no need to plant more. The growths of fear, caution, doubt and censorship (in its broadest sense) are the ones that cause the water to stagnate.

REMEMBERING GOD'S MEMORY

According to the established understanding of medicine, memory operates by recall through a kind of mental library which works to retrieve information from the brain. It is of course the brain that is doing the retrieving itself, not some other biological entity, that is, if retrieval from a memory "bank" is really the way it happens.

But this hitherto relatively simple explanation is today receiving considerable attention for like everything else in physiological research, it may not be so simple after all. For first it must be considered also that, as we have suggested, there may be larger areas of memory such as the cosmic thought-field we mentioned before, that the brain can resonate with.

Secondly there may be memory by "feeling" in which some event or experience of the senses recalls instantly some event from the past. It might be a smell or a repeated scene, a voice or other sound or a touch — anything that happens through the senses and suddenly recalls a memory of some past event which may well have been buried for decades and suddenly reappears without reason. This kind of remembering can of course also operate through the brain but is very hard to recall by the "library" method.

It seems as though certain events are memorized by a method which would appear to require something other than a conscious mental effort, as though the memory were placed somewhere in the brain with a kind of code attached which can only be de-coded by the arrival of a particular prompt.

Probably all readers of this book have had the experience of having something "on the tip of the tongue!" Some memory that is sensed-it's content totally familiar and yet the specific quality or shape of that memory is fugitive and will not be quantified. The more you search the memory for the event the more it seems to escape.

Then you stop and find something else to do — you forget the thing that was on the tip of your tongue and suddenly, out of the blue, it comes without warning.

This kind of memory then seems to have one qualification — relaxation. The moment we give up trying, the sought-for memory pops up. Tension fails, relaxation works.

Standard brain medical research explains memory as something which operates in short-term and long-term fashion. According to the most widely accepted theory new information enters through the senses and first encounters an immediate memory which takes the items entering for just half a second. Those items that are considered not necessary are immediately rejected and like bits of garbage end up on a heap somewhere outside the individual!

Those that are considered useful are passed down the line to the short-term memory which keeps things on ice for up to thirty seconds, only capable of holding 5 to 10 items at any one time. If the filter overloads, the short-term memory box refuses to accept anything more or drives out information that is in the box in preference to new items — in this case something like a child surrounded by dozens of toys — each new one will cause the rejection of the last.

Items that are sufficiently rehearsed or repeated travel on down this line of memory boxes and enter the long-term memory which is very large — large enough in fact to span a whole life-time. This long-term memory is split into three different forms — stimulus response memory, event memory and abstract memory. This is the current understanding. The fact is, of course, that we don't actually know what really happens in the brain. It is like much of the scientific world in so far as there is such a vast gray area in most matters of human behavior that a great deal of guess work is in operation.

There are new theories emerging now that the memory, at least in its long-term facet, is not situated anywhere in particular. Whereas biologists would previously have stated with assurance that the neo-cortex was the seat of the memory, it is still not certain that this is so.

One of the most fascinating research avenues is into the hypothesis raised by Rupert Sheldrake that memory is in fact not a replication by library or computer-like techniques but a construction or re-construction of vast amounts of information that may be drawn from the past into the body, from anywhere in the universe, spatial or temporal.

There has long been a similar idea used to describe this method of memory which was used extensively by Edgar Cayce and derived from the Theosophists view of a kind of vast, celestial bureaucracy which might be termed *Akashic* memory, using the *Akashic Records* as the metaphor. The Akashic Records were said to be the records of *all* time, past present and future existing somehow as a universal memory bank for everything that had ever occurred or would ever occur.

Such a concept is fascinating as it comes close, once again to the same idea of a cosmic memory which is accessible by us all, unconsciously and that our memory system relates to all things. The brain is therefore, within this hypothesis, able to tap into an enormous group record that it gathers information from and the result is the simple item that is then brought to the front of the consciousness as thought.

However, according to Sheldrake's hypothesis, this still doesn't quite touch the true potential of the human memory. The metaphor of the Akashic Records still uses the concept of memory *bank* as its beginning and this fails to touch the more subtle levels of a flowing force of humanity.

If we think, therefore, more in terms of a river of flowing movement that we humans resonate with at each moment, the story expands into something which does not require any bank of records over which the Theosophists would have enjoyed applying their Indian love of organization! What we have in this case is much more like what is seen everyday on the TV screen when live broadcasts are relayed to us — a live resonance of activity that is really happening somewhere around us in the world. The memory therefore would work in this same fashion, resonating, Sheldrake offers, from the past and tapping into a vast flowing experience of life and the universe.

As we have mentioned before, if David Bohm's theories regarding the wholeness of the universe, are an accurate assessment of life, it maybe that each individual memory derives from this massive river around and within the body. That we literally draw upon each other's vibrations of the whole of mankind and his environment. This concept is very attractive insofar as it finally dispenses with the last vestiges of the attitude of divide and identify. And it should be "remembered" that the river within which we remember not only contains us but we also contain *it*.

WHO SAYS ?

We are told that the initial memory system, which can hold events for a very short half second, rejects much of what comes through. So what tells it what to accept and what to reject — who is the censor? Mum, Dad, Society, Me, You, or the memory itself?

Somewhere the super-short memory has learned what it wants and what it doesn't. Before that learning presumably it accepts everything without discrimination but after a period of time, the filter closes down and takes on a number of selection processes that have been provided through experience or parental dictate.

An example might be the tendency that a mother might have to tell her child —

"Don't do that."

In a situation where a child is constantly doing what a mother does not wish her to do — i.e. embarrassing her, bothering her, generally doing "naughty" child-like things, both mother and child have a choice. Mother can either remain permanently anxious and on the child's tail because she believes this is the way to behave, or she can relax and allow the child to go crazy, do everything outrageous and not worry about it.

There will often be a strong element of determined disobedience about children's behavior and clearly if there should happen to be an audience to reinforce the child's determination to be outrageous and the mother's to suppress it, as in, for example, a public place, then the situation can be all the more difficult to remain calm and aware within.

The child then also has a choice — either she can obey or disobey. Either way the short-term memory is going to accept certain filters which lay down tracks of future behavior. But insistence on obedience is no more, after all, than a power struggle. Why should the child obey the parent — why not the parent obey the child? Who gets his own way? Who becomes so afraid to disobey that the filter is securely fixed for all time and in later life applied to all manner of nonsensical matters such as being afraid to do all sorts of harmless things and not know why because the short-term memory has only transferred the *fear* to the long-term memory and not the reason.

The proposal would be that this so-called long-term memory is merely a flowing and responding mechanism that "fits" and resonates with the entirety of existence — we might call it all "foundational memory" — and such a resonance is always accessible and taken from everywhere in the cosmos. That provided the individual is not constantly learning to filter out the information, he or she may have access to this river that is always there, for the children of all generations.

MASTERS OF THE UNIVERSE

Until very recently, in fact until the end of 1988, one of the most basic tenets of biology was that evolutionary variations are made by small changes that occur in individual members of our species. Biologists generally agreed that these variations happen by mutations or genetic changes that are totally random and spontaneous and that they have no concern or regard for their effect on the human race: — i.e. such changes may just as easily be detrimental to us as beneficial. A paper published in the scientific journal "Nature" in September 1988 by John Cairns and two of his colleagues at the Harvard School of Public Health in Boston put forward the revolutionary idea that the structure of the body may be able to receive information fed back from the environment in the form of selective memory traces, which are then integrated into the very foundations of life — the genetic make-up of the body which is then, of course, passed onto the next generation. Put another way, we make our own evolution happen.

The problem in the past has been the idea that there is someone else out there — or worse still nobody out there — making all this happen (or not making it happen according to the persuasion). This neatly sidesteps the need to be responsible for what is happening for if it is random and separate we need not feel guilty if we foul it up for perhaps "Nature" is fouling it up already. If we discover that only *we* are making all this happen, then we have to start figuring out whether what we do is OK and we have also to take responsibility for all our past mistakes.

So, such a foundational memory would be added to constantly, and would exist all over the body and the universe, and around the body in a kind of "morphic" resonance that affects the body and its environment. Such a memory would contain not only those events and stimuli of the life in action but all lives, all events, all existence within the universal environment, both matter-of-fact and temporal. The mystic would assert that such a foundational memory was carried from one life to another and this would explain how children are said to recall previous lives.

In effect, such a memory gives us access to the brain of God.

In this context (and perhaps in all contexts) we are not referring to God as a person but as a presence such as beauty or joy or us. We can therefore think of God as a verb and not as a noun — *Goding.*

Because we have decided at some stage in our existence on this world to filter and distort our environment to fit with our requirements, this Goding-memory is shadowed from our conscious awareness and although it constantly accepts and accrues everything and although it has literally a bottomless capacity for such input, we cannot see it or consciously feel it.

We cannot feel its presence on a day-to-day basis and may only glimpse its power and its depth in split-second explosions of awareness — those human devices which the mystics call satori.

But, during the short time that the child has lived before the social awareness factor cuts out the sun, this Goding-memory is visible and indeed everything to her. She is, as J.P.Salinger would have it, God.

If we "softly assert" then that this Goding-memory exists in all of us — that it "binds us and surrounds us" connecting us with the universe, gives us psychic abilities, special gifts, a perfect knowledge of everything that we are connected with, the fact resulting is quite devastating because it becomes clear that we are, right now, separating ourselves from our world deliberately in order to avoid the very connection for which we exist. And in our new view of children we can benefit so much. For in looking with that child-like perception at the universe around us we can drop the very veil or shadow within which we normally lose sight of everything and relearn the ability to connect — to de-separate.

"Absolute subjectivity (or God inside us all) is one with its universe of knowledge, so that you, in fact, are what you observe.
Thus the split, the space, between the subject in here (i.e. me) and the object out there (i.e. that) is a subtle illusion. The real Self does not know the universe from a distance, it knows the universe by being it, without the least trace of space intervening. And that which is spaceless is and must be infinite."

Ken Wilber

GAMES WITH GOD'S MEMORY

The simplest method of tricking your filters is to employ the imagination.

Let us take a normal situation of memory recall. Suppose that you are sitting in your living room trying to remember an event in the past — it can be anything from your childhood such as the first day at school, for example. You can remember that this day was unhappy or that it was frightening, but you cannot remember whether your father took you or your mother and you cannot remember what your school teacher looked like on that day. Whatever you do, these particular memories do not come to the surface. So stop trying to remember and make it up.

Simply describe the face and appearance of the teacher you first met in as much detail as possible whether it feels right or not — just make it up.

The chances are that this is what she was like. If you could verify it at all by finding a picture of her there is a 75% or more chance that your imagination has selected the precise memory of her appearance. The reason for this is that your mind is so busy with other things — with more recent events, with future worries, with present problems that it is developing — that it does not look in the right place for the memory that you wish to recall. It does not consider it necessary so it ignores your request in favor of getting on with something else. When you employ your imagination you deceive the mind into doing the necessary search. In effect you appeal to the mind through another lobby!

Try it with a child, you will find that she will bring up all sorts of incredible stuff — even past life memories of people whom you knew together and which you will both feel familiarity with.

Game- HAVING NOTHING TO DO

Not everyone is this way, but most are. How many times have you found yourself with nothing to do — nothing to occupy yourself with — no dishes to wash, no clothes to iron, no kids to organize? Not very often. Of course not very often because we all arrange our lives deliberately so that we don't have any times just to sit and stare. In fact, many people have the idea that if you are doing nothing then there is something wrong with you — "stop wasting time, you good for nothing!"

Yet, how about stopping and looking at this wasting of time business. How do you waste time? Is there really so much to do before we die that we must cram the time full from beginning to end?

The game should be created to have a group of people or one or two people wasting time — doing nothing and feeling that agitation that exists when there is nothing to do. The point for children is that they are allowed to understand this adult neurosis — that they do not need to cram their time full and become neurotic like us, for time spent doing nothing is immensely valuable. The mind gets a rest and the whole feeling of the body is to relax. The habit of doing nothing is very important especially to very busy stressed people.

Children will sit on the floor with a single toy just rolling it about with no purpose whatever. Ordinarily we congratulate a child that *does* things with a toy — that builds things and creates things — because we think this is the correct way to be. This is already encouraging the child towards neurosis. Get past the initial feeling of restlessness — wanting to phone someone, to write a letter, watch TV, listen to music, go out — anything to fill the gap. Don't fill it — feel it. Feel that gap — play with the toy on the floor with the child. Watch the small child how she can be perfectly absorbed just doing nothing.

THE MIND'S EYE

We have looked at the mind and the way in which we may remember, but now we need to take a closer look at the input itself — that which is available for the brain to receive and filter.

First, examine the picture opposite. This picture was originally devised by K.M.Dallenbach early in the 50s and this version is improved by Ken Wilber. Very few people can decipher what it represents (actually, the only person I ever met who was able to was Swiss — which explains itself!) until given help.

But once the viewer identifies the representation it is then very hard to un-represent it — i.e. see it as you, the reader, are seeing now — naively and without map or reference. For the moment we are going to leave the picture un-revealed, simply allowing it to remain a featureless and unidentified series of squiggles, because this represents something very important in our understanding of childhood.

 A man of fifty who had been blinded by disease at the age of ten months had his sight restored by corneal grafts. So, for the first time in his life, except for a short period in babyhood, the man could see again. At least, there was light passing into his body through the eyes, but he could not identify the objects that he "saw." For example, the man had some experience of lathe machinery during his life of blindness, but when presented with a lathe he could not identify it at all, except as a series of light and dark shapes and colors. This

was not "lathe" — this was simply a jumble of vibrations and appearances without a name, rather like the squiggles on our unidentified picture, though in three dimensions and with movement and color.

Then the observer allowed the ex-blind man to touch the lathe. He closed his eyes and ran his hands over the lathe from one end to the other. When he opened his eyes again he was immediately and dramatically able to identify the once shapeless and identityless object as lathe. Evidently, according to reports of the event it was immensely exciting to watch. His words were "Now that I have felt it, I can see it."!

If a baby looks at something, anything, she has no identification of it. If she, for example, looks at a tree in the garden where her pram is sitting, she will reach out for the tree without knowledge that it is not reachable because what she sees is a series of light and dark shades, colors and movements without identity and without necessarily the same perspective that she will gain later. Her perceptive indicators may not be arranged yet to tell her that there is distance, shape, comparison, light haze, or necessarily a need to focus the eyes. None of this is present because none of it has been impressed upon her. She is a blank slate as far as "tree" is concerned, and indeed all that surrounds "tree".

The suggestion is that the child is living in a state of chaos without perception of events around her but that the specific identities of items are not ordered in the way that they are for the rest of us. She has no specific labels for these shapes and so they remain simply shapes and shadows and unidentified colors.

THE COLOR CON

To take the story a step further, we presume that colors exist. When we see green or red or purple or blue, we "know" that everyone else sees the same

and we presume therefore that these colors exist. As far as science can track down the content of color, its existence lies solely in the brain — not even in the retina, but somewhere in the brain itself. Certainly there is no color in the world in the labeled sense of color.

Can you tell what this is ?

What actually happens is that every time a proton (one of the particles of the atom) is endowed with energy, it jumps from the level it is at to a higher level. The energy that is needed for this jump results in what is seen by us as a color — each level produces a different release of energy and thereby a different color. These levels are simply vibrations which have an optical effect within the brain — colors are therefore seemingly our imagination only.

There is only an agreement between us that color shall be used to represent the different vibrations that affect us in varying ways. There are various tricks that can be played to illustrate this.

Game - THE OMEGA EFFECT

Go to an art shop and buy a sheet of green transparent plastic and a sheet of red. Cut out of each sheet a piece big enough to fit on a spectacle lens. Stick one piece of each color on each lens, the red on the left half of each lens and the green on the right half. Tape up the sides of the glasses that are open so that other light does not enter. Then wear the glasses for a whole day or better still two days, not allowing your eyes to be exposed to ordinary light at all — taking the glasses off only once the lights are turned out at night and putting them on immediately the next morning in a darkened room.

What you will see, of course, is that everything to the left looks red and everything to the right looks green.

After the two days or so you will begin to see colors normally again even with the lenses on. But when you take them off what you will see is that everything which was red on the glasses before will look green and everything on the green side will look red! This experiment illustrates clearly that the determination of color comes from the brain and not the receptors in the retina. Gordon Ratray Taylor calls this the "Omega Effect."

The Omega Effect is that which we cannot identify, within the brain, as being a mechanical reaction to stimuli. The Omega Effect might be to fall in love with someone or something, or to switch color hues because of changing conditions. It might also be enlightenment, for it derives not from clearly definable computer-like or chemical changes, but from indefinable phenomena — most of which scientists have no explanation for whatever.

136

YOU SEE WHAT YOU WANNA SEE - AND YOU HEAR WHAT YOU WANNA HEAR

So, what does a very small child perceive?
She doesn't perceive identified objects or shapes.
She doesn't perceive identified colors and for sure
she doesn't identify sounds in the form of language

It is not that the child lives without order or reason in her new world for modern research seems to indicate that children are entirely orderly in their environment, but the suggestion is that the shapes, colors and surroundings are un-labeled and derive their existence for her simply as events without reason — not *unreasonable* but *reason-less*. There is some evidence to suppose that small babies have favorite visual stimulations such as the color red, for example, but there can be no certainty that this "redness" is actually the reason for the child's favorit-ism.

Like the blind man who regained his sight after fifty years and could not identify anything until he touched it. The only difference with a small child, and perhaps the inherent danger of traditional parenting, is that it is *we* who touch it and not the child. It is *we* who decide that red is what the child sees as such.

The adult creates much of the environment — the mirrors, the influences, the instructions, the rules and regulations, the shoulds and should-nots. During that vital and sensitive period of life

137

when the child is searching around himself for shape and form, at a time when he is most impressionable to stimulation — this is the time that we create the psyche and the personality that will "fix" the child's nature — very often not a natural state at all.

There are five traditional senses; sight, hearing, smell, touch and taste and if we look carefully at each of them we soon realize that we hardly use them at all — certainly not to their fullest capacity. When we use our eyes to look around us we spend much of the time avoiding what is actually before them. We don't look directly at people because this is embarrassing for them and for us. We don't look closely at our surroundings, our scenery, our environment because we are so busy thinking about our problems that we are blocked from true perception.

We hear perhaps 20% of what comes to our ears, filtering out the majority of our surroundings as irrelevant or not useful, so that the hearing organs simply cease to work properly.

We hardly touch. One of the greatest fears of the city dweller, for example, is to be touched or accidentally touch someone else for fear that the other will think we are sexually interested in them. Sex has become such a taboo that we rarely use our sense of touch, except perhaps with those most intimate with us and then often only minimally.

Our sense of smell is probably the most damaged of all as its greatest skill is detecting sexual input. Of all the senses, that of smell was originally the most active for sexual contact. Since we em-

ployed our determination to repress sexual behavior in society, the sense of smell has taken a back seat. We coat ourselves in deodorants and natural represents because we are afraid to display those natural smells that will indicate to another what we actually feel. Again, how embarrassing that someone should know that we feel sexual attraction. How embarrassing that our body smells of sweat!

And finally, of course, our taste buds are close to death from the input of various and numerous junk foods, tobacco, alcohol, fumes, polluting atmosphere and a generally unbalanced diet.

But this sense-itivity to life and existence is available to all young children from the very moment of birth.

For the very best starter to really get into the senses, try the section entitled *Feeling the Weather*.

There are also a number of very simple tricks that can be played on the senses to demonstrate exactly how variable the received input can be. For example: keeping the face directly forward, turn the eyes as far to one side as possible so that you are looking "out of the corner of your eyes" at some object, preferably a moving object, over to the far side of your vision. In this way one of the eyes must focus at a different level to the other eye in order to maintain the pin-point focusing of both the eyes on the object viewed. Remain looking for at least a minute in this way.

After the minute return the eyes to the front and look at a wall or some other solid object and you will see that it is moving. Very slightly, the surface of the object in front, now the focus of the perception, is moving.

Another trick is to cross the eyes and keep them crossed for about thirty seconds, until it becomes a little uncomfortable. Now uncross them and look ahead. The vision will then move in a circular motion and the object perceived will seem to turn in front of you.

We may now wish to look back at the picture on page 135 of this chapter and once again try to identify it. If it still makes no sense perceptually to the reader, it may be revealed as a large cow — the head on the left of the drawing. Now try to see it as anything other than a cow!

LEAVING THE CHILD ALONE

If you have ever spent time on a public beach, almost anywhere in the world, you probably noticed this scenario:

A small child with his or her parents is playing perhaps with sand castles or digging some deep irrigation in an attempt to beat nature and channel the whole ocean into his lap! Father is reading the newspaper while surreptitiously watching the topless girls sunbathe. Mother is half sunbathing her body and half keeping a watchful eye on Johnny in case...just in case! The child seems quite happy with his play and so long as he keeps chatting and "bothering" mother or father with his noises and questions or spillings of water and sand or whatever other nuisance he normally makes, mother is happy. But if he should cease all noise and troubles and become silent for a moment, staring out to sea or gazing in the direction of nothing, mother becomes uneasy. She notices that there is nothing to notice and in her turn begins to bother the child. "Johnny, what are you doing?" "Johnny, what's the matter, why don't you play with your bucket and spade?" "Why don't you come here and eat something — have a coke, a sandwich, an ice-cream?"

In effect, such concern is destined to cause the child to stay with mom, to remain within her influence and rarely to be free to discover aloneness.

There is a considerable difference between loneliness and aloneness. They are two completely separate and different states of reality. Loneliness is something we expect and feel accustomed to and familiar with. Aloneness is unfamiliar and rare for it supposes a state of being happy alone. Children rarely get the chance to sample aloneness unless they are determined, have a lock to their door and a sign on the outside which says KEEP OUT — BEWARE OF THE CHILD. And it is perhaps in this aloneness that the child is sampling and feeling the very five senses that we have lost, so don't imagine for a moment that a "lonely" child is suffering, for it is equally or more likely that she is having a great time doing nothing — and everything. And this leads us to the sixth sense.

THE SO-CALLED PSYCHIC CHILD

There exists today a great deal of material surrounding the idea of the psychic child, of special powers that exist in "special" children that are not understood by adults and that are currently being investigated by scientists or para-psychologists.

Put very simply, once again the adult observes something strange in the behavior of certain children and wishes somehow to comprehend it for the betterment of human understanding.

The approach within this book is to try to place psychic behavior within a more normal realm — to say from the start that it is believed that psychic behavior is not unusual but simply part of the life of a child and therefore also part of the life of all adults.

Almost all of the best known psychologists of the past and present have touched upon psychic behavior. Freud spoke of a child's instinctual behavior during the first years of life and equated it to what is known as the development of the physical field — i.e. that area of development which is involved in the child's growing awareness of his or her physical environment — from the body out. This time is then followed by a more subtle appreciation of the environment, such appreciation involving areas of understanding which we adults have since lost sight of.

One of the main and most prevalent directions of interest adopted by child psychologists is that of personality growth. The experts tend to look upon the development of the ego/personality as the most important area of growth taking place after age seven and spend much time examining the ways in which a child grows into the social surroundings that he has been placed in by parents and society. This society does not understand the more esoteric suggestions that arise *within* the child,

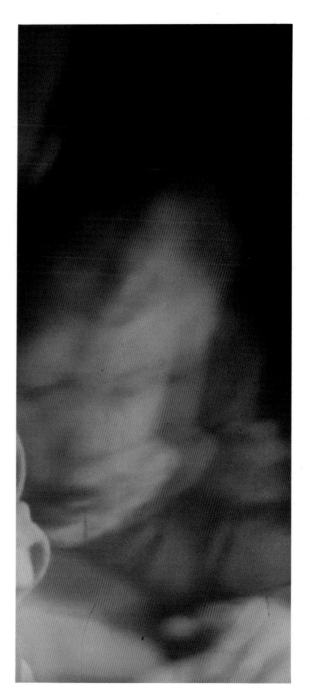

areas of growth which are not associated with accepted phenomena and therefore this society tends to see psychic phenomena as somehow being a bit "weird," unexplained and therefore exceptional.

The chart on these pages is taken from an adapted form originally created by Rudolph Steiner and published in the book "The Radiant Child" by Thomas Armstrong. It indicates Steiner's understanding of the levels which a child naturally grows through and it is most interesting in its proposal that the stages of a child's growth move through the etheric and astral before coming to the ego or mental stage. In other words children are naturally aware of things that we adults do not comprehend *before* reaching the normal social conditioning that society imposes upon them.

It seems fair to suggest therefore that the social conditioning effectively drowns out the esoteric and psychic development of the natural child.

Rudolph Steiner suggested that from birth to the age of seven years is the time when the child is most involved in physical "fixing," i.e. she is learning how her body works in the world. At about age seven the child begins a transition of energy and awareness which then results in the period of her life in which she feels and experiences esoteric phenomena. Steiner suggested that this change in awareness and energy begins at about the time of the loss of the milk teeth and the growth of the adult teeth.

The child might be said to be getting her teeth into another world. But this other world is only "other" because to the adult it is strange and misunderstood. To the child it is a perfectly normal state of awareness and probably a very beautiful one at that.

Piaget's observations indicate that a child operates on an "egocentric" or "paradoxical" basis until the age of about six and then enters a "concrete operational thought" stage which continues into adulthood. Rudolph Steiner maintains, however, that the period from seven to adolescence is a time when children experience a releasing of dormant astral and powerful emotional energies which we nowadays dramatize in horror movies such as "Poltergeist".

Clearly these two possibilities may be in conflict, for if a child is both passing through "concrete operational thought" learning — something encouraged and imposed by society — and at the same time is becoming aware of energies that are much more personal and even "trans-personal," such as flying dreams or out of body waking dreams, the child is probably going to "think" that she must make a choice. In our modern ideas of what is right and wrong, safe and dangerous, normal and abnormal, psychic behavior quite clearly falls, in the eyes of adults, into the abnormal, wrong and therefore dangerous side of the dualistic coin. In short, we discourage anything that looks like trouble.

The choice of the child, who lives completely within the care and protection of the parent, will naturally be towards what the parent encourages. "Don't worry about ghosts darling, it's only in your dreams."

Steiner's proposal is very much the "softer" one and he observes that the child does not naturally need to reach the "concrete operational thought" period until past the age of 21 — i.e. just short of complete adulthood. This proposal gives space for the understanding of "unknown" phenomena *before* the time of entering into the stricter disciplines of the mind and might, if permitted to develop, allow the child to retain the psychic awareness and also enter society as a normal human. But this is generally not how it happens. The psychiatrist Laurence Bendit and his psychic wife Phoebe Bendit offer a perfect metaphor for the stage of psychic awareness in children which also happens to fit well the whole development of children in general:

"...in terms of etheric anatomy, (the child's) psychic-centers — the chakras — are open and unprotected, like the windows of a house before the glass is put in."

In effect then, this indicates that a child is open to anything and everything that exists in his or her environment, including what we adults term psychic phenomena. These stimuli might be other people's thoughts or any other kind of energy that comes from who knows where in the cosmos. The

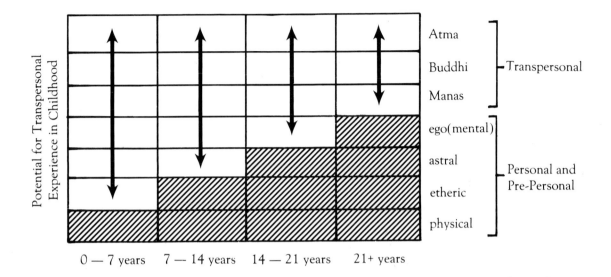

child is not in a position yet to distinguish between what we call real and unreal and the psychic phenomena entering the child might in many cases seem as important and real as the food on the plate.

But this is the whole point. Reality, as we have already discussed, may take many forms and it is only the accepted judgments of the adult world that define those forms as real or unreal. Actually it is all unreal and all real.

Armstrong points out that "as children move toward school age, they receive stronger messages from adults and peers that non-ordinary kinds of experiences are incompatible with what is emerging as the "official" version of reality. In consequence these experiences are repressed, forgotten, or simply kept to one's self."

It is suggested here that the psychic energies of children exist right from the very beginning and continue to function through the early years until about age seven when in the main they are suppressed completely by parental and social pressure.

In rare and unusual cases these energies re-emerge during early puberty in the form of kinetic phenomena or ESP or astral dreaming simply because at the stage of puberty the energies are so strong, due to the growth of sexual awareness, that the suppressed psychic energies come to the surface despite attempts to stop them.

But what is more troublesome is that this social filtering not only filters out etheric input but also most other input as well, leaving the child devoid of much of the magic that exists to be sampled in the world.

In other words, once again, through the unintelligent application of fear we drown our children's awareness.

It should be appreciated here, however, that we are not suggesting that all children are highly psychic to the extent of being capable of "ESP" or major kinetic activity. Human beings are born and grow into many different varieties. Some children are great musicians, others great artists and in the same fashion some children will be gifted

with psychic awareness to a greater degree. But this concentration on the more dramatic abilities of children tends to drown out the subtler ones. The finest and most gentle ability in psychic fields may be present in a child and yet because of our fears of the results we may tend to ignore or subdue such gifts to the child's detriment.

GAMES for PSYCHIC AWARENESS
For the concept "psychic" to exist we need:

1. A human being or other living creature.
2. A phenomenon that we do not understand.
3. An observer.

The same old rules! Without an observer, in this case probably an adult observer, the psychic ability of a child is irrelevant. The child doesn't worry about these gifts — they come perfectly naturally. It is only the influence of the observer that will make the child aware that it is not necessarily natural. The phenomenon, once observed by an adult, therefore becomes misunderstood because there is no convenient pigeon hole to put it in. How do you explain a child who can apparently read your mind?! It's not normal, after all!

For the concept "psychic" to exist we would then need:

1. A human being (forget about psychic animals for the moment!)
2. A phenomenon that we do not need to understand but simply accept and
3. A game.

But how about if we were to alter the perspective slightly — just the tiniest twist — and see what difference it might make.

In this way what we have done is to disperse the one element of the concept "psychic" that causes it to be something that needs suppressing or inflating — we have dispensed with the fear of the unknown.

Now we can begin to approach the subject in a different way altogether. Not only that, but we can begin to re-learn how it is to be psychic ourselves — for we were once, all of us.

Psychic "gifts" are not unusual. They are only gifts in so far as everything we each have is a gift. If you imagine how very very easy it is for some tiny little thing to go wrong with the formation of a fetus in the womb — how many millions of opportunities there are for a growing cell structure to mess up on its way to birth, it is then a totally incredible miracle that we are almost all of us born perfect. You could say — how on earth do we do it?

The existence of psychic abilities, put in this context, is no more of a phenomenon than the existence of sight or hearing or a warm hand.

Drop the idea that psychic abilities are somehow more incredible than anything else and you come face to face with a simple truth — we may all to some extent know how to read minds!

It may be that it is too late for many adults to re-discover the hidden realms of psychic energy that are readily available in a child, but that does not mean it is good to destroy them in new children. The able appreciation of the sensitive and magical consciousness available on etheric planes of awareness, if permitted freedom of expression, could remain in the child through to adulthood. Then such gifts might be incorporated with the stresses and strains of normal social life, providing thereby a magnificent method of living a magical and spiritually satisfying life. A life that the adult has largely been denied by the previous generation.

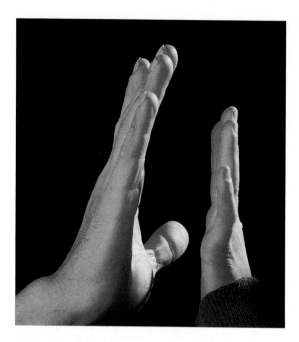

Game-SENSING UNKNOWN ENERGIES

Sit opposite a child and hold up your hands as though you were about to play "patta-cake, patta-cake." But do not touch the hands together, merely hold them a few inches apart. Move the hands back and forth slightly until you feel a pull, a kind of energy shape between the hands. Play with it until it becomes familiar. This is an aura energy — the aura that effectively connects us with the world outside our skins and it is also the aura that receives and accepts all phenomena without filter.

As suggested in the section on "remembering," this energy aura may be the single most potent area of our lives for receiving all cosmic input. You are, therefore, in effect, in touch with the most fundamental part of the child before you. And it is a part which you cannot see, taste, smell, hear or touch. None of the five normal senses are available to detect it. But the sixth sense *is* available.

THE SIXTH SENSE- AWARENESS

We all use the term "sixth sense" on occasions when we cannot explain our awareness of things that come to us. "I had a sixth sense about it."

It is a sense which we acknowledge, perhaps with tongue in cheek, but somehow we associate it with instinct or hunch — that thing which cannot be explained by the mind.

To the psychologist the number six applied to this paranormal sense is wrong anyway for there are in fact, altogether eleven or more senses. They are said to be as follows:

1. Hearing,
2. Vision,
3. Taste,
4. Smell,
5. Touch,
6. Kinesthesis — feeling of motions,
7. Equilibrium,
8. The sensing of warmth
9. The sensing of cold (two separate senses),
10. The pain senses (of which there are at least two).

The sixth sense, i.e. the paranormal sense, would therefore be the "Eleventh Sense", not the sixth!

But who's counting? Well the scientists of course, who are, as always our resident skeptics and whose job it is to doubt all things that do not fit with the existing laws of science — which incidentally the scientists made up in the first place!

Nevertheless, with whatever degree of skepticism exists within the world of reason, we have all had experiences of the sixth sense, on perhaps a less paranormal level than would normally cause any eyebrows to raise. Our everyday experiences are more to do with small coincidences, the inad-

vertent transmission of information to or from others close to us, or perhaps a minor prediction which happens to come true.

Perhaps the most common form of sixth sense experience is that of the hunch. We knew, somewhere inside us, that some event was going to happen and it did.

Our disconnection with life is the biggest reason why we have lost the use of the sixth sense — why we do not often enjoy instinctual occurrences and when we do, we doubt them. Science has taught us to doubt them for if there really *were* a genuine and identifiable sixth sense that could be functional and available to us at all times, most of the scientific dogma would have to be re-assessed. One thing is clear in relation to the existence of a paranormal sense, and that is that it cannot be functional and usable in the same way as the other senses for the sixth sense does not

operate through the mind/brain. In fact, the very moment that we think about it, it is gone. Attempting to recapture any "strange" and unexplainable event through mental activity instantly fails for in the very act of recapturing we chase it away.

To try to make this fascinating element of life into a clearer matter we can compare it with sub-atomic or quantum theory. If we remember the brief explanation of probability theory it states that sub-microscopic bodies cannot exist as certainties — that they have this unerring and irritating habit of moving just as we try to look at them. The presence of uncertainty bumps them away from our available scientific apparatus so that we are forced to admit that life in its smallest elements cannot be secured — it may be there but it may also not be there.

In effect we can play a game with this. Imagine,

for the moment that instead of acceleration chambers being used to "see" sub-atomic particles, you have "thought chambers" (or the brain) instead. If you use your thoughts to observe a tree, you can make something out of the tree because the item tree is thinkable. You have a set of references which you can apply to tree as a subject. At least you think you can!

If you take these same thoughts and you try to apply them to sub-atomic particles it doesn't work because there is nothing to think about, no shape, form, color, smell, taste, sound — no nothing. So you are left hanging without anything thinkable. In this way therefore sub-atomic particles are not only object probabilities but they are thought probabilities also. You have to admit it — the very foundation of life — the building blocks on which everything is supposedly built may not be there.

If we take the sixth sense in the same vein then we can perhaps figure it out more easily. Hunches cannot be seen, heard, tasted, smelled, touched or thought about. You can think about the event and have a hunch about it but you cannot actually sample the mechanism that connects the probability of it coming true with the event when it comes true. You cannot re-make the hunch or the coincidence because existence has this unerring and irritating habit of moving just at the moment when you think you've got it figured. The very act of thinking chases it away, just like the sub-atomic particle when accelerated inside a chamber and (probably) recorded on film. We looked at Hidden Nature in Chapter Two and the Hidden Emotions in this chapter so that we may already have gathered some feeling for things in life that are not so obvious — not so definable as trees and rocks and other people and it is on this same level of awareness that we may sample the sixth sense, for the sixth sense is not a paranormal sense at all, it is the whole sense of awareness.

Notice, when you next feel a hunch coming on. It very often has something to do with a subtle understanding of your surroundings; an awareness of things the way they are. In fact it often seems to be made up of a combination of all the other senses which at that precise moment bring you in touch with something beyond your conscious knowledge — a sort of ultimate sense. And this is the secret of the sixth sense which arises directly out of our conscious, sub-conscious, unconscious, cosmic conscious connections with existence. And this understanding turns a frightening notion of unknown factors into a positive and encouraging notion which might even be a lot of fun.

A child has the ability to *be* a flower, and we shall see later in the book there is an innate ability that a newborn child has after birth to *be* the mother. This connection with existence; with the world that surrounds and contains the child, so that the child is somehow like the stitching of the fabric in a tapestry, is something which the adult mind has a terribly hard time with. We are separate, separated by our minds and our conditioning, so that we must see everything before we believe it and the scientific community is, to a large extent, the pinnacle of this state. If a scientist were able to *be* his experiment then he would be able to see nothing for the experiment would be a continuous one involving him or herself and that very involvement would always have a missing link so that the experiment would be never ending. Without getting too deeply involved in the intricacies of this philosophical meandering, this is in fact how science works, for science is an everlasting search with no final answer.

Scientists like David Bohm and others have even made it clear to the rest of the scientific community that nature/life actually alters in great shifts (which have been named "paradigm shifts") so that science is not a matter of making any progress at all but a matter of total change. These shifts may even happen precisely *because* a scientist has reached a point of conclusion.

But to return to the sixth sense — if we can appreciate that children live permanently within the fabric of existence then it becomes easily clear to us that the instinctive sense or the sixth sense is the method by which a child "talks" with existence.

And if we wish to do the same we can start with a game!

Game - CONSIDER ME GONE

The nature of this game is that the success or failure at it is only a probability. There is no certainty of one or the other. In fact, the essence of the game is that you may have to drop the idea of game altogether — on the other hand, you may not!

Put another way — the essence of game, within this game is not the game! And, as the professor of philosophy said to his students, I am not going to tell you what is.

Play with a friend or a child or both. Take a sheet of blank white paper and as many colored pens or pencils as you like. Blindfold your eyes and those of your players. Feel your way to the paper and with the pencils or pens, in any order or selection, draw something on the paper. Draw for as long as you like and with anything in mind or not. Simply *be* drawing to your fullest extent until you feel that the drawing is done.

Then take off the blindfolds and have a look. Hold the drawings up in front of you, each person in turn make a shape out of your own drawing. Form the shapes into something that you can recognize and name it to your partners in the game.

Once you have been around the table and figured out each drawing, take turns again to hold up the pictures, one at a time, this time to each other and make recognizable shapes of each other's drawings. See how much fun you can have out of identifying different things from each picture — as many as possible so that you reach a point where you are not at all sure what the picture represents.

Now comes the tricky part! Take back your own drawing and re-envisage the original shape and identify what you first made of the picture. Look hard at the picture and concentrate on it. Now — make it disappear. If you need to, it is OK to make your eyes go out of focus in order to vanish the shape you defined. But the definition must vanish so that the original squiggles of shapelessness come back onto the paper.

And here is the point — when the picture forms a shape that you can identify, you are in the mind — your thought particles are working for your known senses — and when the shapelessness reoccurs and the picture makes no sense to you at all, you are in no-mind and the thought particles are shifting the observed nature of the paper and its squiggles into probability.

In both cases therefore, you have both failed and succeeded at the same time. In identifying the shape as something knowable you have failed to be in the state of probability and succeeded in being in a state of probability. When the shapes are shapeless you have also failed to be in probability and succeeded being in probability. You are therefore only in one place — the sixth sense — awareness — probably.

CHAPTER FIVE
THE POWER OF SERGEANT <u>WILLIAM</u>

The Mind's Sergeant Major

It can reasonably be supposed that the **WILL** has something to do with the **MIND**. It is always better to put these **BIG** words in capitals and underline them, or they get hurt! Big words have big egos, you see.

I expect the reader will recall all the times when someone has said the words — "You have no **WILL** power." And how it felt to be so weak (this word must always be in the tiniest letters). The most common users of this particular form of manipulation are parents, ex-spouses, brother or sister or even Sergeant **WILL**iam.

Will power is a fable — there is no such thing as will — it is a perfect invention of the mind to whip or congratulate itself with, and in the same way others too.

If you are a King or a high statesman you can only rule the land that pays homage to you if you have something with which you can threaten it — to command requires obedience and obedience requires threat. The mind acts in the same way — it splits itself up into different power structures. In order to congratulate or chastise itself the mind has created will. The choice of word, of course, derives from where will-power leads us — always into the future — **I WILL DO THIS**, or I **WILL** feel bad. If I manage to do this, because my **WILL** is strong, I **WILL** be happy. Always in the future.

Of course if we do succeed in **MAKING** (i.e. forcing) ourselves to be slimmer or cleverer or better in some way, then the will and therefore the mind is reinforced and becomes still stronger. It will thus, in the future, expect more of itself than before. "I did it last time, so I can do it again". And people live their whole lives in this belief —

that they are driven successfully by their will. These are the sad ones around us with the furrowed brows and the heart attacks and the bitten nails, for will does nothing but cause suffering.

There are of course those who will answer to this that if we did not have will-power we would simply drift in and out of situations without purpose and without aim. But this is yet another mind-method. Actually in this case, such a proposal is the mind's method of protecting the will! And in turn, of course, the will then reinforces the mind — and so on and so on, round and round until we fall over from dizziness. There is no reason to suppose that our propensity to drift without purpose necessarily has anything exclusively to do with mental discipline. If we enjoy something and wish to do it, that act will necessarily be a happy one. If we are constantly forcing ourselves into actions because we think we should do it, for our own good, we are simply playing mind games with ourselves and ignoring the feelings altogether for the benefit of the ego.

One of the biggest powers of the will is to shadow the feelings. If we are so utterly determined to make something happen then the feelings don't get a look in. The mind becomes so strong in that determination that the emotions and deeper inclinations that are natural to us become easily drowned. It is like oil on the surface of water — the oil occupies only the thinnest layer on top of the water, the most superficial covering, but its murkiness is such that the beauties beneath are no longer visible.

In relating to children we naturally use those devices that have become familiar. Such items of our own conditioning, such as will-power, often exist without intelligence. We do not consider what

is behind them. Because we have constantly undergone these systems during our lives and have rarely stopped to figure out what they really mean, so we pass them on to our children, also without concern for what they do to the child. Generation after generation has done this without ever considering what it means. Discipline, which derives largely out of a sort of army-assault course form of will-power, is one of these systems. We consider it, mostly, as something which entails strength and determination and therefore lots of **WILL**. We also imagine that children must be instilled with this power so that they can get along in life the same way we did!!!!!

Creating a better life, empowering the child with the capacity to do good for her or himself does not require will and determination or some kind of internal whip. It requires only one thing — the ability to listen. By listening we do not mean listening to what others tell us, but listening to ourselves and our feelings — that beautiful deep water which lies beneath the top layer of murky oil.

Give this power to your child and she will have all the discipline she needs without ever having to **WILL** anything, for life will happen to her because **IT** wishes to.

Game- WITH SERGEANT WILLIAM

The mind's best friend is appropriately named the Will. This character is constantly at attention ready to exact the power of discipline over any individual and of course children are a perfect group of victims for the big bad whip.

Children need to be kept in order, after all — for their own good! "They have no will-power."

Will-power is one of those strange mirror-images, created by the mind to whip itself or congratulate itself according to whether the extra pounds in weight were lost or not. In effect the mind splits itself in two, one side telling the other side what to do.

This device is, of course, passed on to children — it normally takes the form of obedience, another of these seemingly important words which has actually to do with only one thing — dominance. We adults prefer that our children do as they are told. "Children are to be seen not heard" was the old Victorian adage.

But today — YOU, THE ADULT, WILL DO WHAT YOUR CHILD TELLS YOU TO DO!!

For one whole day, probably best at the week-end, you the adult will follow precisely and to a T, all the rules, regulations and instructions that the child or group of children in the family propose. Sit down first thing in the morning with the children and make up a list of rules. Right them down and do not try to change or analyze them. Allow the child to make them up.

You, the adult may not propose or order anything that day, so that if the child wishes to change the rules she can — there is no overall rule that says you may not do the most unreasonable things.

If you give complete carte blanche to the child without any restrictions whatever, then you will be surprised just how intelligent and loving the child will be. If you impose rules on the un-ruliness

of the child, then she will react and make life more difficult for you. And in any case making rules against rules is ridiculous for it achieves nothing.

Follow everything and just feel what it is like to be told what to do all the time.

Ideally, this game should be played at least once a month to remind the parents what it is like to be disciplined and how foolish it is.

Of course we must create margins for children to feel comfortable within, but these margins need to be flexible and caring, not rigid and demanding.

The original English Public School is the prime example of how to damage a child's sense of freedom and self-care. The schools used to (and in some cases still do) charge large fees to parents to slot their children into firmly established ruts — to iron out the individuality of the child and build him (usually him) into the socially conditioned regularity of English practice — whatever that is.

More unhappy, maladjusted and disturbed human beings come from such training than from any other neck of the educational systems of the world.

WILD KIDS

Of course, there is reason to suppose that amidst all this freedom we are going to give to children, we adults are going to end up in strait-jackets in a padded cell! There has to be space for us too. The kind of question most frequently asked by mothers and fathers, when considering the whole concept of the wonder child and the freedom necessary to encourage individuality, is what happens for example if my child grabs a sharp knife and waves it around or starts to mess with

dangerous chemicals or starts to stick his fingers in electric plugs? We fear, quite naturally, the possibilities of physical damage, so readily available in the domestic home. Domestic harm is still one of the biggest threats to physical well-being.

But essentially, to ask such questions is to miss the point somewhat. The predications outlined in this book are not intended to create a wild and willful creature who is free to cause horrendous damage to his or her surroundings like some monster let loose in a china shop. There is a difference between open and honest margins of behavior and a thoughtless chaotic permission to do what you please, regardless of the consequences.

If we allow a child to run wild, encouraging any kind of behavior without limit, then we are not being caring, we are being careless, for as much as a child will experiment with experiences that are helpful to his growth, he will, in some cases, also search out those experiences which may cause harm to himself or to others.

The proposal is that we simply act honestly and not with ideas of good or bad that are based on conditioned responses.

A good example is actually one that was mentioned by one of the editors of this book — a mother of a young child who asked what would I suggest as the response to a child grabbing a carving knife? The answer is very simple — if a child gets hold of a dangerous implement which could cause physical harm, you take it away with whatever force and determination is needed to make it clear to the child that there is danger. We know, without doubt, that a sharp knife cuts the skin and causes physical pain which is undesirable. Our normal human response to such behavior is very straightforward and should be made patently clear to the child. There is no need to beat the child or scream blue murder! Simply remove the implement and explain quite plainly that this is a sharp knife which is used for the purpose of cutting food. Show the child how it works. Cut a tomato and indicate that the knife will cut the flesh in the same way, that blood is not easily stemmed if the cut is deep and the child should keep well away from such implements until the time comes when he or she can use the knife effectively for its true purpose.

This applies to all such situations and only a little intelligence is needed to apply such conditions.

False discipline comes more from the expectation of dangers that are largely fantastic in their nature. "Don't go outside in the rain or you will get sick," "don't suck your thumb or you will end up catching some disease," "don't touch those tins of food on the supermarket shelves or they will put you in prison," and so on.

More subtle forms of this kind of routine are described in the chapter on education, such as the complex methods that teachers are taught to create competitive attitudes in children.

These methods are unconscious. They have been employed for centuries without question and the author merely proposes that each form of conditioning is looked at afresh, without bias for the personal attitudes that we adults have learned so that we only pass on what is useful for the child's natural growth.

DISCIPLINE-ING

The word discipline comes from the same root as the word "disciple." It means learning and learning is a verb not a noun. It is not knowledge we are talking about but knowing, a continuing process and therefore a living process. Discipline, when used in the form of punishment or rules, becomes stagnated by the previous conditioning of parental "hand-me-downs." In order truly to discipline you have to become a disciple of what it is you are trying to teach to the child. You must know the truth of what is happening by personal experience, not by passing on information which may well be already dead.

Additionally we cannot discipline another person. This is thoroughly operated by the military forces and we are probably aware what results from such forms of discipline. We can, however, involve others in our own discipline, sharing it and enjoying it as a disciple would his Master.

The master is the learning not the learned. And this leads to the final aspect of discipline which we can most suitably touch our children with — that discipline is purely personal and changes from one individual to another. It must come from the heart and will therefore never "fit" another person — it will only fit the person whose heart it came from.

Take a practical situation. One of the children in your family persistently stays out late at night when you have asked or demanded that he comes home by eleven. He refuses or neglects to do so and you feel that he is not disciplined. He is wayward and should be willing to accept your demands.

You have some choices. You can scream at him, make him feel bad so that he obeys through a sense of guilt and fear. You can blackmail him by refusing to pay the allowance unless he obeys.

You can offer rewards to him so that he becomes a business man in the affair. You can simply let the whole thing drop, go to bed and suffer on your own and not say a word, but worry in silence. You can also talk to him sensibly and try to figure out why it is that he needs to be out so late at night without regard for your fears.

All these choices have to do with control. You wish him to obey you, to do what you tell him to do and by whatever subtle or un-subtle means you will manage his life in a way that accomplishes that goal. This is disciplining a child in the age old way because it works towards framing the child's life within your picture not his.

If the child can come home and not find you up, pacing the floor, but sleeping soundly without concern and the following morning he can talk to you about what he did, what fun he had, what girl he met, what movie he saw, then you will be his disciple and he will be yours. He will learn from you and you from him. There will be a mutual trust between you because the child will know that you trust him to do the best he can for himself. You trust him to be also his own disciple. This is discipline.

Create this mutual trust with a child as your friend from the earliest age and there will never be any problems with discipline. In fact the word and its authoritative attitudes will never even crop up in the home.

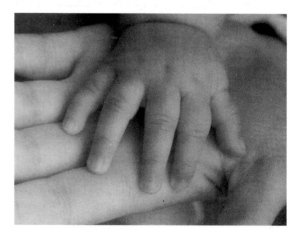

CHAPTER SIX - FATHER FOLLOWS

If you have ever experienced living at close quarters with groups of people such as in a commune or perhaps a boarding school — or even a group vacation, you may have noticed one feature that seems to be common to all groups. However happy and friendly and easy-to-get-along-with the majority of the people are — however much harmony there is in the group generally — there is always at least one person that you wish wasn't there. This one is often either emotionally unstable, super-demanding, depressive, aggressive or unlovable in some other way. He or she will dominate the group much of the time, providing everyone, daily, with all sorts of reasons for kicking him or her out of the nearest airplane door, off the edge of a cliff or into the nearest toilet. By the end of the group's period together, everyone is sad to see everyone else leave except perhaps him!

But one thing that might be noticed after the gathering is over — or in the quiet moments away from the others in the group — who is the one that gets talked about most? Who is the one that attracts the most energy? Being with "nice" people is easy — pretty much anyone of us can manage quite well to relate to others who don't go out of their way to bother us. At the same time, we are happy to forget them as soon as they are out of our lives. But those who cause problems and make themselves visible above the rest attract our interest to a far greater degree. Effectively this "syndrome" has to do with demands. Those that demand most of our energy get it, rather like a magnet, even though the pole of the magnet may sometimes be negative!

Within the family unit - the average family unit, if there is such a thing — the one who generally seems to stand out as the equivalent of this "sore thumb" figure is the father.

Fathers very often have a big problem. They don't "have" the children, they don't primarily look after them. They are more often than not the ones who take on the job of providing the money and the "security" of the household, which is not only a fairly full time job but is also an absentee job. And finally, perhaps the biggest problem of all — they are men!

Men today are having a harder time with their lives than ever before. Men are under fire from every quarter.

Government clearly does not work in the hands of men.

Women are apparently seriously considering firing men from all the domestic and relationship jobs — for men don't seem to be very good at marriage, fatherhood, steady relationships, home-minding, faithfulness, love, tenderness, sensitivity and a whole arm-long list of vital life-affecting activities. Women are finding, in fact, that they do most of these aforementioned things better themselves, without the awkward and hampering presence of men. They tolerate us today, often as a necessary evil — the evil is already defined but somehow they don't seem yet willing to tell us what the necessary bit is about!

Men have proved responsible for all the results, on a global scale, of their determination to dominate nature, the land, the rest of the world, other countries and each other. This "warrior" or "animal" characteristic which seems most prevalent in men has been driving them forward relentlessly in the wrong direction for thousands of years. They have dominated their villages, their cities, their countries in the same way for the whole of history and it is only just now becoming apparent that this may not be the way to operate the planet Earth at all. So men are coming under heavy fire from this angle too.

Being a father is like having an impossible job to do without knowing what the complete job description is, knowing that it is failing and having no other solution, or support in the effort.

What may not be so well known about fatherhood is that it *is* a job — it was created by our society — it was not always there. For many thousands of years humanity got along perfectly well without fathers. The mothers had the children but they did not necessarily know who they had had the child by, so there was no one to call father. In actual fact the word "uncle" is a lot older than the word "father," for if there were many possible men who could have sired the child then they were all known as uncles.

The word and the institution of father arrived on the scene at exactly the same time as the concept of private property. In order to create the whole business of handing down the property to the next family generation there had to be a father and a son to do it with.

Private property created family and father because of the idea of passing a part of the father down to the next family using the son as the carrier. In the original tribal method of society the whole tribe continued the knowledge and the ownership rights of the generation before. The shaman or witch doctor's knowledge was passed on to a designated individual chosen as the next witch doctor and the tribal property was given to all those children who would carry on the tribe's good work. There was no question of private property owned by individuals, it was all shared. The responsibility for the up-bringing of the children, then, was shared amongst all the men in the tribe — the "uncles" of that tribe. Even the female responsibility for the child was shared by all the women, not just one, though mother was always mother.

UNCLING

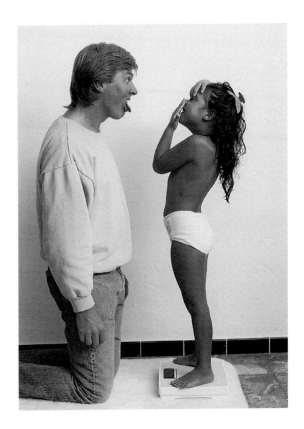

Probably many of the fathers reading this book are already uncles and this will serve our purposes well. For those who are not also uncles, try to remember how your uncles were with you.

An uncle has no responsibility directly for the nephew or niece — he is like a second-position father. He probably has the idea somewhere that if the father were to die he would take on more of the responsibility of the children of his brother, but not all of it, for he is unlikely to be as emotionally involved with that family as his brother. He is a bit like the original "God-Father," not in the mafia sense, though close. The mafia godfather was originally created as the head figure of the extended family in Sicily — the chief of the mafia tribe — with an overall responsibility for the whole "family". He had many "sons" with no focus on any particular one.

The family uncle can have many sons without feeling that any of them are HIS — that he owns them and MUST look after them — MUST be available, MUST be a good example.

If you, the father within the family that you have chosen to live with, became the uncle of that family instead, everything would change in all sorts of interesting areas. You might even begin to see the woman in the family in a new light if you did not HAVE to be there with her, but did so by choice.

In the past of humankind there was a time when there were no fathers and no private property. The time must come, therefore, when this happens again. Sometime in humankind's future there will be no families, no fathers and no private property. It is inevitable, for mankind uses and re-uses the same methods in cycles throughout history.

It is not proposed that you throw away your family ties and dump the whole thing in the garbage. But it is proposed that you try, as a problematic father, to work out a new perspective. Look at and try the following game.

FUNCLING

There is nothing more to the game than this, except that it must be adhered to religiously until it has become as much of a habit as it used to be to call "Father." After the month has gone by the change of name can be continued if it seemed good. If the members of the family have found something special in this new address then it should continue. Don't worry about what the neighbors say. They will just gossip about the new men in the mother's life which will make them happy and shed a new light on the relationship in the house — which cannot be bad!

The point is this — first the father will get a chance to be the center of attention because everyone will have to remember consciously to call him Uncle instead of Father — so he will feel wanted. And second the "old" father is probably taken for granted by now and this new "title" will make everyone look at him again, with fresh eyes.

But most important of all is the effect it will have on the father. He will perhaps begin to realize that he does not have to be a father — with all the heavy duty responsibilities that entails.

The game is very simple. For a full month you and your family are going to act out a play. The play will not have a script except for one word-change. For the word "Dad" or "Daddy" or "Paw" or whatever other synonym has been adopted in your family for father, everyone, for that month, will use the word "Uncle."

If you have the kind of family which uses first names instead of Dad or Father, still change the use of names to "Uncle...." whatever the name is.

This does not mean that he stops loving the children, that he shirks all his important work to make the household function. It simply gives him a chance to relax within that position as his role changes. Uncles do not HAVE to do anything, they do it because they want to. Actually what should occur, if the game is played with constancy, is that the "father" begins to find he can love his children more and with greater flexibility simply because there is no longer any obligation to do so. Simply changing a single word can do all this.

FATHERHOOD

"I am available. Drink as much as you can, take as much as you can. Remove all hindrances — and that "all" is your responsibility. I am doing my work; about my own work I am absolutely open and available, but that's all I can do. I am like a light: I can show you the path, but you have to walk."

Bhagwan Shree Rajneesh.

A father's job is simply to be there, available and completely honest about everything he does. This is the simplest and yet the toughest trick — to be honest. If, as a father, you take ALL the responsibility, provide ALL the answers and push and shove and drive and manipulate the child to DO everything you say she or he should do, then the child is going to give up doing for herself. The child is simply going to say "Daddy what should I do next?" and not learn how to take the responsibility for her own action. The child is never going

possessiveness. We go through our entire lives calling children "My child," "My Tommy," "Our Kid," and then when someone else comes between us and "our child" we become jealous and critical of the person who has come along.

The situation can even reach extremes. Take the story of Mr A, for example: He fell in love with and wanted to marry a woman who was half his age. He was almost the same age as her father! The father hated his daughter's new lover so much that he sent a private detective after him to investigate his background. He would shout at his daughter whenever she and the new man went to visit, having enormous rows with her and refusing to talk to the man. He was so jealous that they feared he might even try to kidnap his daughter and imprison her to prevent her from marrying the older man!

This is an extreme case and perhaps her father was simply firing off his natural Italian passions. But it is not, in essence, so dissimilar to other situations where fathers refuse a boyfriend entry to the house and say terribly critical things about them for months until eventually the daughter's determination is sufficient to make them give up.

The only time that the father is willing to allow the relationship to flower between the daughter and a man is if he, the father, chooses the man himself. Then the father can continue his possessiveness. For thousands of years it has been happening like this in many parts of the world. In Europe it stopped only a few hundred years ago and in India it still happens that way now. So long as the father chooses the man for the daughter's hand in marriage then it does not hurt — the father does not get jealous because the daughter is obeying him and not living her own life. The rebelliousness is not allowed to happen and the parental ego remains undamaged.

Fathers in the West don't chose their daughters' spouses for them but still they exercise their preferences and give superfluous advice as to the best kind of husband! How can a husband ever be the best kind — nobody wants to marry the best kind of husband, everybody wants to marry the lover — the one that is most exciting, most de-

to mature because she does not have to. Humans are like that — unless they are faced by change and growth and learning every hour of every day, they simply stay the same. Eventually you, the father, will look at the child at the age of 20 and still see a kid who cannot make decisions or take responsibility for anything. And it will be because you, the father, have taken all the decisions for the child, never giving enough space for him or her to make the jumps.

One of the classic occasions when the father's "love" becomes evident in its normal form is when a daughter falls in love with a man. The father suddenly becomes possessive and jealous.

It won't be called this because we have such a blockage about jealousy being something sexual. Jealousy is not necessarily sexual, it is primarily pendable, least dependable, whatever the preference may be. It is not the father that is falling in love, but the daughter, so how can the father possibly know what is right.

If you are a young woman with this problem the answer is not to argue about it. You cannot argue effectively with parents, there is too big a gap between the generations. You will say something to him that he will understand in another way and his answer will be understood by you in another way again. The argument will be like talking to an African Zulu native — there are two totally different languages being spoken — it used to be called "the generation gap" and it still applies. The words may be the same but the experience and conditioning makes the meanings totally different.

DAUGHTER LOVE

So argument does not work. What works is a little love. If he shouts and screams at you, don't be affected, simply keep still and give him another hug. He is hurt. He has had you with him, "HIS" daughter, all this time.

So you need to love him even more now because you are leaving. One of the great problems of father-daughter relationships is the fear of both people in the relationship that too obvious a show of love will imply sexual interest. Fathers are afraid to be too intimate with their daughters in case the daughter or other people think there is sexual interest.

Incest is a heavy duty problem in our society. We have created such an aura of horror around it that we are often afraid of even touching our children! One thing should be clear, there is a long way between the love of a father for his daughter and actually reaching a point of making love to her. There is nothing wrong with the fact that the father may see the daughter as a young version of

the wife; she probably looks as the wife did when he first met her and so there are many of those warm and passionate feelings in the father applied to the daughter. This does not mean that they have to go and consummate it or that they would ever want to in reality. Simply admit that the feelings are there and then they cease to be a problem — they are totally normal and natural and not to be denied.

In this release of tension — the tension that comes from denial — the father can freely love the daughter — care for her, touch her, hug her warmly and allow his feelings to be directed towards her. And when the real lover comes along and takes her away from the father, the daughter can be more loving and caring of the father than ever before because she understands the father's feelings.

163

MY SON AND I

The fact is that fathers very often love their daughters and hate their sons (hate may be an exaggeration but the point is made). They cannot talk to the son and do not understand why. The son, in turn, learns that his father is not his friend but some modern version of the Victorian father or worse, so busy with his work that he does not have a minute to stop and talk with the child. The son also notices that the father will cuddle the daughter, allow her to sit on his lap, but will not do this for the son.

With some sons, of course, there may be the opposite problem — my own for example, who is a full six feet and five inches tall, built a bit like a barn house door with the unerring tendency to jump on me the moment he sees me. He plasters me with kisses and generally hugs and squeezes the life out of me on all available occasions. He is, like his sister, one of the great joys in my life. We are not really father and son though — we were, biologically speaking, at one time — but not any more, for about five or six years ago we became friends instead.

The big problem for fathers is the conditioned belief that was given to the previous generation and the generation before that, that men should remain at arms length from one another. If we see two men hugging in the street we presume that either they are gay or foreign! It is so that in many foreign countries, Italy, for example, there is no such prejudice against bodily contact. Men are happy to hug each other and kiss, even lip to lip, without any sense that they must inevitably thereafter hop into bed together!

Sexual indifference, prejudice or fear is yet again to blame for the lack of love and tenderness between men. And sons really suffer from this.

Fathers are so full of *shoulds* that they can hardly offer anything to a boy beyond the age of five years old so the answer is to become so busy

and so preoccupied that nothing needs happen because there isn't time for it to happen. The boy then grows up with a mother fixation and the idea that only women can bring love and not men. Men are for drinking and telling dirty jokes with.

And this leaves a huge hole in the young man's natural appreciation of other people. Try the following game.

SONING

First — take your son with you to work. It does not matter what your job is, there is always a way you can arrange the trip with him around for one day, especially if he is over ten years old. If need be you can explain to the boss that he is interested in following in his father's footsteps.

Everyone else at the office or factory will love it — people adore young boys around the office, it takes some of the drudgery out of the boring day.

Take him with you and tell him about everything you are doing for that whole day. Watch yourself become irritated with him because he interrupts what you think you should be doing. But do it anyway — it's only one day and for sure this day will change the rest of your life together.

Next, at a weekend, go for a walk with him alone — just the two of you. If at first there is no conversation don't panic, just remain silent for awhile and then search around for something to talk about. If it doesn't come, tell him you are having difficulties and cannot think of anything to say. Tell him that this is a problem you have with him and talking because you don't know what he is interested in. Ask him to tell you about his interests.

In any event, the conversation you might have with your mates at work — with your colleagues and the older men with whom you spend time during the day, would do equally as well for your son. If he is over fourteen years old he will welcome your views on women, on love on sex or anything else. Just natter with him the way that you have seen your wife nattering with your daughter or her friends. Tell him your fears too.

The extraordinary thing about father/child relationships is that the effort to change them is only needed at the very beginning of the change. It is a bit like that jump that we need to take when we want to change our work situation. The daring is only needed at the beginning — a push in another direction and the one change alters everything.

In the father's relationship with his children, one push towards the child is enough — children are invariably receptive to more intimacy with parents — especially fathers and there is nothing in the world that a child likes more than to be able to tell his or her friends what a wonderful father he or she has — this is such an unusual thing.

CHAPTER SEVEN
EDUCATING OR DE-EDUCATING
PUTTING LEGS ON A SNAKE

The original schola (Greek) or school was a place of leisure where the rich spent their time in the casual pursuit of the arts and learning— we have become so serious about educating our children into survival that we have forgotten that there may be other ways.

FORMATTING

Modern education is largely confined to systems which intend from the outset to teach a child to think. In effect this is like formatting a computer, i.e. creating the basic conditions within the brain and body so that the child may receive the programs of the culture. These cultural and social systems can broadly be described as competition, examination, ambition and fear of failure, the last being the most important method of manipulation that the child learns.

In this book we are not concerned with the subjects of education such as history, geography and the rest for these are not the real education that we provide — these are merely the side-issues which somehow bulk out the true formats. It is also clearly necessary for a child to learn information — nobody is denying the need and the ultimate pleasure of gathering knowledge — it is not the knowledge that is wrong, it is the method by which it is gathered.

The methods are, by necessity, group oriented and do not make so much allowance for individual tendencies. Some educational systems do have a greater emphasis on children's natural individuality but it is hard for schools to give special attention, especially those schools that depend on local authority or central government grants for their existence — i.e. state schools.

Fundamentally there are not enough teachers, that is professional teachers and those that there are, are not necessarily the best people for the job.

167

LIFE'S ATLAS

Education is, broadly speaking, maps. Maps that are inscribed within the child's memory and sensory systems, which ultimately paint a complex picture of the land from which they have been drawn. In effect, therefore, education tends to be abstract and not experiential. You cannot take a child to the 15th century and show him the Renaissance directly. You cannot spend the fare needed to make a direct discovery of the Alps or initiate him into the microcosmic aspects of Quantum Mechanics — not even the scientists can do that — so how can a teacher? The experiences of education, therefore, are largely vicariously vicarious for even the teachers do not *know* the stories directly. They are not Masters of the world, they are merely story-tellers.

Their re-telling is at least secondary in nature, for they were not shown anything except by others with the same backgrounds as them. Also, in more cases than not teachers do not love the pupils they teach.

The net result is a lot of attitudes, methods and manipulations which result in more attitudes, methods and manipulations which not only organize the child-human into a way of life but strongly influence *all* his perceptions in the future. In effect the child learns to edit and translate reality into terms that do not necessarily suit him. They suit the society into which he must inevitably step, making, therefore, no allowance for individuality.

"...a person is in society when society is 'in' him."

KEN WILBER

This is why we sometimes suffer the black sheep of the family, or the rebel child who refuses to live in accord with the social maps but goes his

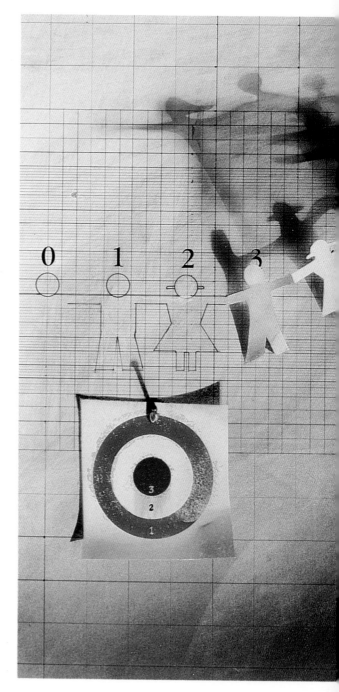

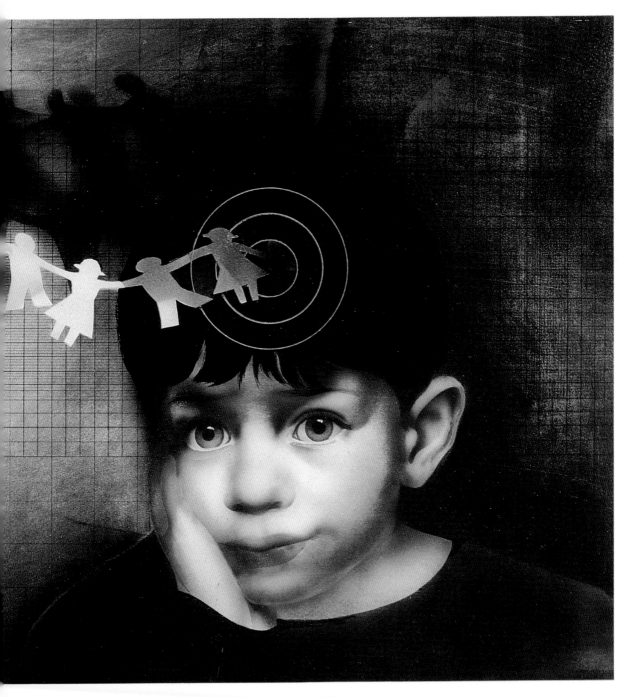

Language is our method of agreeing with one another. Even if the agreement is to disagree, it is still an agreement because it is formed through the use of terminology the meaning of which has been agreed among us.

We have, for example, decided that a thickish white liquid which comes from cows and is used for our tea, coffee or cereal enhancement shall be called milk. Even in the description of this item of human consumption I must use words which describe the described — "thickish," "white," "liquid." If I did not have these devices to make the shape, form and color of milk I would only be able to point. If the milk was not within pointing distance, I would have to do a lot of work to get it there. Language, therefore, is about the most important form of social instruction that we have.

But it is good for us, in the context of re-learning about childhood, not to take anything for granted. The word "milk" means nothing whatever of itself — it only means something because we have implied that meaning. Just to illustrate this, as a small game on the side, repeat the word milk over and over again for half a minute and you will begin to see that it has no intrinsic meaning whatever.

It is yet another abstraction in the same way that money is an abstraction of wealth. Every single word we utter is one step removed from the real thing (incidentally the word money is of course two steps away from wealth and the credit card is therefore three or four steps away from it; thus the way in which we tend always to overspend when we have credit cards instead of cash) and signifies effectively only a form of correspondence — a method of pointing out to one another that this thing is so. In effect then what we are doing is splitting the universe around us into parts — actually, with the advance of science, into ever diminishing and more precise parts. On the simplest level, though, we are splitting it up, into two parts — the object that we are referring to and the referral — the real thing and the word used to describe it. And we do this because we need to give meaning to our lives. And in giving meaning we also give fragmentation — we split ourselves also in two.

or her own way, colliding continuously with parents, teachers and, perhaps later, authorities. An increasing number of parents have to face this problem and generally take the view that a rebel child must be disciplined into conformity because otherwise the resulting trouble and unhappiness won't be worth the battle involved in going against the rules and regulations. In effect, this is like saying I am punishing you with these restrictions but it is for your own good.

Behind this extremely complex interaction between human individuals and the social organization there are an extraordinary number of items, not the least of which is language.

And this brings us soundly back to the old story (at least old in terms of this book) that we humans consider ourselves somehow outside our universe and distinct from it — separated.

But the world is not separate from us, it is only that we choose to point at it and give it names, therefore making it separate. The Buddhists, Taoists and many of the modern-day gurus and masters continuously tell us of the "suchness" or "isness" of this "unspeakable" world. We are in a state of everlasting present-ness surrounded by positive and meaningful nothingness.

It is not that there is nothing there. If that were so, we would not be there either. It is much more that the meanings, terms and references that we have given to the universe around us may not be an accurate description for what is really happening. In fact, the truth is that it is rarely if ever accurate and it is only a mixture of our forgetfulness, our seriousness and our egotistical ideas that we think, naively that we know. And out of this gentle and sometimes comical arrogance comes the average child.

It should be clearly understood that it is not the problem of language that we are concerned with but the problem of taking the language seriously. The maps that we have provided for our children's and each other's education — social maps — are not real, they simply represent something which may or may not be real. And the basic dilemma is that we have forgotten this and become so identified with the abstractions of the real world that we no longer see anything beyond those abstractions. We will unhappily spend our whole lives struggling and full of anxiety to fulfill something which does not exist at all.

Commerce, business and the making of large sums of money, which represent the greater part of the purpose of modern education, are a perfect example of this. The basis of social commerce is programming for failure. Even those of us who "make it" to the "top" generally want to climb higher, make more money, get further up there. And when we stop to consider our situation or look for praise from our peers or betters the likely response is "fine, but now you can do better."

Fortunately, facing failure is enough to cause many people to drop out of the race, but often not before all health, happiness and emotional stability has been already destroyed.

Some direct experiences may improve our chances of appreciating the theories — take *Kinetispheres* for example.

171

KINETISPHERES

A Kinetisphere is very simply a circle around a part of the body. The body is a kinetic energy machine; in other words the body creates energy around it. The psychic would call these energy spheres "auras". So, for this game, which is intended to provide a different form of abstraction from the normal one, we are going to become aware of the reality of our kinetic energies.

For the game to work at all we need a very large sheet of paper, color pencils or fiber tips or crayons — at least six different colors. The piece of paper needs to be at least as tall as the tallest player and at least three times as wide. Probably the easiest way to get such a huge piece of paper is to buy cheap wall paper and use the back of it.

Or go to an art store and buy the largest pad of drawing paper and then tape the pieces together until the size is achieved.

Stick the sheet to a wall (or lay it on the floor) and take off your shoes. Lie against (or on) the paper and stretch out an arm as in the illustrations on this spread. The other arm is tucked in at the side.

Take a colored pen and draw a circle using the wrist as the center point, twisting the hand to make the circle.

Then, from the same starting point draw another circle, the center of which is the elbow — much bigger. The next circle should center at the shoulder and the next circle should center at the naval, thus surrounding the whole body.

Now that the circles are drawn the person lying within them can test them. Turn the wrist

and notice that the fulcrum for this joint remains roughly within the circle drawn. This is the kinetic sphere of the wrist — i.e. it is the sphere of physical/static energy influence of that part of the body. Revolve the elbow joint and it will operate within the larger circle. Move the whole arm from the shoulder and you will notice that it has a kinetic influence within the circle.

Now rotate your whole body on the paper as though you were pinned to the ground at your naval and you will turn within the largest circle on the paper.

Here are your basic, two-dimensional spheres of energy power and you will realize that these spheres influence everything that happens in your life: whether you touch people, how you remain during times of contact with others, what your limb muscles do in order to operate in life.

But there is more to it still. Now the person on the paper should turn on his or her side and stretch over and point with the hand that was extended, say to the right of the body — still remaining on the sheet of paper. The first pointing should touch the edge of the biggest circle — you are still within your normal static body sphere. But now move your right leg over your left and "step" to the edge of the largest circle, as well as stretching the right arm out beyond the circle.

In this position you have created another circle — another kinetic sphere and you should then draw this new circle, using the side of the waist as the pin point.

With this simple act you have stepped out of your static kinetisphere and into a new one — an active kinetisphere. This is the beginning of your approach to the mobile world — you are no longer inside a static circle but can now create any number of new circles which could take you across the whole globe.

Another place to play this game is at the beach where the sand provides a very convenient drawing board. Follow the drawings on page 173, and you can create "mandalas" — patterns — with your body in four directions. Here you are an energy source and you are creating a perceptual pattern on the face of the world.

SUCH AS IT IS AND THE DOUBLE BIND

Many readers may be familiar with the term "double-bind." It sounds, on the face of it, rather like an unpleasant torture which might have been imposed on religious heretics during the Spanish Inquisition. In effect this is what it is, except that the victims are not long in the past and have nothing to do with religious heresy, but walk our streets today, very often wearing school uniforms.

The existence of the double-bind today relates to a simple difference of life-form; that which exists as a dilemma between the processes of becoming human and the requirements of the social order that we live in. Ken Wilber, in his study of consciousness *The Spectrum of Consciousness* calls this strata of awareness the *Biosocial Band*, i.e. that part of our lives which relates us to our social environment, or the area which is concerned with "I and you."

The story starts young. Put through the simplest possible example, the double-bind occurs when society instructs that a child should become a part of the social norm by becoming an individual. "If you want to make friends, stop imitating Peter — be yourself." Another example might be the tendency among parents to force children into believing that there is no pressure on them — "Johnny, surely you don't think I would ever make you do anything against your will?" Another common double-bind is that of family love — "Ann, how can you not love me, I'm your mother after all." Perhaps the "after all" says it all.

The bind is in the accepted fact of *having* to love one's mother and the double comes through the rule which says that you are evil if you are unable to do so — guilt being the main source of anxiety. It does not occur to the perpetrators of

CLASSROOM POLITICS

In a classroom a child is faced on a daily basis with what we can call the "Get-to-the-top" game. It goes something like this:
Jenny is asked by the teacher to answer a question concerning the name of the capital of Italy. Although she may have known the answer before being put on the spot, she is unable to give it at that moment. The grilling that she is given freezes her mind. The rest of the class, not under any pressure but seeking reward and superiority over Jenny, is waving hands and making eager sounds, hoping that teacher will choose one of them. Teacher concentrates, however, on Jenny telling her to "think hard." But the answer does not arise from the "hardened" thoughts and so teacher turns to James who gives the answer easily. Jenny is thus put in the wrong and James in the right. Jenny is put down to James's advantage through the toughening process of success over failure. And this is reinforced day in and day out.

such idiocy that the words they utter to their impressionable children are both ugly, unloving and ridiculous because the purpose of the words is neither to extract love from the child nor confirm love to the child, but to manipulate the child into a mode of acceptable behavior which is nothing to do with love.

It is not suggested here that parents are somehow brutes who set out to damage and disturb the child. It is much more that this kind of behavior has always been the way and socially engendered habits die very hard indeed, unless we operate with intelligence.

It is very simply that we seem to have taken a wrong avenue some time in the past and that avenue has led us to a labyrinth of complexity which we are busily attempting to justify. The safety of numbers — that there are so many of us agreeing to do it — further enforces the mistake as an acceptable reality.

As a final example before we launch into more games and changes we can make in order to accept the buck and change the pattern, it is worth looking at the contrast of human behavior in the average Western school against that of the behavior amongst, for example, the Hopi Indians. The following pattern will be totally familiar if you or your children have had anything to do with elementary education.

Three aspects arise from this common scenario. The child first is taught, not what the capital of Italy is, but the process of how to compete with others, how to fail at this competition and how to relate to other people without love.

How many of us, perhaps particularly the men, have continued to live unconsciously on this plane from the departure of schooling right through to the top levels of management, where the dreams of a good life include fear of failure, instead of

joy from success. And to take it still further, despite our knowledge of the psychological and physiological ways that operate within life, this kind of stress can take its toll on us. Few of us ever stop to realize that this getting-to-the-top process is a task which can easily result in misery, dissatisfaction and heart attacks. And yet we not only continue to do it but we continue to pass the method of doing it onto the young.

The Hopi Indian child knows nothing whatever about competition. If the child does something successfully there is no reward, no congratulations, no smiles. Equally if he does something badly and fails to complete it in anyway that is useful, there is no admonishment or punishment. The state of movement within the social structure is simply what it is — without judgment, without need to do better or worse and a situation in a classroom as above described would be torture for the Hopi child.

To us it is normal.

To a Hopi child the whole aspect of "mistakes" is taken from a different view point. Mistakes are normal and receive as much interest as successes. There is no discrimination of value between good and bad. They simply are parts of life rather than being made into value judgments. It is not that we make mistakes and this is unfortunate — it is that we make mistakes and we make successes and they are the same except that one will produce one result and the other another result — without problems in either case. So much of the Western child's life is oriented towards the value of success and the disgrace of mistakes. For a Hopi child there is no dis-grace in failure.

The basic reason why we feel the need to get up to the top is that we consider our environment to be different from us. We say things like "facing reality" and "getting the better of things," "beating the game," or "winning over the next man," without realizing that in beating the environment we are essentially beating ourselves. And of course beating ourselves is exactly what we end up doing — witness the growing instance of heart disease, cancer, AIDS and other self-unrealized discomforts.

Once again Ken Wilber has a succinct way of putting it:

"Not realizing the problem is nonsensical, however, we are in the position of the poor drunk, who, leaving his favorite bar and heading towards home, collides head-on with a lamp post. Staggering back several paces, he looks around, tries to re-adjust his course, and proceeds to smack into the lamp post once more, this time with such force that it knocks him flat. Resolutely, he picks himself up and charges forward again, only to repeat the collision. Defeated, he cries out "Oh, it's no use. I'm fenced in." There is no physical barrier, no actual basis to our problem — the difficulty lies in the tangle of our thoughts, not in reality."

THE LEFT/RIGHT PAINTING GAME

Take a large sheet of white or colored paper, a large thick soft paint brush and a hard lead pencil. Place the brush in the right hand and the pencil in the left and paint/draw with them both together.

This should first be tried by the adult and then by the child and adult together. The point is very simple. The left side of the brain operates the ordered, sequential and structural aspects of life — it is the hard pencil side. While the right side operates the broader, more poetic and conceptual aspects of life. The right side of the brain operates the left hand and the left side the right hand — thus the switch. Stop and figure it out, if it is not clear as understanding this is important.

If we are forced to operate both implements at the same time and they are opposite to our normal practices we at once confuse the social structure of the mind — the learning process is thrown into confusion and you will be amazed what beautiful and original artistry will emerge.

Game - SENSELESS ART

Still on the same track, take a pencil or a felt tip pen — any color. Close your eyes and on a blank piece of paper — preferably large — draw something with the eyes closed. Do it with a child — both together on the same table but on different pieces of paper.

When you are satisfied that the drawing is done, open your eyes and sit with the child. Look at the picture and make shapes out it — formulate a design of something that it is close to — adjust it a bit if necessary so that it becomes closer to what you can see it is meant to be. Make pictures out of nonsense.

A MOMENTARY LAPSE OF REASON

The old professor of philosophy who was retiring addressed his class: "Men, I have two confessions to make before I go," he said. "The first is that half of what I have taught you is not true. The second is that I have no idea which half."

One important part of the education which the parent can give to a child is an appreciation and encouragement of *un-reasonableness*.

The mind is man's master and very often even his God. The mind has been fulfilled and nurtured as though it were the creator of all change and improvement. This condition probably arose originally out of an industrial need — i.e. that man believed he had to master his environment. The inherent fear that he would fail produced a situation whereby instead of the environment mastering man, his mind mastered him instead.

The result of this is reason as manipulator, logic as ultimate dictator. Science lives by this dictum — or largely, at least until the 1950s when the difficulties of quantum physics put a spanner in the works of certainty.

Now that science has to entertain the likelihood of probability as opposed to certainty, things have started to change.

Perhaps science and logic will cease to be our religion and a momentary lapse of reason will inject the world with a breath of fresh air.

Children are unreasonable creatures — indeed they are in a permanent state of unreason, until we, the adult and reasonable ones, bring the logic of society and culture into their minds. Not only do we bring reason but we bring OUR reason, our particular brand, certain that it's the only brand worth considering.

"They have to learn after all, otherwise how can they survive in the logical world?"

One of perhaps the most rewarding and deeply felt games ever created was originally a Zen Koan and has been recently used in various similar formats throughout many Eastern therapies by such as Sri Ramana Maharshi and Bhagwan Shree Rajneesh.

THE 'I' GAME

A little explanation first.
Our thoughts come directly and invariably out of
the I-thought — that is we think everything through
the concept of me. This is the central pivot of the
ego and the complete source of all our identification
with ourselves and everything that relates to us. It is
also what is so deeply enforced by normal social
conditioning and the seat of reason.

It is therefore only possible to look in other directions, i.e. away from "I", if we suspend the I-thought, and this is actually easier than it seems. It is merely a matter of tricking the mind into turning inwards and finding that there is only a limited amount of available things there. We cannot suppress the "I" because the only thing that can suppress the "I" is another "I" so we must set about the task by suspending it instead. The method employed in the Eastern tradition is called "nan yar" or self inquiry. It's a bit like taking a vacuum cleaner and turning the suction hose on the motor thus sucking up the sucker (so to speak!). Try this method for a two hour stretch.

Sit down somewhere comfortable, preferably cross-legged on the floor on cushions, sitting opposite a child, between the ages of eight and eighteen years old — i.e. a child that has already undergone much of the educational instruction that we are trying to supplement.

Have other members of the family remain absent for the duration of the game and do not drink or eat anything during this time.

Ask the question of the other — "Who are you?"

The next five minutes will be spent by the other answering things like — "Well, I am Joe Doe, I go to school, I live at number such and such, I am American, blonde haired, ten years old" etc. etc.

Your answer is — "No, that is not what I am after — those are perceptions, ideas — who are you?"

Then will come more personal things like "I am alive, a human being, I am made of flesh and blood etc. — is that what you mean?"

And the answer will be — "No — those are still words and abstractions — still ideas — who are you?"

As we continue to ask the same question what happens is that the mind runs out of ideas — runs out of things to say and comes back again and again on itself — it has to turn inwards. As it does so, it finds there is nothing to say — nothing left in the store of ideas that works. The result is silence and an active silence that is awake and vigilant — looking for something but finding nothing. The mind, or the consciousness, is fully aware and awake but in a state of silence because it cannot work the way it is meant to. The result is truly magical, for at the very moment when the mind shuts up the being becomes suddenly aware of a flash of something else — a flash actually of reality. This is our natural state.

The game will not work with a very small child because small children are already in a state of "Bodhimandala" — a state of no-mind and would therefore simply laugh at an adult for playing such a silly game!

Game - GOING BY SOUND

The silver is white, red is gold;
The robes they lay in fold.
The bailey beareth the bell away;
The lily, the rose, the rose I say.

The words themselves are the meaning — no sense needed. No continuity. No explanation. Just listen.

THE ART OF BOREDOM

Boredom is usually something which arises in a child after about the age of six or seven. Children start saying — "Mum, I'm bored, what shall I do?"

Before this age there is rarely any problem with what to do — they are constantly doing; either running or breaking or sleeping or eating or whatever is available — they are never bored. But then they start being bored and asking those awkward questions which make their parents feel guilty — "must find something for them to do or they'll be bored." As though boredom were in some way a crime and if they aren't busy a van will draw up at the door and two little men in green uniforms will get out and take the bored child away.

Let the child be bored — boredom is what makes people discover new things, new methods, new sciences, new ways of life. If a child's boredom is constantly activated — if things are constantly given or provided for the child to do, by way of gifts or toys or sports equipment or computers or bicycles or whatever, then the child will not get the chance to discover ways of dealing with that boredom.

It is a very subtle thing, boredom. It happens only to the most intelligent and active children and if you say — "Oh yes?" when the child cries "I'm bored" and return to what you are doing, then the child will think — "Hmph, so *he's* not going to fill the gap: either I shall have to remain sitting here restless and bored or I shall have to find something new to occupy me." And so the problem is solved by the child not by you.

And you stop feeling guilty too! What a deal.

HAVING

I live in a house that overlooks a valley about 20 kilometers across. In September especially, when the light takes on that translucent, pastoral texture, and at other times of the year, the colors of that valley are so extraordinary that when I take a camera and look through the lens I know that any attempt to capture the scene is fruitless.

Equally, to try to write a description here is also a pointless undertaking. It would not benefit me and it would do nothing for the reader by comparison with the real scene.

But it does not stop there — this human desire for having. Even when I look, I do not see the extent of the beauty for my eyes are only one step better than the camera lens and two steps better than the pen.

Since childhood, those isomorphic filters in my brain have created a barrier between me and the valley that I see.

We have already touched on this view of the surrounding universe in several parts of this book — to the extent that it may have become clear that we are *not* clear about what we see or feel or touch around us. The purpose of this was only to point out that there should be doubt and not certainty in reference to our surroundings. With this doubt in hand we may then approach children and their view of the universe with the knowledge that they may see something quite different from us. Once we understand this we may open our minds a little to other possibilities rather than close them and apply our own view as somehow a discipline. Such discipline is by nature a closed shop.

But here, in this section, we can look at something else that touches upon adult blindness and its application to children's awareness.

The need to have everything that surrounds us, especially everything beautiful or desirable, is a need that we can easily experience, for the Western world of acquisition and fulfillment by ownership is well established.

THE UNSPEAKABLE WORLD

"In the year... 2000, the United States of America will no longer exist. This is not an inspired prophecy based on supernatural authority but a reasonably certain guess. "The United States of America" can mean two different things. The first is a certain physical territory, largely on the North American continent, including all such geographical and biological features as lakes, mountains and rivers, skies and clouds, plants, animals and people. The second is a sovereign political state, existing in competition with many other sovereign states jostling one another around the surface of this planet. The first sense is concrete and material; the second, abstract and conceptual.
If the United States continues for very much longer to exist in this second sense, it will cease to exist in the first."

Alan Watts

The Western world's dream of wealth is twice removed from the unspeakable reality. The desire for the abstraction of wealth is the fundamental content of the dream. Or, to put it more simply: we want to want to have the symbol of wealth — i.e. the banknote. The chase is more important than the catch and the bill is more important than what it can buy. This is, of course, only realized once the chase is over — when the riches and glory of finding large cash rewards are discovered.

When the key is turned in the lock and the door opens, the average rich person discovers that the goodies on the other side aren't all they were cut out to be and that actually he prefers to go on desiring to make more money. There is no wish to stop because the fun is in the chase, and very often there isn't a lot of fun in that either.

This amazing state of affairs helps to provide us adults with many of the methods which we apply to children, for if we are occupying our lives with a chase and indulging in all the rules that this requires, we naturally live this life in all aspects and apply it to our children.

"You gotta qualify son!" "You must make a niche for yourself in the tough world out there." "Career is everything."

The degree to which this applies is sometimes so extreme that the child will suffer the most terrifying nightmares and waking anxieties in order to fulfill what often are the father's ambitions for his son. Many children today end up on the psychoanalyst's couch even before they are teen-agers, and there, very often, they receive further confirmation of how insane and abstract the world is.

I can remember one brief period of my life when my father, in every respect a kind and loving man, pushed me headlong into a professional career that was so alien to me that when it came to taking the examinations during the university course, I would sit crying on the telephone to him, unable to express my depression, anxiety and failure at not being able to fulfill *his* wishes.

It is not that parents are bad — hopefully this has not been the impression of the reader — it is only that adults often cannot look beyond their own abstractions of the universe. It's as though, peering through a camera lens at everything around them, they wonder why the resulting picture is not what they saw when they pressed the shutter button.

To most of us this is one of the greatest eternal mysteries — that our hopes do not conform to the results we get. And yet we continue to hope and pay little or no attention to the results. Actually we forget the results so quickly that they rarely form part of our progress for change.

The existence of this unspeakable world is constantly hidden by the simple fact that we try to conceptualize it at all. In our attempts to speak it, to reasonable-ize it, we actually make it all the more unavailable to us.

A child, especially in the early years, does not attempt to do this. Children are quite content to sit and stare. You may have seen your child sitting, gazing out onto a beautiful scenic horizon, literally consuming the incoming data. You can sample this too if you realize that the child does so without comment, words or any kind of comparative conceptualization. The words are not *there* to quantify or divide — there *is* no divisiveness available to the child in the mind until we, the adults, provide it.

Pointing a child toward a specific career, then, is perhaps the epitome of the parental conditioning by which we encourage the abstraction of real wealth. We say to the child "what do you want to do when you grow up?" at about the age of 14 or slightly older, if the child is lucky, and in this simple and common instruction we tell the child to ignore the actual wealth that can surround him and aim him toward the secondary abstraction of making money. Once he gets involved in that game and begins to take it seriously the abstraction jumps back again to the state of desiring to make the money and so he is twice removed from the appreciation of true wealth, and thus lost as we are.

Put very simply, children do not need to be encouraged into any kind of career identity. Most young children, around the age of 12 will begin to play the game of imagining what they are going to "be", career-wise, and may well change their fantasies about the future any number of times. "Dad, I want to be a fireman," "Mom, I want to be a dress designer." And it is more than likely that the eventual result will be something totally different from any of the fantasies enjoyed as a child. The fact is that these *are* fantasies, simple dreams that the child can have tremendous fun with in early life, provided the parent doesn't immediately jump on the nearest career guidence councellor and drag him to the house for ready advice on fire-fighting equipment!

Wait for the child to start playing the game and play it with him.

Back in the sixties it was possible to buy uniforms from toy stores that suited most of the general career fantasies — a nurse's outfit, a cowboy outfit, a fire-fighter's helmet and jacket. These "fancy dress" packs were a lot of fun and I can remember getting through at least five of them in one year, charging around the garden fighting every fantasy fire I could imagine. Within a few weeks I was fighting the local "Indians", still wearing the fire-fighter's outfit!

In a child's mind a fireman can so easily turn into a John Wayne and the game brings such joy to the child that it would seem always a pity to take anything of this kind seriously. Play the game with the child. Be a store keeper — set up a table in the garden or the front living room and deck it out with Cornflakes, jams, teas, cakes and then get involved in the great game of trading with your child.

And remember the common maxim of the wealthy career person: "I spent the first forty years of my life destroying my health to make money and the second forty years spending the money to get back my health!" This is work as pain and it begins in the playroom.

To bring the theory once again into practice, perhaps we may look at a simple game.

THE SUPERMARKET GAME

Visiting the food store is a common game that we take very seriously, but this method may help to bring the story back into its real state. Normally what happens is that we take our pocket book and visit the local supermarket for the week's household food requirements. We push the cart around the aisles and pick from the numerous shelves of goodies those things that we have previously listed as necessary or those things that we cannot resist!

The pleasure of doing this is maintained if we keep our eyes off the prices but many of us carry along a calculator in order not to get too big a shock at the end of the line. We go to the check-out counter and the cashier adds it all up, usually resulting in a sick feeling at the pit of the stomach when the total presented is more than we had reckoned. It does not occur to us that the money we are parting with is not lost — it is merely replaced by the value of the goods we have acquired.

We now have vegetables and meats and liquids and fruits that will enter our bodies and make us (hopefully) healthy and strong.

We have simply exchanged one form of wealth for another. Actually the foods we have bought are worth a great deal more than the paper bills we have given, for in a state of starvation (as for example the 1930s depression in America where there was no shortage of food, only a shortage of cash) you cannot eat hundred dollar bills.

On this occasion, take along a child for the weekly shop. Before going sit down and go over the planned food requirements of the week — the meals that you wish to cook, the dishes or cakes or whatever that will form the week's consumption. Allow her to be familiar with this list and then give it to her and once in the supermarket let her do the whole job. Do not look at the prices, simply accept that this week you are totally unconcerned with the financial value of the shopping.

Emphasize to her that it is important to choose items, where there is a choice, that are economically worthy — not always the most expensive, but always the best value — and allow her to make the value judgments. Once you are through doing the buying, at the end of the game deliberately ignore the cash total — do not look at the cost. Hand the purse to the child and let her do the reckoning and the paying. The cashier will not short-change a child, she will be too much involved in the unusual pleasure of having a child do an adult's job

and will carefully count out the change to the child's satisfaction.

Take the goods purchased and throw away the pay slip.

Concentrate on the goods/wealth you have acquired and savor it in the form of what it can do for you and your family. Even if the child has got it all wrong and bought things that were not what you wanted — no problem, simply go back another time and give her more precise instructions. It will not break the household purse, it will do enormous things for the child's confidence and sense of play in work and you will for once (or more) be free of the anxiety that results from financial abstraction without real measure.

TALKING IN STRANGE TONGUES

As a final game to try to exemplify the ideas presented in this chapter, for a whole morning or afternoon the family must each choose another language to speak in. Each language chosen must be spoken by all the family for the duration and of course it does not matter if you do not speak the language genuinely. Take French for example — everyone knows how the French sound when they speak — sort of "heehaw heehaw heehaw" or "comontalivoo!"

Speak whatever language chosen all the time and with as much drama and totality as possible. Ask questions — real questions about having a cup of coffee or eating lunch — in the fake language and you will get the greatest laughs out of trying to make yourself understood.

Another day, chose another language and do it again. If you feel that the tongue chosen needs emphasis with hand and arm gestures then accompany your speech with lots of French gestures or Italian gestures to add to the flavor.

In the East, they call this the "Gibberish Meditation." It's a lot of fun.

CHAPTER EIGHT
HABITS – THE STAGNANT POOL

TRUST ME!

The epithet "Trust Me" has gained a bad reputation. It is largely through its use by second-hand car salesmen and politicians that this reputation has come about for generally, today, if someone says "trust me" to you, you don't. Actually politicians have recognized this and rarely say it anymore, not because they are trustworthy, but because if they do say it people won't believe them anyway. Distrust is a complicated thing, a little like lying, though not quite.

We generally look upon trust as something we feel for others — "I don't trust you because you never do what you say you're going to do." It doesn't often occur to us that we can trust that person completely, knowing that he will not do what he says he is going to do. We can trust him not to do it! Instead we prefer to distrust him, which means in effect that we have to sever relations with him completely or remain in a state of paranoia whenever he is around because we are expecting any moment that he will fail us.

Such relationships of distrust occur most readily in areas where money is involved, because money is a very convenient abstraction for almost all our feelings. We love others because they give us money, we hate them because they don't. We think we are being tricked, one way or the other and the real problem is that we don't know whether we are being tricked or not. In any case it is important to us that we should not be lied to because people who lie are not reliable — we cannot tell if they are worthy of *our* trust.

So, in actual fact, if we look a little more closely at trust, perhaps it is more that we do not trust ourselves. We do not trust the knowledge we have of the world and other people. It is not really a matter of trusting or distrusting others at all.

And we can take this problem with trust to its final level — trusting ourselves to survive — or in other words trusting existence to provide us with what we need.

And this brings us to the point of this part of the book, for of course small children are born with this trust, completely intact and working like a dream.

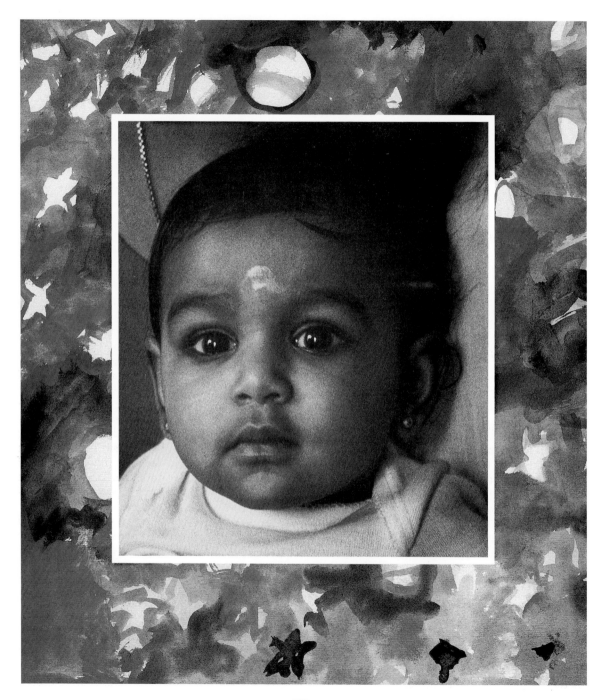

CHILD OF EXISTENCE

Most of modern civilized reasoning is based on dualism. The Greeks invented it a long time ago — primarily Aristotle, who said that if life is to survive successfully it must be based on opposites — i.e. good vs bad, love vs hate, life vs death, truth vs untruth, sadness vs happiness and so on. Look around you, most everything functions in this manner — especially humanity vs the universe, we and them (or it).

Effectively this basic concept has divided man against himself. We are in the world and we believe ourselves to be separate from it, but another reality is becoming clear in recent scientific and philosophic thinking: we are existence, one with our surroundings and un-separate, which means that if we see ourselves as separate from existence we are necessarily separate from ourselves.

This accounts for many things — for fear and uncertainty, for ego, for anxiety and stress, for disease, loneliness, cancer, AIDS, insanity, nuclear war, power, politics, ecological chaos, indeed for all life as it stands today. Thanks to the ancient Greeks!

Science is now awake to the fact that there is no object and subject. Scientists have begun to see that they cannot be objective about experimentation, though there is still lip service applied to objective reality.

The trouble started some two or three decades ago when a few very bright people such as Eddington and Schrodinger came up with the startling fact that if you tried to look at a sub-atomic particle it moved! In other words, the very act of "looking" or the existence of observing particles in the area of sub-atomic particles that you were trying to look at, changed the particle's position, thus indicating that the universe responds directly to the observer — that in effect the observer is as much part of the experiment as the thing he is trying to observe.

The discovery has so far only really been digested within the area of physics concerned with tiny particles — in other words the microcosm of the universe. Few people have yet woken up to the fact that if you look at a rock it also changes, simply because of the human presence. That a tree is something different if you are beside it or if you cut it or strip it of its leaves. The scientist will say that the difference of human presence in a tree observation is not substantial enough to affect the tree, but that may be because science cannot yet measure the difference. The day that it can, physics may realize that perhaps there can not be a Unified Theory of the Universe because we *are* the universe and we cannot measure ourselves in relation to ourselves without there always being an unknown factor. This dualism is learned, not natural. A small child does not think in terms of opposites — she does not either hate you or love you, she does not feel sad or happy. To her, they are the same, part of a constant flow of energy and life which exists inside her. It is not even that she is connected to the universe for to use the word connection also separates — making us sound like we have a rope around our necks that is somehow tied at the other end to some God or universal consciousness.

The very concept of *being* the universe is immensely hard for us to come to grips with because it goes against everything we know. In particular it goes against the mind, for the mind/ego flourishes out of division, as we have seen in other parts of this book. The ego stands tall because it

maintains this Greek understanding of the universe. In fact one could almost say that the Greeks invented the ego, or if not invented, seriously boostered it. "I am better than you," "I am wealthier than you," "I hate you one minute and love you the next," "My feelings keep changing and I am confused by them, so therefore I don't trust them, I prefer to trust my thoughts."

All these and many more such motives for living are false and based on something passed down from generation to generation over thousands of years. It is no wonder that dualism is so strong in us and it is equally no wonder that we cannot conceive of being at one with everything around us.

Imagine what it would mean if we really knew of our oneness. Take a few typical phrases first:

Instead of saying "Life is a bitch and then you die," you would say "I am living and dying all at the same time, every moment of my life/death!"

Instead of "I hate that guy because he is rich" we would say "I *am* that guy so I am also rich — so unless I hate myself I must also not hate him."

And it is clearly true if we look closely at our own feelings. Hating someone else for whatever reason is extremely painful. In fact, we often hurt ourselves much more through hatred than we hurt the person who is the target of the hate, for that person may not even be aware that we exist!

And if we can imagine being in this state of oneness, whereby we are totally "into" everyone and everything around us, it will become quite clear how a child exists, because this natural state of oneness is how a child is *all the time.*

We are extraordinary creatures. We create solid items around us in order to make us feel that we are real. We then label them so that we can set ourselves apart from them, wonder why we are lonely and then destroy the solid objects we created in the first place.

The child of existence has none of these problems. He is not interested in form or shape until he comes in direct contact with it. He is a flowing and integrated whole, connected and part of himself. He has no judgments about things or people around him, they simply *are* and that is enough. His feelings flow through and around him perfectly, just exactly as they should. He is completely willing to be happy, sad, frustrated, angry, desperate, alone for these are his natural gifts for communicating with existence and others whom he considers must be the same as he is.

He receives signals and information from the whole universe, without filter. He is in touch with you and me on a level that we are no longer familiar with and he is part of nature to the extent that he *is* nature and is therefore able to feel everything and everyone around him. Because he has no way of communicating with adults in ways that they can recognize, these gifts and natural skills are largely lost to us until it is already too late for him to tell. For the moment he receives our conflicting signals of division, duality, dishonesty and all the other social misinformations, he has forgotten his own purity. You cannot remember something that

you have forgotten that you have forgotten. And with this forgetting goes also innocence.

Trust, it would seem has to be re-learned through a reliving of childhood.

Game
ACTING ON IMPULSE

Most people are very frightened to listen to the first thing that comes into their heads. They consider this to be impulsive, "thoughtless", etc., and prefer to give matters "serious consideration" before acting, especially if the matter is important — like buying a car or a house, or choosing a school for the kids or getting married. Some people will "consider" these situations for so long that the whole pleasure of the initial idea has gone by the time they reach a decision and suddenly they no longer want the thing after all.

Others act quickly and then find that they have not quite got what they thought they had and can therefore feel remorse and regret, or guilt because others feel a better choice could have been made if they had given it "some thought." There are plenty of familiar adages such as "look before you leap" which well-meaning people feel may stop the impulsive person from acting too quickly and getting into trouble. So, in this coming game, you are going to get in a lot of trouble! Because you are going to act on impulse all day long. Everything you first think of in every situation, you act upon. It doesn't matter what it is (except of course doing yourself physical harm which is not impulsive but stupid), whether it is a thought that needs verbalizing and will upset people, or an action that will get other people angry at you because it is not convenient for them. If you feel like doing it, do it at once. No consideration, nothing sensible, only impulse.

Follow your feelings for the chosen period and what you will find will open your eyes to many other forms of being alive. What you will notice is that the sensible mind will object constantly — telling you that this is a silly game and will only cause trouble for you but let the mind chatter, ignore its secondary responses. Once you get used to follow your feelings you will begin to recognize the power of them and how rapid they respond to life. Give the heart a chance — follow it for a day and the world that appears before you will be varied and exciting.

MUMMY'S BOY

The small child awakens into life with an unquestioned certainty that life will care for him. He accepts existence as his mom, his ultimate protector and there is no fear of that mother ever letting him down.

Once the human mother has induced a sense of uncertainty after the first few months of his life, by insinuating a thousand different doubts into his mind, he forgets the certainty he'd had.

He then spends the rest of his life trying to find his original mother again and the reassurance that she provided.

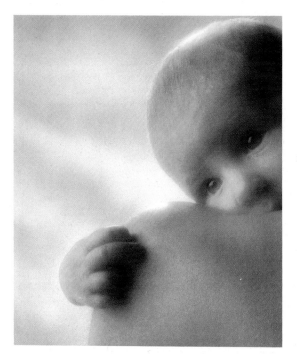

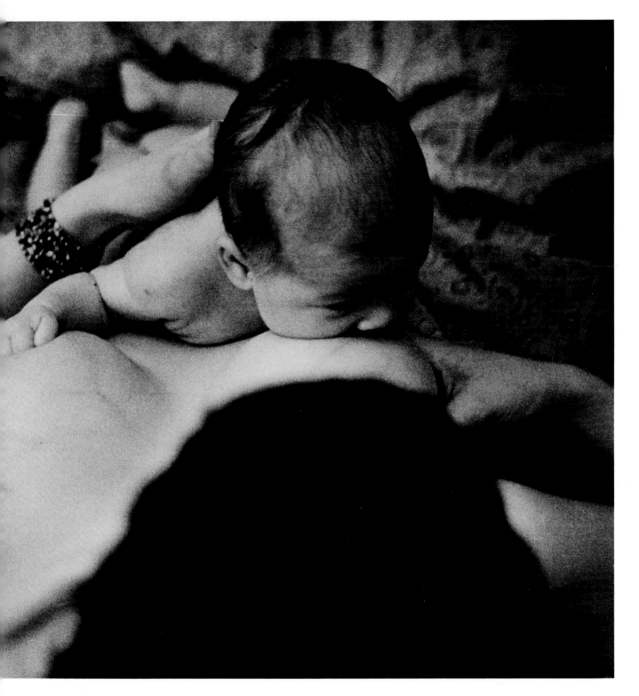

All work, acquisitions, possessions, relationships are an attempt to rediscover this undivided state of oneness and most of us fail ever to find it again. In the relationships that most of us form there is the greatest example of this loss of security. It takes many forms such as the grueling and complex "arguments" that we share with our loved ones over matters that afterwards seem to have been totally irrelevant. Anyone who has been involved in a long term sexual relationship will be familiar with such encounters.

We have many ways of dealing with these occurrences — but mostly they amount to us avoiding pain, either by walking away until the energy has died down or simply cutting off from the other partner and remaining remote or even silent. These arguments derive almost invariably from a basic fear that the relationship is coming to an end.

This too derives from the basic dualism which is death vs life — our dependence on the idea that we are living until we die, a misunderstanding of life which once again we can blame on the Greeks!

As we have mentioned before, fear is non-existential. It is an emptiness which we can do little or nothing with, for it is like floundering around in a vast empty space full of pain. The last thing we feel like doing under these circumstances is love the other, but in fact this is the answer to the problem. Love is existential — it is a constant remedy to fear. If one can inject it into that empty space called fear, it creates a reality which can then be worked with.

The willingness to "remember" love, comes from awareness of the possibility that it is there, somehow hiding behind the anger and frustration that accompanies most disagreements. Perhaps a cooling period will be needed but ultimately it all relates to how much each individual has invested in the anger.

In the case of young children, the very presence of constant love, i.e. honesty, allowance and care, accustoms the child to life in that form. In other words if the child has grown used to being loved under all situations in childhood, then she or he will have learned how to apply the same "techniques" later in life. The other essence needed for this early plus-conditioning is a willingness to undergo constant change without fear.

TELLING ALL
For adults together.

If you are two parents within a relationship then this game can help to provide the answer to any fight or disagreement between you. Perhaps the disagreement is regarding how much one loves the other, or derives from a small sexual conflict. In any event the disagreement is not a superficial one but tends to arise constantly over a period of time. The couple's argument tends to take the same format even if the initial reasons for it are different or forgotten. Such disagreements between couples arise because of some fundamental difference in the characters, needs or ideas of the people concerned. Arguing over the reasons for the disagreement does not help, as this is only the mind perpetuating anger and resentment and the basis will be more difficult to sort out.

This game is designed to bring to the surface the very essence of why the couple are at odds on each occasion. It takes a great deal of generosity and self-awareness and therefore is best undertaken in circumstances where the couple is alone and preferably in a stress-free environment, such as on vacation or at the week-end when the children are either asleep or somewhere else. Other games will follow with children present, but this one is only really playable with two adults of the opposite sex.

It is not necessary for there to have been a recent disagreement, but this would be ideal!

Go to the bedroom together and close the door. Light two candles and place them one on

either side of the bed on bed-side tables. If you have some incense light it and place it in the room. Turn out all other lights in the room and sit opposite each other on the bed with the covers turned back so that you are on the naked sheets. Sit in a meditation position, back upright, leaning slightly forward, using your hands or fists as support to the front so that you are both leaning slightly towards one another.

Close your eyes and breathe deeply for a few breaths together making sure that the breathing is the same in each of you. Allow it to continue until it feels fairly natural, even if this is difficult to begin with and keep going until the rhythm is working together.

The atmosphere of the bedroom should help this to happen and the vibrations that exist there will give you an additional chance to be in harmony,

even if you have just had a heated row.

Open the eyes and decide who will be the first to speak. If there is argument about this, then the woman should be first. There is one basic rule — that the one who is speaking has full freedom to speak and CANNOT be interrupted for any reason. He or she must be given the floor for the full duration of the talk. If necessary, set an alarm clock for a minimum of ten minutes and as much as thirty if you wish, to complete the monologue that will follow.

Now tell the other absolutely everything that is in your mind about how you feel about the other but choose deliberately as many bad things as you can find. Call him an oaf, a chauvinist, a pig, then be more specific about his "faults." Tell him ALL the things that you have always wanted to tell him about his faulty character — the things that you hate most of all about him but have kept back for fear of making him angry. It does not matter how terrible they may seem to you — speak them at him and speak them as calmly and simply as possible. There is no need to dump on him, no need to yell and scream and froth at the mouth! Just tell him calmly and simply what you hate about him.

The other partner will remain completely still during this quiet tirade of hatred and abuse — absolutely quiet, even if it means taping up his mouth and tying his hands behind his back. No response whatever. Just keep in mind, you who are being attacked, that your turn comes next!

When the alarm goes off, or when the words simply cease coming, stop and close the eyes, both people. Breathe again and notice that the breathing between you is no longer in harmony for you have created a mass of energy that is firing in all directions. Bring the breathing back together again. Do not open your eyes, do not speak, simply breathe together. If the recipient of the abuse is feeling angry, sad, hurt or is crying, just allow it. If the mind is going crazy with answers, justifications, reasons etc., just allow it. Do not verbalize it openly. Remain silent for the time it takes to bring the breathing back together.

Now the other can do the same as the first. Call her names, point out her worst features, get into the depths of all the things that you have always hated during the whole of your relationship. Remember and speak as much as you can in the time you have, while the other remains completely still and silent, regardless of the pain and discomfort.

Then, when the second tirade is over, close the eyes again and stay silent while the breathing is brought back together. This time it may not be so hard to do because perhaps some part of the game element may have become apparent. If you are already laughing or crying then the next part of the game will be easier for you. If you are both still taking the whole thing very seriously then it will not be easy at all. But nevertheless, this second part is most important and should be followed as diligently as the first part.

The first speaker should now tell the other all the good things — all the qualities, the pluses. Everything you can find that you like or love about your partner — tell it now and keep the eyes open as you do it. Once again, the silent partner must remain still, silent and un-commenting. No jumping into each others arms yet!

Then silence, breathing and the silent partner gets to tell the story from her/his point of view.

Then silence and now come together in each others arms, either sitting or lying and breathe together once again for at least as long as it takes to be naturally together. If there is a feeling to make love then now is the time.

After this game there will be a sense of freedom, as though you have both unloaded a great weight off your shoulders and off the combined shoulders of the relationship. It also achieves another result — that all the worst possible fears that are engendered by not telling the truth of what you feel are dispersed — you have said it and he did not die or leave you (I hope!), so next time you feel something, you know that you can express it whatever it is.

This is not to say that couples should not have secrets from each other — secrets are healthy and happy things if they are kept out of love.

TELLING THE KIDS

With children and adults together.

The exact same game can also be played with children. In this case it is good that there be an equal number of adults and children in the game — two and two or one and one or three and three (more difficult). The children should sit opposite the parents first and be permitted to tell the whole truth of their feelings about what the parents are not doing, should be doing in their eyes, and what

faults they have. The parents absolutely MUST remain silent and not get into a superior, "I know better than you" mode, as this will seal the child's lips and spoil the game.

When it comes to the adults' turn there is no need to hold back or protect the child. Tell him/her everything and allow the tears if they come. Then go into the positive mode and tell it all again — with as much joy and laughter as you wish this time. No need to remain silent or serious with children in the game.

You will find that this particular game releases more energy than any other in this book for it gives the child all kinds of new things to look at. He will see that his instincts about the true feelings you have, both good and bad, were correct for all along he knew that you felt "that way," but denied it because children believe in the idea that parents are somehow perfect — at least until the child reaches the later teens.

It is ideal if this game can be played at times when there is maximum conflict between family members. Do not try to do it on a regular basis, like once a month, for this will kill its power.

CHAPTER NINE
THE ART OF LISTENING

THE NOISE BLOB

Mankind has long since lost the art of listening. There is so much information around that literally floods the senses into the mind, that there is no room any more for us to hear what is really there. It is somewhat like being in a densely filled party room with people shouting and talking, laughing and singing, and trying to hear your own heartbeat — you can't, of course. And it is especially difficult because we are constantly being told to listen to all the shouting and music and talking and forget about our own heart beat — the shouting is more important, it is being done for our benefit, after all!

It is, in fact, a fascinating experiment to regard all sounds that come to us as a sort of "noise-blob."

Next time someone is talking to you (though it must be admitted this is rather a disrespectful thing to do!) allow your ears to go fuzzy, as though you were doing with your ears what you can do with your eyes when you let them lose focus and stare blankly. With the ears "staring blankly" no one can tell until they expect a response (and in any event most people prefer to talk than to listen so you are probably safe for at least a few minutes!) let the sounds come at you without making sense of them — don't listen to the words, only the sound.

Then repeat the game elsewhere, for example in a traffic-filled street or a busy office. Let the sounds converge into one social blob of noise and you will appreciate that this is another way of looking at your surroundings — a mass of continuous noise, even when there is relative silence there is still noise (this is incidentally a corollary of the concept that there is never silence anywhere in the world at any time — only within yourself). You will also appreciate, purely for your own sense of play, that everything everyone ever said to you was gibberish! The only thing that actually makes any sense in your life is the sound of your own heart beat.

THE SILENT DIET

A good example of the phenomenon of social-noise is the whole curfuffle that surrounds dieting. There have to be at least a thousand books on dieting available at any one time and there are bright people thinking up new diets almost every week, in magazines, articles in newspapers, books. There is the Fiber diet, the Scarsdale diet, the Protein, macro-biotic, vegetarian, vegan, fruit, grape, sea-weed diets, every possible kind of diet. And they are all based on two human tendencies:

1. The inability to diet effectively
2. and the pleasure that's involved in *believing* that we are going to lose weight and will therefore look better than we do before the diet.

Even if we don't follow the diet for more than a week and therefore fail to lose the weight we want to, and give up the fantasy of looking better until the next diet comes along, we still keep trying. Diet writers are lucky — dieters forget fast!

So, now, here is the simplest diet that ever existed — a diet which requires no more than one page of one book and works every single time. Here is the diet that all children have naturally linked to their digestive system. A diet which, if allowed to flourish will permit the child to remain young, beautiful, clear skinned and in perfect physical shape throughout life — and not looking like Disneyland fatties.

It is called *The Silent Diet* and the one and only pre-requisite is that before you eat anything you follow this routine:

At a meal time or a time when you feel like a snack, sit down somewhere quiet, even if you have to lock yourself in the bathroom, and close your eyes. You have already felt hunger, a faint recognition that you would like to eat, and directly be-

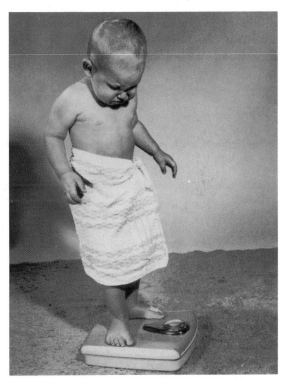

hind that hunger sense there is a knowledge of what you "need" to eat — actually what your body needs.

For there are two kinds of food — there is the food that you smell or see, but don't need — and there is the food that your body tells you about — the food that the body really does need.

If you left a child completely alone in a room full of different foods, all kinds of foods, and the child had never been told "eat this, not that," the child would choose exactly what she needed for her body without the slightest hesitation. She would choose to eat at the times when food was required by the body and she would eat that which her body told her to eat. Children, like animals, know precisely what they need. If the child were sick with some illness and a particular kind of food was good to heal the sickness, such as fruit, then the child would choose only the fruit and nothing else, even if all kinds of cakes and buns and rubbish are thrust at her.

But our surroundings are constantly full of desire for food that does not satisfy us, but rather satisfies the pockets of the manufacturers. The consumption of food and its effective use in the body has to do with a need-of-the-body-factor. If the body does not have a genuine need for the food, you can eat as much as you want of it and it will not satisfy the body, so the body will simply get fat. If you eat that which your body tells you you need then you can eat all that you want and the body will be fulfilled, satisfied and you will remain at the right, trim shape always.

Some people have this gift naturally and you will notice that they remain at the right weight whatever they eat. This is because they listen naturally, and probably unconsciously, to what their body wants.

Dr. Leonard Pearson has given names to the two different kinds of food — he calls the food that the body needs "humming food" — i.e. the food literally sings to you. And he calls the other kind "beckoning food" — i.e. when the food is available, we become interested in it, even though there is no need for it.

So, stop, be silent somewhere, and listen. The mind will identify for you the kind of food you want to eat to satisfy your body. Go for this food at once. Do not hesitate or discuss it with yourself or others — just prepare that food at once and then sit down and eat it very slowly. Look at it (somehow like the original prayer at the beginning of meals which was intended — once upon a time — not as thanks to God but as a chance to meditate on the food so that the body would consume it without discomfort — another word for prayer is meditation), examine the plate of food from all sides. Possibly those around you will think you are completely nuts, but do it anyway and encourage them to do it too. Touch the food with your eyes closed so that it is not only the sense of smell that

is at work in the consumption of the food, for smell is a very powerful sense in the act of food appreciation and very often the other senses are drowned out. Let your hands get a look in. Then eat slowly, chewing lots and eat small amounts at a time. Your appetite system works from the stomach up. Signals from your stomach tell the mouth and hands that there is enough food in the stomach now and you should stop eating.

Unfortunately we have developed the habit of eating so fast that by the time the stomach's signals have been received in the mind we have already eaten twice what we need and more, so that we feel full and uncomfortable, even suffering from indigestion. If we eat slowly and little at a time, the body will give the signal and we will be able to stop at the right time.

And don't worry about what is left on the plate — keep it for tomorrow or throw it — putting it into your body when it does not need it is worse than throwing it away.

Mothers beware! Children do not need to empty their plates, like your mother told you to — they need to eat what their body tells them to and no more.

There are periods of a child's life when she or he does not need to eat at all, even for more than a whole day at a time. Mothers panic when this happens, thinking that somehow the child is rebelling or does not know what is good for her. Allow her to do as she wishes. When she is ready to eat she will eat. Pressuring her to eat when she does not wish to will kill her natural appetite which may need to grow slowly for some reason best known to her body.

Do not imagine that you know better - it is her body after all, a body that is likely to be far more in touch with natural needs than yours is.

SOUNDING OUT

It is not that we need to listen to the body's sounds in the sense of actual sounds — in fact, the reason why we don't "hear" what the body has to say is because we have learned to accept that the body doesn't speak to us. In early life, probably our parents have told us not to worry about physical responses — not to pay attention to the distant hints that repeat themselves over and over again in our lives.

There is an ancient Shamanic saying that if you want to know the central issues in your own life, you should be conscious of those items in life that repeat themselves — those things that happen to you over and over again.

Unfortunately, very often these repetitive aspects of life are not heard simply because they are repeated and we have become accostomed to them. Take a simple example. Some people are apparently accident prone. They are always cutting themselves, breaking bones, experiencing bad luck with material things. Adolescent children are much like this — frequently seeming to fall into every hole or trip over every stone in the road when others easily avoid such pitfalls.

We say about such people that they are clumsy, accident prone or simply adolescent and discard the entire matter of their constant experiences just like that because we have already formed a "Box Judgment" about it. Even if we are the clumsy one — the one that contiunually behaves like Charley Chaplin tripping over everything in sight, we will simply accept this aspect of life, curse each time it happens and pay the hospital bills. It rarely occurs to us to stop and look over the whole business of our accidents or those of our children and see if there is an avenue of interest that tells a story.

In the adolescent child we can say — "Ah well, she's still growing, her legs lack muscular development, her feet are too big yet, things will change." With an adult we can say "He was always that way, never grew out of adolescence, he lacks coordination." And the matter is done.

Perhaps some of us will have noticed, for example, that on certain days we tend to do more physical harm to ourselves than others. Perhaps we cut our finger with a knife while trying to slice bread and then later on we burn ourselves with a cigarette, cut another part of the body with scissors,

stub the toe on a table leg, drop a hot cup of coffee down our front — all this in one day.

This is a message from the body. It is trying to tell us something.

The adolescent child or the clumsy adult is continually receiving such messages — every day and because they are coming so frequently, the recipient doesn't listen.

An incessant nail-biter is receiving messages from the body — bite me! Take parts of the skin from the nails or tear the nails themselves from the finger! Some of us will notice that we bite our nails only at certain times — perhaps during high concentration at the office, during long TV watching sessions. We don't do it all the time but only when certain conditions are prevelant. Here again, the incessant nail-biter will have created a box judgment about the nail biting. I'm a nervous person, or in many cases there won't even be that much awareness. The nail biter who bites only on certain occasion may have a clearer view of why it happens but still it is more likely to be a box judgment — I bite my nails when I'm nervous, when I'm concentrating, when I'm anxious. We even talk about nail-biting situations. But this is not listening to the messages.

Many more examples can be found and most of them have to do with habits — smoking, masturbating, a need for constant noise, a need to be constantly talking, workaholism, alcoholism, drug addiction, hypercondria, telephonolism (some people reach for the telephone in times of high stress — they make great salespersons or high level executives!)

These are some of the more obvious "olisms" but the body has ways of speaking to us also in much more subtle areas of life.

Perhaps you talk to yourself when alone. Perhaps you tell lies about things that you don't need to. Perhaps you never look at yourself in mirrors.

Which part of the body do you twitch or tap when there is rhythmic music playing? Is it the feet, the fingers, the muscles at the back of the knees, the heels?

When you get into stressful situations that are not totally obvious ones what happens to your body? Does your stomach blow up like a balloon or ache even though you have only eaten normally? Does your head ache? Do you sleep badly or excessively deeply? Stress can be found simply in memories of past events such as visiting a city in which you once lived and experienced unhappy events. The body may react in different but consistent ways in such moments.

But there is a message happening. These physical responses tend to be the same ones. We always get stomach pains or headaches or our eyes hurt or our right shoulder becomes stiff. Messages messages.

Every habitual response is telling us something and can be used to advantage to improve life. Our children will speak to us using similar messages, rather like our bodies in time of stress. A child will come to a parent in need of extra hugs or will ask the same sort of question many times until we are irritated by it.

A child that needs a lot of physical contact is simply saying she feels insecure. At an early age this is easily remedied by an open willingness to hold and touch. Later in adolescence the same sense of insecurity may have developed into much stronger messages such as always tripping over things and breaking bones. The hugs may have been refused in early life and the message now needs to be a stronger cry for attention. The ultimate scream of horror from a child is suicide attempts. We notice this one while having missed all the previous ones that, if answered, would have diverted something more extreme later.

A child that constantly bites the nails is trying to destroy the body, literally trying to eat it! This is an extremely intense activity and carries an equally strong message. It may be, for example, that the child is frustrated with boredom or by an inability to express extreme anger. Or it may be that she is bursting simply to tell you something and afraid to do so.

We can listen to these messages in ourselves and in our children and the result will always be a correspondence on a level that is going to lead to happy answers.

THE ART OF LISTENING

And the art of listening is the simplest thing! The first thing to remember is that the listening does not happen through the mind but through the heart. The heart is the body and has the first question and the first answer to all matters of the body. Listen to the feelings not the thoughts.

Many of us will be in doubt as to which answer is which — which little voice is which! All you have to do is hear the first answer. The first answer is always the heart's and the second is the mind's for the mind can only comment on something that has already happened — on the past, whereas the heart originates.

Listen to your feelings and believe them — they are the only right thing in you. Judgment through the mind has its place and can be most useful but it will never hear what is happening to you.

CHAPTER TEN- HOMES

**The purpose of this chapter is to travel through the whole "home" that we adults
have made for children and to see it, perhaps, in some different ways.**

*"The natural state is not the state of a self-realized
or God-realized man, it is not a thing to be achieved
or attained, it is not a thing to be willed into
existence; it is there — it is the living state. This
state is just the functional activity of life. By "life" I
do not mean something abstract; it is the life of the
senses, functioning naturally without the
interference of thought. Thought is an interloper,
which thrusts itself into the affairs of the senses. It
has a profound motive; thought directs the activity
of the senses to get something out of them, and uses
them to give continuity to itself. This constant
demand to experience everything is because if we
don't, we come to an end — that is, the we as we
know ourselves and we don't want that at all. What
we want is the continuity..."*

U.G. Krishnamurti

COMING HOME

Perhaps the most delicate area of our existing idea of child is encompassed by the further idea of family. And the centerpiece of family, after well over a thousand years, is the still further idea of marriage.

Let us consider history as a kind of theoretical story-line in order to map the possible sources of our modern social structure.

Shortly after the break-up of the Roman Empire the establishment of a new organized society was of primary importance, for the wreckage left by this giant social influence had to be cleared away. Those in a position to create a social structure had several major problems to solve. They had to form something on which they could base their power. The Roman Empire had crumbled perhaps partly because the methods of manipulation employed had permitted too much leeway to the common public and the result had been decay. Any new national formats needed to be more structured at the foundation, i.e. at the people themselves. If you want to make your operation function you have to give it order and the most convenient kind of order lies in manipulation by law.

The most direct method of touching individuals is to go for the heart of the matter — or the soul — that which creates conscience — and religion is the best possible weapon for this strike.

If we can envisage a small group of people in the most powerful part of the world — geographically speaking Central Europe and Middle Asia — we can surmise what their plan might have contained. There had to be a father because God was the Father of mankind, so the patriarchal structure was workable from the viewpoint of the powers that were.

This patriarchal system was based very simply upon family with a head-boss who had the authority to do what he wanted and the Church and Monarch could impose the details on this power and therefore govern the people within this system.

Father was given certain workable rules within which to operate his power:

1. He could chose the woman who would marry his son. That dealt with love and morals.

2. He could dispose of his property to the first son and the chosen woman. That dealt with wealth.

3. He could actually "make" the marriage in all its format. There was no need for a priest in the last millennium, the father conducted the ceremony, saw to it that the son and his wife made love on the nuptial night and that the resulting child was nurtured within the Church and the Law.

4. He could control the legal aspects of life by seeing his other daughters married off and his other sons converted to the priesthood.

By this method the social structure was such that marriage meant faithfulness, property, power and honorable or moral behavior. The married man was bound (at least in theory) to have sexual relations only with his wife and only for the purpose of making babies. Women had to be completely chaste and could only indulge their base and immoral behavior in the presence of the husband. Anyone committing adulatory was in direct disobedience to God himself in the form of the Church and the King, for the King was the Earthly representative of God in heaven and master of all Law, administered through the thousands of sub-Fathers in all areas of the land — the land which produced the wealth that the coming sub-Fathers would take over when the old man died. And to be without land and therefore without wealth meant a pretty poor existence.

A perfect system and it worked. For hundreds of years it facilitated a very successful and ideal cultural growth throughout civilized Europe, giving the authorities a method of exacting any kind of murder and mass slaughter in order to keep the people in place. The leaders could get on with the happy business of ruling and effecting the increase of national power.

But of course it had little to do with love or mutual concern. It was a pure and simple abstraction and we are still employing it as though the same rules applied.

We are still, within our family and marriage systems, operating on precisely the same basis as the people of the last millennium. In fact, the patriarchal system is largely responsible for the nature of our male dominated social structure at the end of this millennium. Habits die hard!

It is not only the superficial aspects of this system that dominate us. We are still willing to make our marriages through a sort of father-dominated appreciation of life. Father's approval is still largely required for the marriage of the son and daughter. Father still gives away the new bride at the wedding ceremony, still nags the son — "when are you going to have children?" — still commands the rules of the new family and still produces the cash necessary for the daughter to get married.

In Italy, for example, the system is frequently operating almost as though the country were still before the Middle Ages. In a marriage to which the author was invited, the bride-to-be spent almost three months persuading her father to allow her the choice of locality for the reception. The father went to "case the joint," choose the food and decide upon the time when the gathering would take place — choose the list of guests and generally oversee the whole operation. He "gave away" the daughter, who had incidentally been living "in sin" with the bridegroom for over two years before the wedding and he stood up at the dinner and made an elaborate speech about happiness and family future.

It is not intended to imply by this that the father was in anyway stupid or unloving in his behavior — he was in fact an extremely pleasant and compassionate man with nothing but concern and care for his daughter and the new son-in-law. The giving away of his daughter was literally, if unconsciously, the passing on of a "lover" to another man; a kind of unbonding ceremony in which the ropes of fatherly love were untied in favor of new bondings to the new man, the daughter not being allowed even one minute of freedom between the two owners. This is what the system of family and marriage has meant — keep the woman in bonds all her life. That way she will not only behave herself according to the Church, the Law and more importantly, the determinations of the MAN, but she will not have the opportunity to step outside these bonding systems for one minute and show herself in her true form — a dangerous character!

For man, unconsciously, woman is un-"seen", unpredictable and the source of all sexual immorality. She is emotionally dangerous because she constantly diverts man's attention from the important business of doing, or more precisely she diverts man from his exacting and important need to avoid himself. For women, by their very nature, must constantly stay in touch with the earth and the magic of existence.

We will look a little more closely at the female connection with existence, a little later in this chapter, but suffice it to say at this point that it is

most interesting to note that the time of the month when a woman is most trouble to a man is the end of her menstrual cycle — the time of the pre-menstrual or post-menstrual tension when she becomes, very often, like a crazy creature tugging at the man for reassurance and feeling the dread depressions that men and women have so much difficulty with. It is suggested that this is the time when woman is most in touch with existence, with the pull of the natural order, but because of the demands of society and the male need to do the organized things in life, such as make money and business, the woman is being pulled in two opposite directions — towards the Earth and from the other side, towards man's God — money (or more precisely all abstractions). And this is strengthened by over a thousand years of conditioning, making it no wonder at all that neither the man nor the woman understand what all this is about.

There is a simple Sufi song which is conducted with men and women together, and the words are as follows:

Women — There's no door, there's no door.
Men — Keep on knocking, keep on knocking.

Somehow, in the typical simple Sufi manner, this song says it all!

OVER THE THRESHOLD

Our habitual process of child-bearing stems also from this patriarchal process so that if we have married, i.e. chosen our partner, we have done so very often in order to have children. This is not to say that all marriages are eventually defined in that way but the vast majority still are. All the subtle and not so subtle environmental pressure pushes us to suppose that the woman will one day come home and say "Darling I have something to tell you," and we, the men, will look surprised and delighted at the prospect of having a child — suddenly we jump from being a couple to being a family.

We think in terms of this identity change. And we feel guilty if our responses are perhaps not so positive as they should be according to the TV soap operas. Actually, the majority of male responses to the announcement of a coming child, contain a considerable degree of apprehension. Such a change of identity is a tremendous shock both to the woman and the man, in different ways.

We have it in our power today to make a natural choice in this matter. We do not need to bring a child into the world and in the majority of cases we had better not. I hope that the degree of emphasis on sensitivity and vulnerability in matters of children outlined in this book will have put off a lot of people from having children at all. For, in balance, it is better not to give birth to children than to give birth. If we consider child birth in the light of its present habit; if we take children for granted as something we do just because we fell in love and got married, then we have already started the seriousness of present day child-rearing and made our very first mistake. The

child that will follow, will follow in that vein. There are so many traps and pitfalls in the unhealthy business of modern day child-rearing that if we are already in the *habit* of having children we will fall right into every one of them.

As a specific example, later in this chapter we will look at the criminal state of hospital child birthing techniques — the way a doctor will create the environment which is basically designed to damage the child. If we have not made a conscious decision through natural understanding, we will simply believe that this is the only way because our psyche/patterning for child birth is unquestioning.

Giving a child space on this planet is a major undertaking and one which requires the highest intelligence and the greatest amount of energy.

And the methods employed by those that are supposed to know how to help you do it are, for the most part, catastrophic. If it were in the hands of the public hospitals, for example and especially in the United States, no wonder child would ever survive the delivery room intact.

So, with that in mind we start what is intended to be a practical summing up of the whole of the preceding chapters in a down-to-earth story, running from the moment your decision to bring a wonder child into the world has been made to when that child leaves you behind.

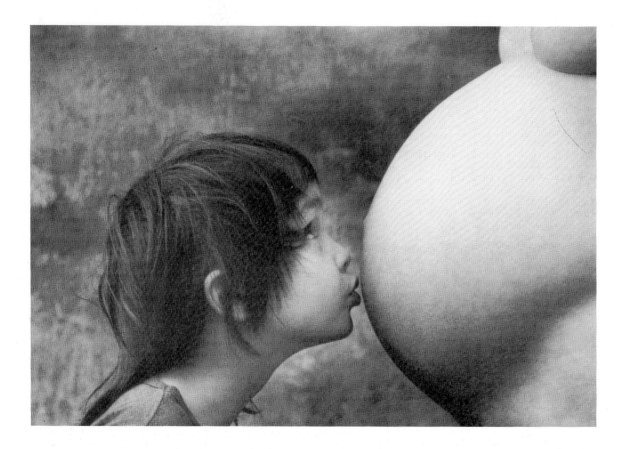

THE LOVE CHILD

As we will see when we reach the point in our story related to child birth, there is much information in book form that deals with the sensitivity of children and their total awareness of their environment during pregnancy. We can no longer say that a child is not aware until she is born or even several months after birth as many doctors would maintain.

It is not a matter of a fetus or unborn child knowing what is going on in the sense that we, already born humans, know. It is that the unborn child is sensitive through other forms of communication of everything going on around her first home, the mother's womb.

All this, we will sample shortly. But there is something to be considered long before this point of the process, for the process of giving birth does not begin when the child is already in the womb, it begins in the bedroom of the two adults who will cause this eventually to happen.

If you have arrived at the conclusion (despite all the discouragement to the contrary!) that you both wish to give birth to a child, and the preventative methods have been abandoned — deliberately — try during the coming days and nights to play the following game.

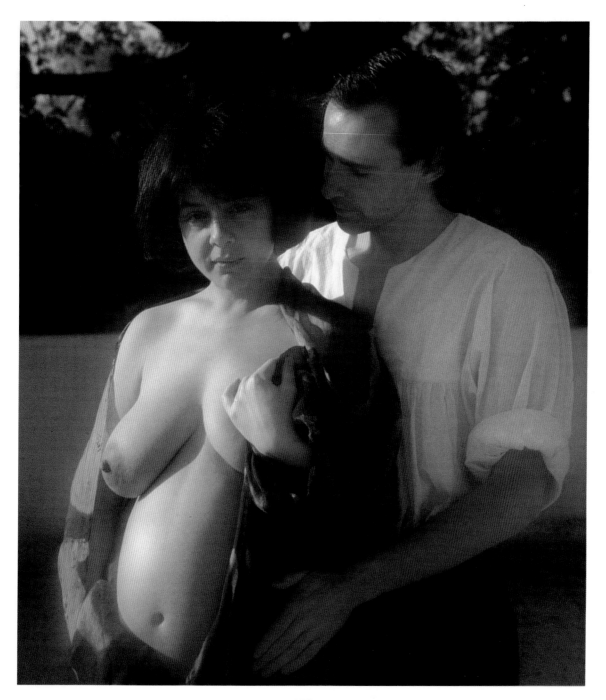

Game-THE ULTIMATE LOVERS

Essentially this game is to understand that we are now leaving the patriarchal society and entering existence. We are not abandoning male domination in order to enter female domination; we are not transposing patriarch for matriarch for this would simply be to drop one idea for another, both of which are meaningless.

What we are proposing to do is to create a harmony between man and woman which will tend to be somewhat female in emphasis. When all is said and done it is the female in us all, men and women, which gives the lead in matters of child conception and birth — if you like — the romantic pattern of life. The man, therefore, needs to bring himself in touch with the female energy that he contains and in this way come into contact with the woman in himself and in his partner.

This may sound tough for some of us but it is quite simple in practical terms. During these days and nights of potential conception accept the woman's lead. If she is unwilling to make love do not force it, pander to her and her needs. Bring her flowers, play her game, be the caring and serving husband/lover. Make the bed, do the domestic chores etc. Follow her.

This does not mean that as a man you must cease to be manly. Few women enjoy a soppy man! But allow the flow of her emotions and her instincts to guide the love-making patterns.

A sensitivity to female seduction will arrive at the best result in terms of a happy and harmonious love-making.

Play the knight in shining armor. Treat her as one hundred percent number one. It follows, of course, that the woman should do the same for the man. He is the one who will provide the love and thereby the seed of this child and the whole matter is somewhat holy in nature — almost like worshiping in a temple of love.

Try to make love-making a continuous process. It begins first thing in the morning with rituals such as bringing breakfast in bed and helping with bedroom chores and it continues through the day with phone calls, flowers and presents, culminating in love-making (or a tender acceptance that this night is not the time for love-making) at night or any other time of the day. And remember that early time, when you first fell in love, when you both enjoyed that feeling of astonishment which arises when someone falls in love with *you* — how can such a thing be, that someone would fall in love with *me* — when you have spent most of your life thinking that everyone dislikes you! (This attitude may not apply to everyone — living some time in Italy, for example, I was continuously astonished at how many Italian men presumed that every woman would fall in love with them!)

You may wish to entertain more complex forms of Tantric or Tao methodology, for which there are books available, the names of which may be found in the bibliography to this book.

The most important aspect of this game is to appreciate that the child to be born starts in the home.

PREGNANCY

The relationship between the man and the woman during pregnancy is a continuous ritual — a holy preparation for the coming of a spirit from God. I cannot put too high an emphasis on this religiousness. Do not think of it in terms of church or Pope or some other organized concept, think of it in terms of a pagan ritual.

The woman is a channel for the child to emerge from outside her; from a place in existence which is not physical, to a place that is, and the process is one of total wonder and amazement. It is not down-to-earth at this point, it is heavenly, magical and worshipful. All races and creeds in the ancient past and many that are still alive today, regard child birth as being akin to the mightiest of religious feelings, a matter for Godliness in its purest and most glorious form.

What's more, become accustomed to the feeling that you, as parents, are not the owners of the child. You do not own the child that you are giving birth to. Never call the child "my child" for this will only bring problems later of possessiveness and jealousy which in turn bring only anxiety and anger. You are nothing more than a holy temple through which the child's consciousness will emerge and your whole effort is to prepare your body for this task.

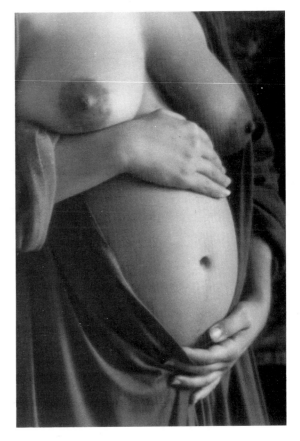

So- in practical terms:

1. No alcohol, no drugs of any kind. This means no aspirin, no analgesics, no hallucinogens, no uppers, no downers, no valium. If you get headaches, allow them to tell you what is wrong with your body. Listen and follow the chapter in this book on The Art of Listening. In the last analysis, if there is no other way, go to your local doctor or the natural doctor you have chosen.

No cigarettes or other forms of nicotine. No coffee and only the gentlest of teas such as herbal teas.

If you get morning sickness, be sick and then be gentle with your body until the nausea passes. It is perfectly normal and though tiring and problematic, it will normally pass. If it does not go find a herbal or homeopathic doctor, an acupuncturist or other natural doctor.

2. Find a natural birth doctor somewhere close enough to your neighborhood. There are many of them and if you have problems refer to the back of this book where you'll find places to call which will help you locate a natural birth doctor in your region.

Avoid at all costs a hospital doctor whom you sense has no feeling for child birth but who will inevitably treat you and the coming child like another piece of meat to be cut up and slotted into a pigeon hole. You may be lucky and have a local doctor who understands what you want. If necessary, give him a copy of this book and simply ask him what he feels about the whole process you have in mind. Test him, he is there to do *your* will not his own. Ask him about the natural child birth methods that he uses or suggests, and if you are not happy, go somewhere else. Follow your feelings in this matter for you are the boss. If it is necessary, move during the latter part of the pregnancy to a different locality for the birth rather than submit to a standard hospital birth.

It is important, of course, to make one note to this aspect of child birth. Not all doctors are bad! And not all situations can be managed without a doctor. It is not the author's intention to state that the child or the parent will know all the answers because there may be conditions in which a qualified and caring doctor's presence is needed. The point being made is much more not to take the doctor for granted as being the only person in the exchange of child-birth. There are three or four people who come before the doctor — the child, the mother and the father — then the doctor or midwife.

3. In terms of food, once again follow your feelings. Stay with the "Silent diet" system suggested in this book. Eat as often as you wish but only those foods that "hum" to you. If you have cravings for food, follow them.

4. Keep your body fit all through the pregnancy. The best possible method is swimming as water provides a soft and strong element for the body and also gives you a sense of the child's feelings in the swimming pool of your womb. Do not strain or overdo any part of the physical exercise. Only exercise to a point of satisfaction and comfort, but keep it regular.

5. Classes for natural birth are a must and should be attended by both father and mother.

6. Follow the chanting methods outlined in this chapter. They have been proposed and are taught by Frederick Leboyer, the Master of natural child birth and form the single greatest method of retaining your natural state during pregnancy and birth. The method and understanding proposed in this chanting is a preparation for the actual birth which may then be undertaken without drugs or medical aid.

7. Love making should be a gentle and loving ritual, the man always giving way to the woman, never pressing himself upon her. If the woman is not well and not able to make love there are always other ways for her to help the man find some satisfaction. The task of the man is to be mature and to give as much freedom and space to the woman for whatever her needs are. If he cannot manage this then he should not be fathering a child in the first place. The love affair between mother and child has begun when the woman has conceived — let her go. If she is free to have her child happily, she will come back to the man all the sooner and be more loving than ever before.

8. The process of the relationship between the man and the woman — mother and father to be — should be one which will draw the beginnings of the map for parenting. Try to make space for one another during the time of pregnancy as has been suggested at the beginning of this section on pregnancy — treating it somewhat like a kind of holy ritual with all matters observed with clarity and concern. You may be surprised how quickly this can become a habit too.

And lastly, remember one thing — this whole period of pregnancy and child-birth is not a serious matter — not heavy or dangerous. It is a dance of life and nature of which you are both part.

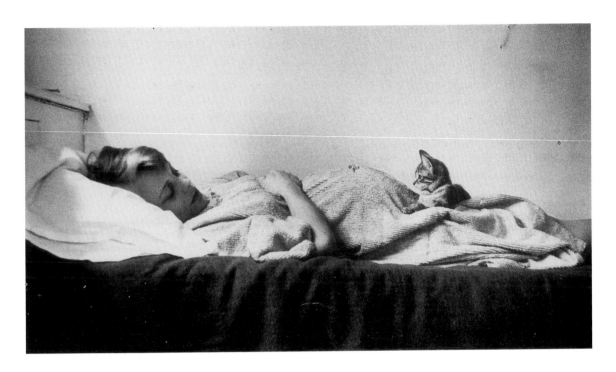

THE SIX-MONTH ENLIGHTENMENT

Frederick Leboyer has noticed, in the mothers-to-be that he has worked with, that many of them experience an extraordinary feeling during about the sixth month of pregnancy. Feeling may not be the best word but the English (and all other languages for that matter) language is inadequate to describe experiences so close to the heart.

During this time it is said that the child's spirit enters the fetus and takes up residence and that for mother and child there is a time of such joy and elevation that the mother becomes transformed if she is open to it. The spirit has, after all, arrived from existence; from a merging with oneness and a place which we living humans can have little awareness of. It is often felt, by the mother, that this time is the most beautiful of all the pregnancy. In the Indian Upanishads it is said that the coming child knows, shortly before birth, that he or she is arriving once more into a life, after perhaps many lives, and is aware that if he retains a knowledge of all the good and bad of the past he may pray to God that this be the last life in the body and never come again to such suffering. But once the birth takes place with all its trauma and catastrophe, the experience wipes the memory clean away and the new human begins once again in memorylessness only to make all the same mistakes. Perhaps, given enough care and tenderness, enough real love, it may be possible for mothers to guide the new child towards a state where the birth and early life is not so traumatic and the prayer to God is answered.

THE FIRST HOME-BIRTH

One of the best recent eye-openers related to modern hospital child-birth methods can be found in the books of Joseph Chilton Pearce. Mr. Pearce has no doubts about the way our current social order makes its mistakes in dealing with the business (!) of children. The chapter, for example, entitled "Time Bomb" in his book Magical Child *will help us to recognize something in us all that makes us take for granted the way in which the average hospital doctor "gives birth". The unfortunate state of hospital birthing is such that we have become intoxicated (sometimes literally) by the mighty medicine into accepting whatever the degree of suffering we and the child undergo during birth, because the doctor says so.*

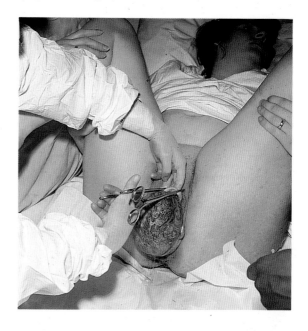

"All the anxiety-ridden fallacies of our day seem to congregate in the hospital delivery room, where they bring about a disaster that remains largely undetected because it works like a time bomb. None of the parties of the crime ever has to pay, for the explosion takes place in slow fusion over the years and creates such widespread and diverse havoc that few bother to trace it back to see who lit the fuse."

The essence of Pearce's proposal is that the starting point of this astonishing human confusion lies in the hands of the hospital doctor, what he calls "the medicine man," whose task it is to outwit nature and impress the world with the complex array of machinery and drugs at his or her disposal. The fundamental excuse for this astonishing and often inhuman behavior lies in the belief that the small fetus/newly born child is unaware of what is going on around her/him. In effect the child is considered so much meat because it is believed she cannot feel anything.

A typical and unhappily still common scenario

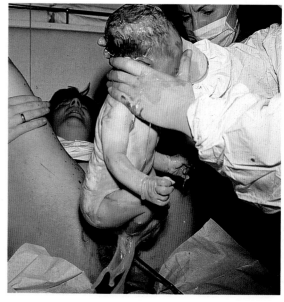

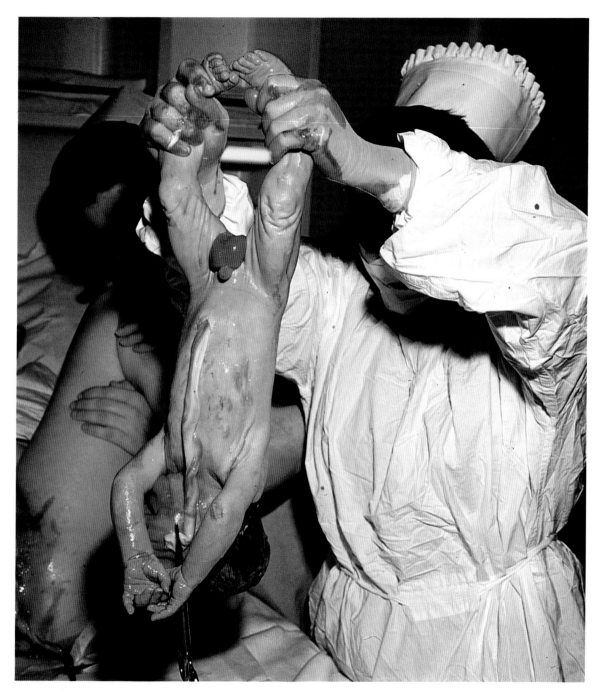

is one that occurred to the first child of the author in a London hospital, one well known for its professional facilities. It is worth the mention, even though the event has long passed and the child appears not to have suffered greatly from it — this factor allows the author to observe it without resentment for those who operated the drama.

The hospital was extremely busy and mothers (often with the fathers present) were queued in the pre-delivery room, where contractions were happening in most cases. The staff had evidently some list drawn up of the timing of the proposed births which seemed to have little or nothing to do with any natural process being experienced by the mother and child. Drugs were administered by student doctors to reduce the pain of contractions and the attempts to inject into the back of the mother's hand were so pathetic that she ended up screaming at the student who had punctured her hand, in the midst of contractions, no less than eight times before successfully finding the correct blood vessel. The mother was given a saline drip to encourage the contractions but the child to be born had clearly decided that he was not ready yet and despite nearly 24 hours of inducement no final stages were reached. Instead of removing the saline drip and allowing the mother to recover from her extended ordeal, she was taken to the delivery room and further drugs were administered to bring on the birth, regardless.

To cut a long and extremely painful story short, the child was delivered by forceps, accompanied by episiotomy, spinal puncture and other deadening drugs (the spinal puncture did not work the first time and had to be repeated) following which the child was delivered and the umbilical cord cut so that his lungs did not function properly in the first moment and he had to be rushed to an incubator where he spent the first three days of his life. It is astonishing that he survived the ordeal at all and that he appears not to have suffered subsequent physical ill effects. He is now seventeen years old, large and strong and perhaps the sweetest young man that one could ever hope to meet. But, were the occasion to repeat such an operation to arise again, it would not be permitted to happen in the same fashion.

Other children, still being born in this exact same way almost two decades later, are not so lucky.

Joseph Chilton Pearce, in *"Magical Child"* explains to us in some detail a few simple facts:

1. The natural process employed by the child's body during the last parts of life in the womb involve the secretion of hormones between the child, through the placental fluid, to the mother in a direct conversation which prompts the mother to know that it is time for the birth. The mother's hormonal response returns the message that this is OK by her body and the child then responds with further hormonal messages that begin the whole delicate and magical process. The two are then in direct communion with one another and the subtle human correspondence takes place naturally.

In effect the mother and child are the directors of the pattern that follows.

2. At the critical point of birth, when the child is moving down the birth passage, there is a very large secretion of adrenalin within the child's body and a corresponding outburst in the mother which facilitates the trip into the world from the womb as quickly as possible and with the minimum amount of disturbance and discomfort to both parties. During this operation there are many things happening in the child's and the mother's bodies but one major factor is the conversion of life's most vital force — oxygen supply. During the entire pregnancy the child has been receiving oxygen through the placental fluid blood supply which passes back and forth in a continuous movement and this, obviously, must change when the child emerges into the air.

The umbilical cord is exactly the right length so that the child may be placed, after birth at the mother's breast and it is intended to be so; should the switch over from blood/oxygen to air/oxygen not take place precisely according to plan, there is a back up supply. For nature is aware (or rather we are aware) that if the child's brain is deprived of oxygen for more than a moment, severe damage will result. At the point of birth there is a great rush of blood which is diverted from the umbilical cord to the child's lungs in order that, once the child's head emerges, the lungs will function perfectly and breath will be grabbed for the first time. The lungs are given this task with all the force that the body can muster, but if it does not occur precisely as it should, the back up in the placenta is still there so that there is no deprivation of oxygen. The mother holds the umbilical cord after the birth and when it stops beating from the flow of blood she cuts it herself at her leisure. There is no hurry.

3. The child is fully aware, physiologically and perceptually, of what is going on. As we will see shortly, the process of growing within the womb also includes brain activity which actually includes an absorption of information from outside the womb, and the employment of all the senses.

Unfortunately what actually occurs in the majority of hospital or medical births is that the doctor takes over, drugs the mother and forces the child into the world. The drugs of course also deeply affect the child's ability to perform his own birth as well as making the mother's task of responding almost impossible. All the natural processes are therefore virtually destroyed and the result is a panic situation in which the child is heaved out of the birth channel, the umbilical cord cut too soon, the child's body whacked on the back side to bring air into the lungs and often a failure to do so causes blood deficiency to the brain and other parts of the body.

The physical result is one clear factor and we can easily examine what this can become. The child's lungs are damaged. The brain is damaged, perhaps in ways that are not recognizable until much later in life, and the general manhandling of the child will possibly result in a severe trauma which may take months to reduce.

The other effects are less obvious but still manifest. If the child is not immediately placed upon the mother's breast, encompassed and encircled within the mother's body, the child must inevitably suffer a severe withdrawal. Pearce quotes a doctor who was aware of the methods of Frederick Leboyer:

"What the newborn needs is to be kept warm and quiet, and that's what we do, we wrap them carefully and put them in a well-heated, quiet and restful place. The rest of this stuff is just nonsense."

As Pearce points out, what in effect happens under these conditions is that the child's first contact is not with the mother's body, flesh to flesh but with a blanket, having gone through a severe and traumatic experience. It is not therefore at all surprising that the growing child will equate suffering and stress with human beings and look for comfort from any human discomfort by making contact with material objects. This may well ring true in our adult psyche when we realize the extent to which we need to acquire and live with numerous material objects — we are in most cases much more at home with things than we are with people.

This resume of the points made by Pearce regarding birth is not intended to cover the whole ground, for there is much detail to be followed which can best be fulfilled by reading the books *Magical Child* and *Magical Child Matures* It should also be noted that Pearce has written several books on themes of child care, all of which are well worth examination.

But what we are more concerned with here are the practical and positive methods of changing these conditions before they are ever permitted to occur. Hopefully readers will already know something of these things and if not, will be suitably shocked and made aware by this information.

So far as the wonder child is concerned, there is only one method of giving birth and that is the natural way. There are a number of different forms that this method can take and they all derive from the founder of natural birth methods, Frederick Leboyer.

In the writing of this book the author and editors have had the privilege to spend some time with Frederick Leboyer who has kindly given much information and many suggestions of how to present the material involved.

Leboyer's books are now world famous and can be acquired in most good book stores. The author recommends that "Birth Without Violence" be one of the first books acquired before child birth.

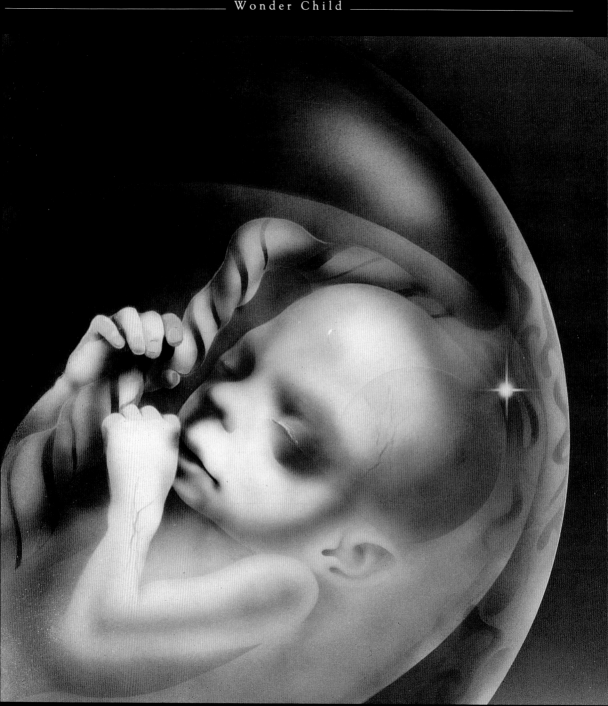

NATURAL CHILDBIRTH

Frederick Leboyer, until the mid 60s, was Chef de Clinique in the Paris Faculty of Medicine with a past history of specialization in gynecology and obstetrics.

"I was delivering babies at the normal rate and in the normal way without any strong realization of care for the child. The medical profession was then doing much as it is now, creating the birth environment in favor of the mother, making sure that her comfort was the utmost consideration and paying no attention whatever to the comfort of the baby."

Leboyer, in 1959, first visited India and became interested in the Eastern approach to life and it was shortly after this new view that he began to work on his now legendary Natural Child birth methods. His continuing development of "Birth Without Violence" seems now, to those who understand the simple basis of it, completely obvious. How can we possibly concern ourselves with everyone involved in the birth except the very individual who is being born?

The following lines, quoted from the beginning of Leboyer's book, epitomize the attitude to child birth that still prevails:

"Do you believe that birth is an enjoyable experience...for the baby?
Birth? Enjoyable?
You heard me...do you believe that babies feel happy coming into the world?
You're joking.
Why should I be joking?
Because babies are just babies.
What is that supposed to mean?
That babies aren't capable of intense feelings.

What makes you so certain?
Babies don't have fully developed feelings.
How do you *know*?
Well, don't you agree?
If I did, I wouldn't be asking.
But everybody knows they don't.
Since when has that ever been a good reason to believe anything?
True. But newborn babies can't see or even hear, so how can they feel unhappy?
Even if they can't hear, that doesn't stop them from crying their hearts out.
A baby has to test its lungs. That's common knowledge.
Nonsense!
Well, that's what people say.
People say all kinds of stupid things. But do you really believe that babies feel nothing at all while they're being born?
Obviously they don't.
I'm not so sure. After all, young children suffer overwhelming agonies about things that seem quite trivial to us — they feel a thousand times more intensely than we do.
Yes, I know, but newborn babies are so tiny.
What does size have to do with it?
Well...
And why do they scream so loud if they're not in some kind of pain or misery?
I don't know — a reflex I suppose. But I'm sure they're not feeling anything.
By *why* aren't they?
Because they have no conscious awareness.
Ah. So you think that means they have no soul.
I don't know about the soul.
But this consciousness...why is it so important?
Consciousness is the beginning of being a person.
Are you trying to tell me that babies aren't fully human because they're not fully conscious? Tell me more..."

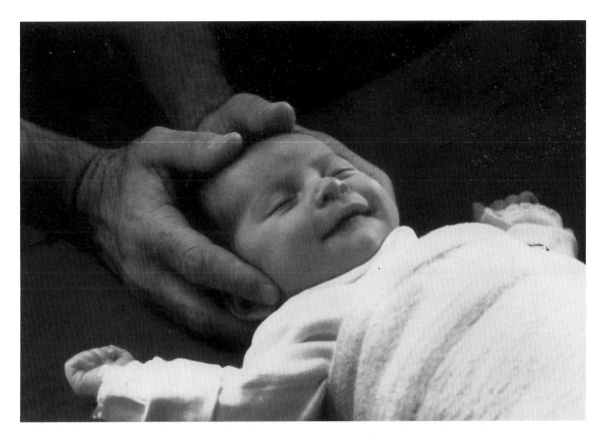

This conversation was first published in 1974 in France and then translated into English the following year and it is now perhaps well known to thousands of readers of Leboyer's books. And yet it still forms probably the most common belief amongst most people who are involved in having babies.

We still think that children are somehow dumb animals without feeling, without consciousness and without pain. They scream like blue murder in order to test their lungs! The fact that the hospital doctor holds the child up by the feet and belts the living daylights out of *it* is normal and acceptable to the majority of people. The fact that the newborn child is snatched away from the body that *it* has lived as part of during the past nine months, and dumped, wrapped in a blanket, somewhere else in the hospital, we believe to be correct because the hospital staff have a schedule to complete and order to create.

It is clear now, hopefully to all of us, that a child can both see and hear and feel. That a newborn baby is intensely aware of everything going on around him or her. That this new edition of consciousness has such a sensitive knowledge of the environment that any event that occurs during the first moments of arrival into the outside world is powerfully imprinted on the internal and external instruments that the child possesses.

We can no longer ignore the child for if we do we will give birth not to a wonder child at all, but to a potentially disturbed and unhappy individual who will eventually end up in the kind of neurotic mess that most of us are in.

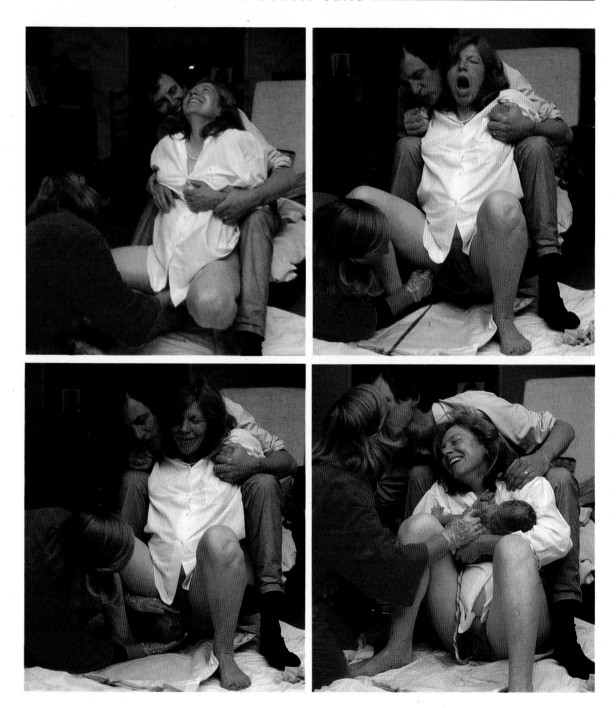

Game - RE-BIRTHING

Re-birthing is a technique to be undertaken with immense care. It is more than a game and should only be experienced by those who have some considerable courage for it carries us back to the moment of our birth. It is suggested, therefore, that adults who wish to try it do so in the company of the nearest and dearest person in their lives and that they do so knowing that it may result in highly traumatic reactions. If there is any reason to believe that this process will cause severe trauma, i.e. that the individual is somehow unbalanced emotionally, then it is better not performed. In many cases even the reading of the method will provoke emotional responses and this simply shows just how powerful our birth trauma may have been.

The game played in the introduction to this book was a mild form of re-birthing and it may then, should the reader have tried it, have provoked powerful feelings.

Take a lot of cushions and spread them in a half moon shape about the floor. Take off all the clothes and lie down amidst the cushions. Curl the body up into a fetal position and bring your partner or partners around your body so that you are effectively contained within this cocoon of warmth and love.

Relax and breathe slowly and gently until you feel calm and at ease. Talk to your partner if you wish and achieve some confidence in their helping presence. Do not be afraid, this is still a game, however apprehensive you may feel. You are not going to die or go crazy and any strong feelings you may experience will pass and leave you with a beautiful result. You may even achieve a state of realization that will last for ever thereafter.

Slowly increase the breathing rate higher and higher until you are breathing unnaturally fast. After a few minutes push your breathing to a state of hyperventilation. You will perhaps begin to feel dizzy and distressed. Continue the process without stopping. The purpose of this part of the exercise is to bring the body's adrenalin output to a maximum level, as does a baby's body before birth. The amount of adrenalin combined with the rapid breathing and the position of the body literally provokes primal memories in the brain to suppose that birth is once again taking place. You are, in effect, tricking your brain and body and mind into a state that fires off memories that you would not normally have access to.

If the process is undertaken with courage and determination and you bring the breathing to a point where hyperventilation is happening, all sorts of extraordinary things occur. You will feel immense panic and fear. You will find yourself crying and perhaps even screaming. Your body will start to jerk and respond in troubled ways and your mind will even perhaps disappear altogether as you begin to cathart violently.

Your partner should continue to contain your body, adjusting pillows and stroking and reassuring you, regardless of what happens.

After awhile the catharting will subside and the breathing and crying will slowly relent until a sense of immense calm overcomes the body.

Once it is all over, you should remain still and comfortable for as long as you need to. At this time you may have memories of birth and immediately, after birth that will be immensely valuable to an understanding of how it all happened. Whatever the feelings and responses, allow them. If you wish to suck your thumb or cry gently, do so. Anything is fine right now for you have been reborn.

The above "game" should also achieve another result. Perhaps your awareness of what it is going to be like for the child you will eventually give birth to, will have been heightened and perhaps, under this new knowledge you will determine to give birth under new circumstances.

It should be added that mothers-to-be should not undergo re-birthing during pregnancy.

LEBOYER'S CHANTING FOR BIRTH

The following chanting methods are those of Frederick Leboyer and should be employed as the full and only sound technique surrounding child birth. Water birthing techniques with special low light facilities and other environmental conditions should also be employed and full published information may be acquired from the purchase of books recommended in the bibliography at the back of this book.

Frederick Leboyer's chanting for birth methods are being enjoyed by a small but ever growing number of people around the world. During his seminars in Europe, the author attended and at the early hour of 7 a.m. a group of some ten people sat overlooking a Tuscany landscape and chanted a whole range of vibrations that created a completely new response within the body.

The result of these chants is to create varying vibrations, higher and deeper, in the body which put the mother-to-be in touch with her physical responses to the coming birth.

Because we have largely lost touch with the effect of sound within us, the whole thing comes as something of a surprise and the result is quite dramatic.

The following is a translated version of Leboyer's chanting with some small additions by the author. The original version can be acquired on audio and video tape, the details of which may be found in the bibliography at the back of this book. The very best, of course, is to acquire the tapes because the chanter can then listen to the sounds directly and get a better feeling of how it works.

But for the purposes of this book the following suffices to give the necessary flavor.

Get together with your partner and other pregnant mothers and the whole thing can be lots of fun.

BREATHING AND SINGING

In the same way that an organist cares for the pipes of his organ so that the instrument works perfectly, so also must we care for our "art of breathing" — our breath of life.
With the right care we can give back the breathing power and fullness which was totally natural to us as children. Breathing and the sounds of our voices carry with them far deeper meaning than we can imagine, for they are both messages and messenger at the same moment with very clear and simple things to say — beauty, joy and perfection.
Breath is very much the music of the universe, of existence, and is given to us in a simple exchange —

that we then breath back into life. So the first thing is to listen to the sounds that we have inside us.

In order to find the best notes, without the use of an instrument we can use the "sol fege" — "do re mi fa sol la si do". Most people know these sounds and if we follow the chart on these pages we can pick up the notes easily enough.

Hold the notes that you are going to sing only as long as they are comfortable and at the end of each breath stay empty for a moment and then fill with air naturally.

Do not wait until the labor has started for then there will be too much thinking going on — the chant needs to be a habit without thought so that it can be felt in your body.

A

E

O

First try the sounds that come from the following phonetics - Ah Eh Oh EE OO MMM - pronounce the "M" as a sound with the lips pursed, as though humming.

One of the first sounds that a child utters is "ma" which arises from "A". So it usually echoed either as "mama" or "papa". So now practice the sound of "A" but keep the mouth full open, relaxed and without the desire to bite.

Next comes "E" which is a smile after the mouth has been open.

The "O" is the first step towards doing something. The passivity of the "A" and "E" is passed and the lips are closing again, the eyebrows raised in surprise!

With the "I" the eyebrows drop and the mouth opens wide once more for this is not the English "I" but the European "I", pronounced like a wide "EEE". Give this new smile its full seductive power.

After this festival of expression we come to the "U" which is decidedly inner, though to be shaped much like a tender kiss — releasing a secret, the brows up once more.

With the "M" the mouth closes but the teeth are not closed behind the lips because the sound needs resonance. Relax the face consciously and allow it to be expressionless as it has now transcended the world of movement.

I

U

M

Use the solfege in the following way for each of the sounds:

1. Ah 2. Eh 3. Oh 4. EE 5. OO 6. MMM

```
                    la la
            sol sol       sol sol
        fa fa fa              fa fa fa
      mi mi mi                    mi mi mi
    re re                             re re
do                                          do
```

Repeat the sequence for at least 10 minutes.

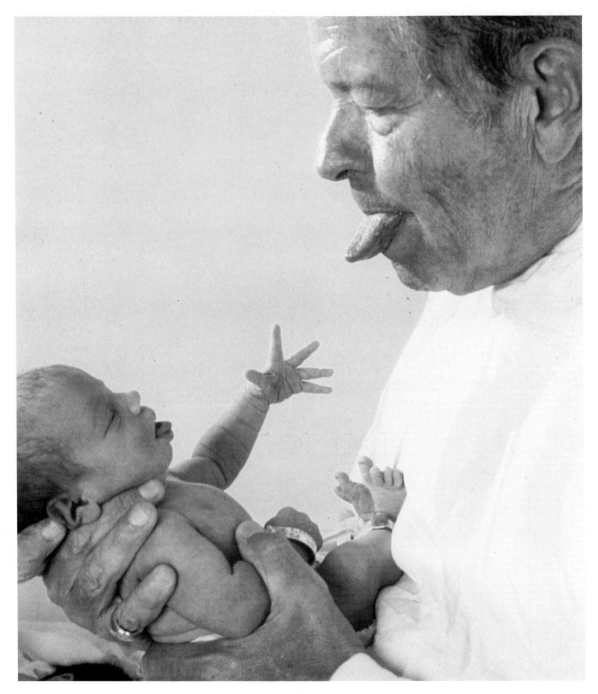

FACE TO FACE

One of the most fascinating new preoccupations of early child life is that concerned with inherent knowledge. And one of the areas in which this is of most current interest to child experts is concerned with the human face.

It has been shown with some convincing tests by Marshall Klaus of Case Western Reserve Hospital in Cleveland Ohio, that a newborn child cognizes the general shape of the human face without any prior imprinting of the memory. These tests basically show that a child will smile at a face, probably first the mother's face, through a natural recognition of facial shape (not the mother's facial shape, for there is not seen to be a precise knowledge of specific faces in the child's perceptive capability) which must exist from or before birth. In other words the child does not have to learn face, the imprint is provided by nature within the memory systems of the child and all that is needed is that a specific face, i.e. that of the mother, needs to be sketched into that memory once the child has the chance to examine it.

245

All those who have watched a breast fed child will be familiar with the way the child continually stares at the mother. The child's eyes will be literally glued to the mother's face, as though examining the eyes, nose, mouth and other features and only occasionally will be diverted by other sounds or influences in that environment. All activities for the child are thereafter related to the presence and the necessary bonding to the mother so that life literally becomes a relationship between child/-mother and everything else around that bonding.

If we remember earlier in this book, we discussed the recent findings of a British scientist who suggested in 1988 that we are capable of receiving feedback from the environment — i.e. perhaps there is a cosmic memory which can be tapped into by the child. Such a cosmic memory would carry within it the information for that child to recognize face.

This, as yet unproven, proposal opens up whole areas of possibility which may not yet have been examined in any detail but for our purposes it is something which may prove extremely exciting and meaningful. If a child does in fact have access to information regarding the appearance of the outside world already by the time birth has occurred then it would seem to follow that the child may well be totally aware of mother, from the "subject/object" standpoint.

The child experts tell us that the early perception of the child is a roughing in of information about the outside world. That in effect the child has certain formats in the brain which give a start and then the learning process, which begins right from day one, fills in the details until at around age seven the child is fully aware of the physical world.

This supposition is based on the operation of all the senses, i.e. that through sight, hearing, smell, touch and taste the child figures out what is going on around him and comes to certain conclusions which fit with the way the rest of us also see the world. The child is then in accord with human behavior as far as his environment is concerned.

In all these findings and conclusions we draw about children we operate always from an adult standpoint — i.e. we not only express our findings by the use of adult tools such as language and tests but we think about them in that same way — the way which basically examines children as the subject to be observed and we, the observer, as the objective one. It is in this method that we make our primary and greatest mistake, for we expect children to be like us in their behavior when they are not at all like us. It is only later that we make them duplicates in their behavior to the adult world — we make them little adults but before this social inculcation takes place they are different in the way that they operate.

Take the whole question of the face recognition. We pay attention to this aspect of child perception and we say that the child contains a map of the face — through whatever means at his or her disposal at birth, perhaps through cosmic memory. We choose the face as our object of interest because probably this is the only part of the mother's body which is readily exposed. Mothers, especially no doubt mothers in experimental conditions, don't expose so readily their whole bodies. But you can be sure that the child has a knowledge of the whole of body so that if he or she, upon birth, is placed upon the mother's body at any place, he will recognize everything — the smells, the tastes, the sight and the touch and certainly the sounds, because these sounds may have been one of the most prevalent aspects of sense reception while inside the mother. So the child emerges from the inside of the mother's body with already a pretty good sense of what is on the outside. But still, this does not reach the point for the child does not regard himself as the subject observing the object mother.

The child is the mother.

If we go back briefly to our explanations and examples concerning dualism, we remember that the creation of opposites and separation are human creations and have nothing whatever to do with reality. This child/mother set up is a perfect place

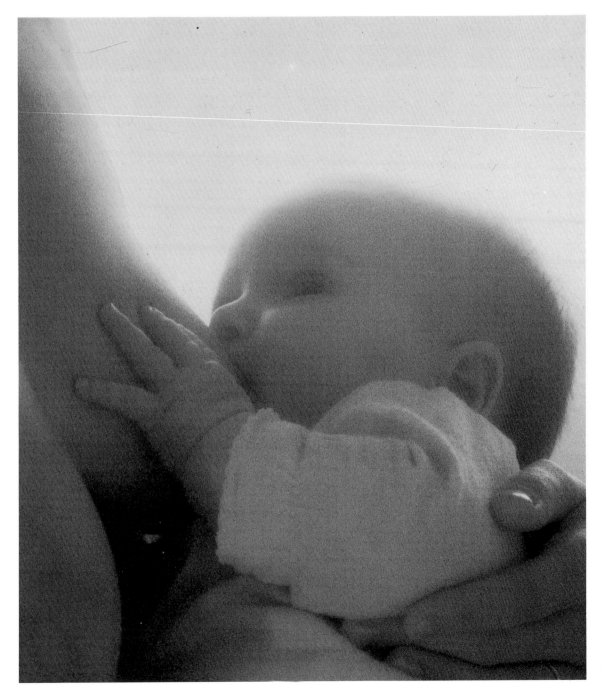

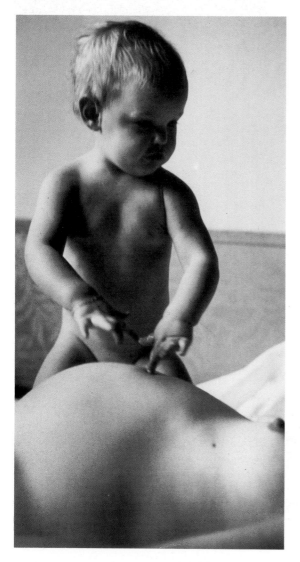

having gone through all the dualist training of a whole lifetime, will not be so readily aware of this. But ask any new mother how she feels about the child during pregnancy and after and she probably will say things to you which show clearly her connection with the child. Society doesn't give us the language to express oneness with life, nor do we find it easy to mentally conceptualize such an existential life-ness, but it's there just the same.

And certainly it remains in the child.

It is therefore not a matter of looking around inside the brain of a child and wondering where the map of face might be — this is adult talk and meaningless in terms of understanding the way a child operates. The child does not need any maps of the mother's face or her body — the child knows the mother completely, inside and out, in every possible detail — of course he smiles at her when he is born. It is like saying that you stare in a mirror at yourself and you smile because you like what you see. The child smiles at himself, the most intimate partnering that he will ever experience.

And this alone is why the hospital and medical treatment of child birth in its most common form is such an appalling crime. For in effect, when a baby which has just been wrenched from the womb is taken away and put, wrapped in material, in another room, the doctors and nurses might just as well have ripped off his leg and removed that to another room, wrapped in material. Mother and child are born one, and to separate them for long periods during the first weeks of life is possibly to create a trauma in the child. And it is reasonable to suppose that this may be responsible for a large proportion of the unhappiness, dissatisfaction, crime, anxiety and fear that we possess and trouble over for the rest of our lives.

So, put very simply, when a child comes into the world she/he possesses a complete knowledge in an instinctual form of *mother*, not as a separated item of human behavior, but as *child/mother* or *mother/child* and without, of course, any use of the words. The child's conceptual aliveness encompasses a completeness with mother which should remain unseparated for this is her or his world and all and everything of it.

to re-examine the problems caused by such a divisive view of the world, for the child, until birth, has been an intrinsic and intimate *part* of the mother's body. She has achieved all her life up until that point from the natural nurturing of the mother's existence. The child inside the womb *is* mother as much as the mother containing the child *is* child. The mother, of course, being adult and

THE LEARNING LIBRARY

"If you look at...young children, movement is primary in perception. They see movement first and its unfoldment as time, and only perceive distance later. They have a tendency to say that if something went further it must have been going faster. They only learn later how to do it right. They are carrying some deeper perception into the ordinary explicate level, where it is appropriate."

David Bohm — Dialogues with Scientists and Sages.
Renee Weber

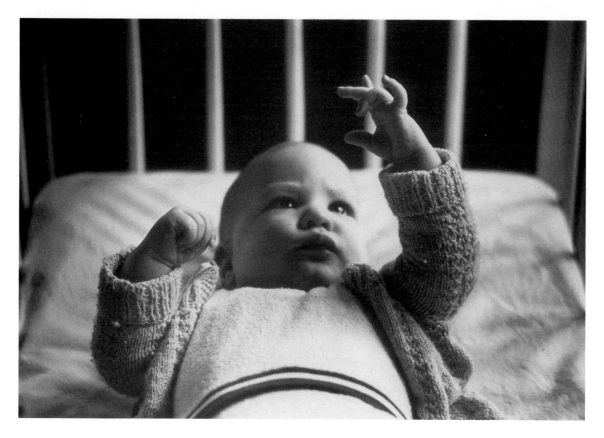

Going back, briefly, to Joseph Chilton Pearce's writing we might take a look, in the light of the previous sections of this chapter, and the earlier parts of the book, at the process of learning in childhood.

Pearce suggests that when a child is born the brain contains a built in program for naming objects and the conscious requirement is to become aware of her or his environment as quickly and efficiently as possible — i.e. to learn about life and the world.

The process begins during pregnancy and continues right through childhood.

Perhaps a familiar scene to us all might be the sight of a small child standing in a garden examining a flower. The concentration of the child is total on that subject — its smell, its taste, its look and perhaps its sounds and of course its touch.

The child will be absorbed in the item until another item, perhaps a jumping cat, passes into the vision of the child, in which case the flower or whatever will be dropped completely in preference to the new influence.

Many child experts and psychologists observe here that this process is rather like a library cataloging system. The new input goes into the brain by whatever sensual perception has been directed and the brain passes the information around looking for comparison, places to slot, compartments to identify this flower. Does it taste like this morning's corn flakes or mother's breast. Does it look like mother's face or smell like her skin. The comparisons produce a reference which is then filed away as flower and this influences the child in the future as to what the next flower will represent.

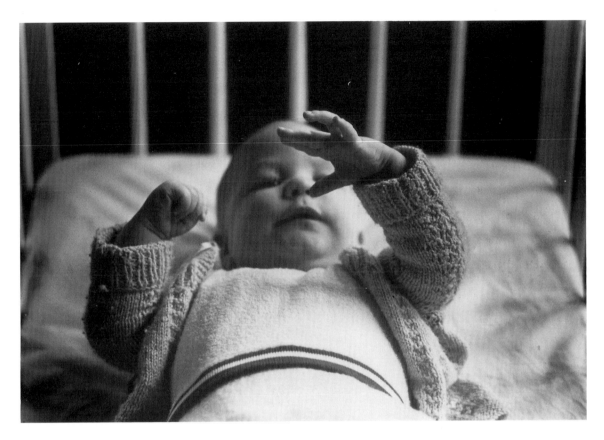

Here again we observe the adult mind at work. With all the greatest respect for scientific minds, they are likely to be lacking in one item — the child's actual form of perception which probably has nothing to do with library catalogs or comparisons. Let us look at it a different way.

One thing we know about children and something once again that we have examined in earlier parts of this book, is that children are timeless. They have not yet learned from the adult world what it is to be continually in the past or the future — they are totally in the present, or, as the masters would have it — in the now. They move from one moment to the next without concern for recognition of what they have done or what they will do. If you ask a child, a small child about some past event then that event becomes present to the child in all its implications. The memory will pass from the brain's recollection system into the present time — it will be examined in that moment and then discarded once its fascination is no longer of importance to the child. This is one reason why children jump from event to event so readily. Similarly, the promise of something to happen in the future is also in the child's present, which is why children are always so insistent about having promises fulfilled, because the event promised is totally in the child's present consciousness and therefore urgent.

This understanding brings us to another important recognition. That when a child examines a flower in the garden the child *becomes* the flower. She takes the flower in her hands and smells, tastes, touches *feels* the flower throughout her whole body.

and it is this process that enables her to know flower. The next flower, for her, will be different altogether for that flower will be examined in a different present, a different now.

Certainly it would appear that the recognition factor exists, in so far as the brain's job is to place the concept flower into the mind/brain's memory cells. But the concept of flower also touches her everywhere else.

It is only when the adult world imposes the word and the labels attached to flower that she moves in preference to adult viewpoints of objective examination and delineation of flower, at which time she ceases to *be* flower and in effect her comprehension and oneness with flower cease.

We can extend this through an example and then through a game.

Very often we may notice that children have a tendency to imagine, in our eyes, that everything has a life. A child sitting on a favorite chair will state readily that this chair is alive. Or to take a more obvious example a teddy bear. "Why doesn't teddy speak to me Daddy?"

In our adult point of view we associate this with the fact that in the case of a teddy bear the child thinks that it is alive because it looks like a real bear and in the case of a chair that the child is mistaken in his supposition that a chair lives. But if we see the oneness of children with existence, their mutual respect and association with all life as *living*, we may realize that everything to a child *is* alive. Why should a chair be any different to a teddy bear, an aunt or mother for that matter. Life exists all around children and if we return to the chapter which includes the section entitled "Childhood Light," we might realize that the very power of all objects given life by existence literally glows with life around the child and quite literally looks and feels alive.

For, in any event, we are, as usual referring everything about children through the understanding of adults — considering the child's view of life through only five senses and forgetting one other sense — the sixth sense that we discussed in previous chapters.

She does not simply allow the event to pass into her synapses, into the brain cells, for recording and cataloguing. She permits the flower to enter her whole body, into every holographic cell of her

LEARNING WITH THE INNOCENT GUEST

We read sometimes in New Age publications that the New Age mother must in some organized fashion imitate the African native mother. The most popular aspect of this new determination is concerned with physical contact on a twenty-four hour basis — that the child should be strapped to the mother all day and sleep with her at night. That the mother/matrix formed in the baby's brain should not be allowed to be interrupted, regardless of the effect this may have on the mother and indeed the poor father, who under these circumstances would have to effectively separate from his loved one perhaps for as long as six months. And, having spent the two or three months prior to birth in a similar physical and probably sexual separation, these new circumstances might appear to be grounds for divorce, or at least estrangement!

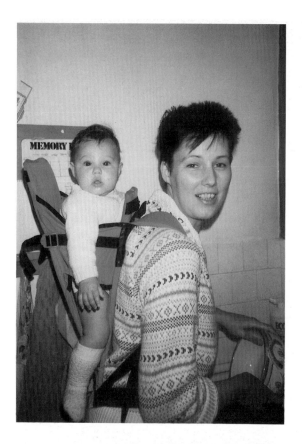

routine and her bodily rhythm. The child will happily sleep or remain without disturbance or discomfort whatever the mother is doing. If she is really heart and soul involved with her child to this extent and does not push the situation into any kind of conscientious dishonesty, and if the child appears to appreciate this treatment, then this is the best way for the mother and child to relate in the early months.

The confirmation of the child's world radiates out from the mother's presence. They are inseparably joined in physical and spiritual and hidden form — they are one and should enjoy this extraordinary oneness while it naturally lasts. The mother will know when it is time to move slightly apart if she has been one with the child till then for her correspondence with the child will be complete.

Some parents worry about the child peeing or generally messing up the mother's clothes. This will not be a problem as the mother will develop, as part of *her* sixth sense, a knowing of the child's needs. She will know if the child needs to go to the toilet as easily as she knows when she needs to go, before it becomes messy.

One can even reach a point where those baby dirt-traps called nappies or diapers are not needed at all.

Another important factor for carrying the child during the day on the body is that the child should generally be on the back of the mother, less the front. The human body radiates energy in circular motions moving from the back over the head and down the front of the body, around and up the back. This means that if a child is continuously strapped to the mother's front she receives the energy flow always downwards and this will ultimately cause the child discomfort and anxiety. Face the child the way that you are going. This is the way most animals do it and certainly African mothers.

It has been said before in this book, but it is worth repeating that we are dealing with and relating to children as highly precious and sensitive creatures, but they are not made of porcelain or rice paper. They are strong, healthy and powerful

It must first be stated clearly that if a mother enjoys her connection with the child on a 24-hour basis then it is a much happier state of affairs if she can keep the child on her body at all times, as she works during the day and throughout the night.

The purpose of this is not simply to retain the connection between these two young lovers but also because the child will benefit enormously from the mother's rhythm and warmth, both in her daily

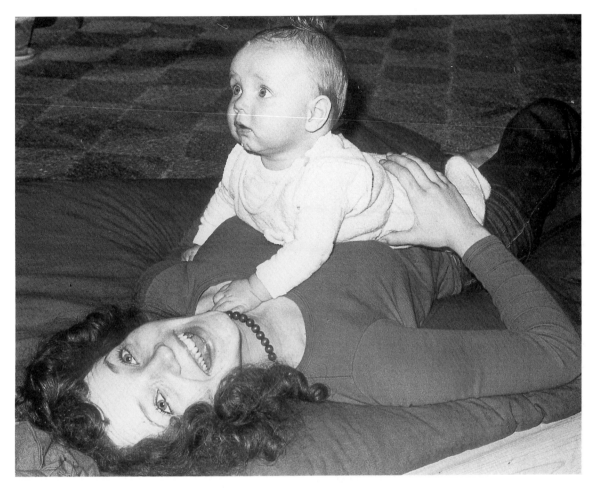

creatures who need the opportunity to be free and joyous, not smothered with over-care and over-protection. The position of the child on the mother's body is an allowance of that child to be joined to the mother in all her feelings, doings and life. The child will learn more from this period than all the maths classes or language classes that will come later, for during this period the child will learn how the mother feels and how these feelings, if honest and clear, are part of life, also the child's life. So this keeping the child close is a time of living not protecting.

Cultures and individuals differ, one from the other, and it is the most essential part of child contact that all relationships within the vicinity of the child are honest. A response can be furiously angry, full of fear and dynamically ambitious for every human failing, but if they are honest they can be loving too and the child will flourish.

Love does not mean constant attention or constant concern and positive behavior. Children pick up fake behavior faster than any adult and then imitate it. Love is allowance and honesty.

And the most effective way of appreciating the enlightened guest in your life is to play with her.

Game - HOLY SLEEP

In the East they say that sleep is a very spiritual activity. It is the one time in the twenty-four hours of the day that the mind is at rest. There is a period of the night when we do not dream, when we are in deep sleep and this time is as close to "samadhi" — the state of ultimate enlightenment — as we can be. The dreamless state of sleep is called "sushupti" and is but one step away from enlightenment — that one step being awareness. Those that are fully awakened are also aware during sushupti.

This was the original reason for prayer taking place just before sleep. Most of us have lost prayer also, in its original form, for the modern organized religions have diluted this pleasure. The original reason for prayer was to bring the mind and body close as possible to God because during sushupti the last thought of God before sleep would enable his aura to remain around the sleeper until waking, and upon waking God's aura would still be there and this state of meditation would then continue during the day time.

Nowadays there is too much to do to be aware

of such niceties. But if you watch a child before sleep, she is naturally ready for this state of purity, the state which will result in her return to the original, natural state in deep sleep.

Here again we can learn from our children. Last thing at night, before the child goes to sleep, sit down on the bed beside her and hold her hand silently. Stay there, quite still until she is sleeping. Keep hold of her hand even after she is asleep and you will feel her silence, her perfect stillness and the natural state of prayer that she is in. You can then go away yourself and remain in this same state until you sleep too. And the dreamless sleep that you will have will be far more relaxed and pure than before. Do this every night and it will become a habit for both of you that will bring enormous joy and contact. Very simple but very powerful too.

THE FIRST YEARS—
ACCEPTANCE AND CHAOS

The first months and years of a child's life are traditionally a period of change and discovery, of course for the child, but also for the adults in and around the child's life. Many new relationships are formed; uncles and aunts, maybe brothers or sisters, certainly mother and father.
In effect the child is jostling the world for space, for his or her new body and for the fresh consciousness which he or she brings to us. The story can be either the arrival of a magical and wonder-full presence with wide open eyes and startled vision or it can be a constricted and squeezed psyche that receives nothing but problems from everywhere around. It should be clear which story we prefer, for a happy childhood is undoubtedly the precursor of a brilliant and delightful adulthood.

How many times have we heard people excuse their poor or unhappy behavior with the phrase — "Oh, I had an unhappy childhood" — it is almost a cliche.

The primary effort on the part of the adults around the child is not protection but allowance. As we have seen in earlier parts of this book, we do not need to constrict the child with rules and regulations which we happily term discipline. A child does not need discipline, a child needs flexible limits within which to live. These limits are bounded by love and understanding, not by mind and belief. Our purpose is not to pass on what we have been taught — "It was good enough for me, and my father before me, it should be good enough for you." Our purpose instead is to see what is going on in the child and to constantly adjust our position through honesty and intelligence so as to allow the child to develop in what ever direction is needed.

Alan Watts had a good metaphor for the desire all of us share to package things into set limits. He likened life to a parcel of water. That as a young man he would always want to put a bucket of water into a brown paper parcel, wrap it in string and send it off in the mail. But of course the water would soak the parcel, refuse to take the string and end up in a puddle on the floor before it ever reached the mail box.

We can liken children to water and their refusal to be packaged with string is fundamental to their need to experience and flow through life like a river. But rivers flow between banks and the banks change their shape and their direction according to the force of the flow and it is in this way that we adults must adjust our positions around the child but still permit the banks to move or even burst if necessary.

FINDING OUT

Walking down any busy street or in any large store you will undoubtedly see the traditional baby carriage or stroller with baby inside and more than likely some string of plastic rattles or other stimulators across the child's face. No sooner is the child able to identify life around him than we adults are thrusting stuff before his eyes, nose and hands that will divert him towards our own passion for things. The purpose is presumably to keep the child occupied so that she does not bother us when we are trying to deal with the all too important matter of acquiring things ourselves.

Children do not need this treatment. The plastic rubbish that can be strung across a child's stroller is useless and disturbing to the child. Imagine that you had to walk around the streets with an elasticated string across your face with colored rings bobbing up and down continuously! Why do this to a child?

We do not need to thrust experience that is somehow imagined as necessary, in front of children. They will find their own stimulation readily enough if given the space to do so. Don't worry about the child getting bored. As we have already mentioned, boredom is only another spontaneous method for children to learn to make life progress for themselves. If we constantly provide stimulation for the child then the child will be far less likely to look to himself for change.

Finding out about the world can be a continuous pleasure and excitement for the child. She will move about a room with one purpose — to touch, smell, taste and feel every single item within her reach. If you do not wish something to be damaged or to damage her, simply put it out of reach. But everything else that is available will be

examined and the parent who constantly says "don't touch that Johnny" is cutting down the world to a size that is smaller than the child. And the child will eventually turn out to be just that — small.

The result will be chaos and at times the adults around will be appalled at the mess and muddle that a child can create. But nobody is going to die. The whole house is not going to collapse and even the most terrible mess can be made into a game. And if it all gets to be too much simply show the child that you are exhausted and don't want any more mess for awhile. Who knows, you might be lucky for a few hours!

In any event you can expect that any healthy child will pass, if permitted, through a period of dismantling the new home he or she has entered. After all, how can you find out what it is all about unless you take it to pieces?!

SEVEN TO FOURTEEN— THE INDUSTRIAL AGE

At age around seven, as we have discussed, the child has begun to earth herself. She has done much of her physical experimentation and worked out some of the limits that occupy her life so that it is now time to show the world what she is made of. The years between seven and fourteen are rather like the Industrial Age which hit Europe and America in the early 1800s. Specifically this age began when the Steam Engine, the Rifle and the Telegraph were invented — all within the space of one decade, the 1830s.

Children enter the age of industry with a well equipped body which contains, in a manner of speaking, a steam engine, a rifle and a telegraph! They rush about the house or park or garden or anything else that is available as space just like a steam engine, firing off their output senses — the voice, the body — like a rifle and communicating at length with a telegraphic determination.

They shout in public just when we least want to be noticed. They point at old ladies and say things like —"Isn't she like an ugly old witch mom?" They cause calamities, break things, fall over and damage themselves as though they had an inbuilt kamikaze instruction inside the body. But they don't

normally do real bad harm. Some kids get scratched and broken-boned. Sometimes they even end up in hospital with stitches but in the majority the accidents are not calculated to destroy the flailing body.

As a child I catapulted myself through many windows, off walls and out of trees, down holes and into various disgusting messes and all between the age of seven and fourteen. I still have the scars to prove it and it seems now, when I recollect this time, that I was in a constant state of testing myself against the world, with a body which still did not quite work properly and which always had that tendency to move in exactly the opposite direction to that which I had supposed it would.

Children, both girls and boys, have a great deal to handle during this cycle of their lives. And the closer they get to fourteen the worse it gets

for them, as during the last three or four years they enter also a full, conscious awareness of sexual energy and there is almost invariably no one around to discuss it with.

The author's son, at the age of twelve, came to his father and asked a question that perhaps all fathers most dread being asked by sons — "Dad?" he said, slightly uncertainly, "Dad? Is it OK if I masturbate?" At fourteen, his sister came and asked: "Dad? When he (a new boyfriend) touches me I shake all over — what can I do about it?"

Most adults quickly enter a kind of autistic state, a catatonia which results in the child quickly deciding that Dad or Mom doesn't like talking about sex — so better go find someone else who does. Worse still the parent, often the father who is relegated the task of talking about sex (which is strange as most men know far less about the heart

than women) give some appalling lecture which skirts around the most important aspects of the subject, neatly or clumsily avoiding the central issue altogether.

Perhaps the days of instructions on the birds and bees are over, at least in most parts of the world, but we still refer to such delicately metaphorical headings as "the Facts of Life" in order to describe the basic and most fundamental subject of all our lives. This part of the second cycle of growth is a good example to indicate to the adult how a child feels during those years.

Game - A NEW WORLD

You, the adult, are living a normal life in a neighborhood that is familiar. Your job, perhaps, has been yours for some years and even though you may have moved from one position to another, the environment is familiar. Even if you shifted to another company, the work is still the same sort and based on qualifications or understandings you have had for years. In other words, you have made your bed and you sleep on it, comfortably.

So, for one day (or as long as you can manage) you are going to change all that!

Leave the house without a packed bag, without tooth brush, without anything, and take a train to a local town. Don't take the car.

Check into the sleaziest hotel you can find, for one night, and take off all your clothes and climb into the bed. Remain there and feel that unfamiliar sense, that insecurity and doubt. That fear that perhaps some monstrous person is going to invade your privacy, invade *you*, that you are going to get bitten by all manner of bugs or robbed or worse by god knows what. Feel it all — this is much the way a young boy or girl feels in the world most of the time between seven and fourteen years of age.

The result of course is often aggressive and angry behavior towards parents, especially parents

but also anyone else who comes along and represents an attack against this highly strung and delicate new mechanism which has only just been discovered.

How does the body work? Why do the emotions keep changing? How come I feel so depressed? Why do people bother me so much? I hate everyone. What is masturbation? What are these shivers I feel? How come no one understands me ever?

The very truth is, of course, that the child does not understand herself and therefore this reflection of no one else understanding her is like a mirror covered in dust looking at another mirror covered in dust and wondering why nothing shows up.

And the way is simple enough. Once again total open and available honesty.

To the boy's question about masturbation the answer was "Of course it's OK, why not? Does it feel good or bad?" Answer — "Good". "Then why not?" "Just one thing though — I promise you that later it will feel better when a lover does it with you."

And to the young woman "these feelings are normal, this shaking is energy in your body that wants to be expressed. Don't hurry with it, just let it be there and follow your heart and your caution. Don't be *talked* into anything, men are very good with their minds, their desires. Just allow the feeling and keep the deeper female softness to yourself."

PUPPY LOVE

Most of us have owned or had experience of small animals such as cats and dogs when they are still "babies." They attract some strong responses within the adult which tends to move us to stroke and fondle, rub the tummy, roll the animal about on the floor and make allowance for all the free-peeing and messing that can happen before the animal is house-trained.

With children we also have this response — at least when they are very small — when they are still "puppies" — before the passing of babyhood.

With animals and children alike this puppy love tends to pass, at least as far as our own responses to it. Animals still get rubbed and stroked but less frequently and with more of an emphasis on friendship. Children also, in our eyes, pass out of the puppy love stage and quickly grow into creatures that we cease to roll about with on the floor. We think that they must grow up and that puppy love is inappropriate after a certain age.

But in the period between seven and early adolescence or puberty, children need puppy love as much as they do when they are very small. They need ruffling, hugging and stroking. Both boys and girls, particularly, before they come to a physical grounding, appreciate the rough and tumble of the adult body.

Some boys will shrug you off because they are now getting into the boyish tough stage and some girls will feel uncertain of too much physical contact, but this does not mean that we have to withdraw from them. Fighting and tumbling is a great game. When my own children were around eight or nine years of age we had a wonderful, almost daily game to play. Father would stand at the end of the bed and swing first the boy and

then the girl between outstretched legs, back and forth two or three times and then hurl the child onto the bed.

Each one would come back time and time again until all three of us were totally exhausted. The physical contact of the throw and the return of the child, jumping from the bed into father's arms, reinforced many aspects of love between the adult and child and the laughter was evidence enough of the pleasure involved in this puppy play.

Physical fighting between parents and children is just another way of hugging and holding and it also provides the child with ample opportunity to test strength and physical capability.

269

CHILD ABUSE

And of course this brings us to a very unpleasant and criminal part of our lives; a part which has grown recently in the United States and Europe

more than any time in the past.
Child abuse has become a disease and this disease is, as usual being dealt with in the time honored way - not by cutting the roots of the problem, i.e. the society which has created the problem in the first place, but on the surface with punishment, repression and generally a shut down of all the things that people think are the reason.

We read articles in newspapers and magazines about taking pornography off the streets, about censoring written and pictorial material in magazines like Playboy and Penthouse, to say nothing of all the other more lurid material freely available on the newsstands.

None of this is going to make any difference. It is not going to stop people growing up unhappy and sick with anxiety, fear, repressed sexual tendencies and violence. Sexual abuse towards adults and children will increase so long as there is a standard of life which proposes that we repress sexual feelings in our children from day one, that we project anxiety and disgust onto sexual activity and we look upon human sexual energy as something dirty.

People who cannot stop themselves from abusing children are essentially those that have been banged around since childhood, have been abused themselves by their parents and other adults and have grown up hating all other humans. These are the ones that were dragged out of the birth canal and spanked on the backside and then shoved into an incubator, later to be left without love and warmth for the first years of life. They are the ones that were hit by the mother or father for touching themselves to try to find some remote and pathetic comfort in the midst of a dirty and depressed world which they probably wish they had never entered. But of course the true criminals in these cases; the doctors and nurses, the hospital staff, the parents, the brothers and sisters and all those other people who refused to give love because they too received similar attention or lack of attention when children, these people will rarely be the ones to go to jail. For society forgets their crimes and does not blame them for what happens in some dark alley way or the back seat of a car at night, leaving a small child psychologically and spiritually damaged for the rest of her life.

As always, we attack the problem from totally the wrong place.

And for the troubled parent with fears that the child will grow too softly into a society if these

protections against abuse are not given, there is no doubt about it. A child must learn what to avoid.

So from the practical point of view: HONESTY AND AVAILABILITY

One of the main problems for a child who is faced by threats of abuse or actual abuse is yet again the double-bind. Very often, the reaction to some attempt on the part of a stranger to touch intimate parts of a child's body are firstly surprise and secondly shame.

Children who have not been given a freedom of sensual and physical expression tend to reserve their feelings as private even from the parents. They detect that the parents feel the same way, that sex is not discussed and that "those private places" are avoided. This understanding by the child comes from many subtle influences: hugging avoids genital contact, television programs about sex or intimate matters are turned off or talked over, the programs themselves are not direct but strangely complex and twisted, parents seem embarrassed when any subject regarding sex comes up in the home etc. etc. Children may not know why this is so but they do get it. They receive the feelings and associate them directly with their own responses. In effect they take up the mirror of the parent and then respond to life in the same way.

If the parents have not had the benefit of understanding this in the early life of children in the family then it is probably not too late to start changing the situation. Children up to the age of puberty are always open to changing influences.

Follow the suggestions and games in the earlier part of this book regarding "Child Sexuality". Try to understand that this tender heart that you live with needs openness and understanding at least from one person in the world - mother or father or better still both. The point of this is that if the child suffers any approach from outside madness, any kind of offered abuse, the child needs first and foremost to be able to come to the parent and tell the whole story.

It is like a child that falls down outside and hurts the knee. There is blood and pain and a feeling of foolishness and discomfort. The child comes to mom and cries. Mom comforts, child recovers quickly. Child abuse is a more extreme version of the same thing except that in this case there may be secrecy and dishonor attached. There is perhaps a sense that the child is somehow to blame for what happened and is therefore bad, because the feelings attached to the abuse touch an area of misunderstanding and confusion. The child therefore keeps the whole thing to herself or himself and cannot release it.

This is where the most damage is done. The repression brings lasting damage which could easily be healed by talk, care and love from an open parent. The primary concern is the healing of the open wound, quickly and thoroughly. The child may wish to tell the whole story, or not. There is no need to force the truth, only to accept the child without reproach or anger. She will have learned to keep away from such influence in the future so reprimand is unnecessary. Just love her or him and give protection and acceptance. The problem will then not last into later life.

LEARNING TO AVOID THE SITUATION

Of course, none of us wish to have this situation occur in the first place and there is a need to give the child information and understanding about the possibility of such abuse.

If the child is given a free and open awareness of love and sensuality from the beginning then he or she will have developed a sense of trust for others. This does not mean an unintelligent trust. It does not follow that the child is a babe in the woods that will fall into the arms of any insane person.

Having provided an open and intelligent environment which is based on free discussion, it becomes very simple to talk openly about anything.

You can even make something of a game out of it all. Explain that we live in a society which is imbued with an undercurrent of sickness. That certain people are not given love and a happy life but grow up in a state which is full of hatred and anxiety. Make the sort of people that you imagine being responsible for acts of violence into a charade of drama and provide the child with an understanding of them as ogres or monsters. Show the child that such people can very easily be avoided for they are essentially afraid of the world.

The method of presenting the face to the world as cold and aloof, untouchable and superior, is one that any child can learn. Simply give the child a vision of the way to look, the face, the body, the position, and practice it. It is much easier for a child to learn how to shut an open door than to have the door permanently shut and only open it occasionally.

There is no reason for children to respond openly to strangers in a city street. This is just stupid. A child will very quickly learn to know who is worthy of her attention and who is not. Intelligence and awareness are the greatest weapons against any abuse, far stronger and more effective than repression and suits of multi-layered armor.

THE THIRD THIRD - ADOLESCENCE
The age of information.

"Adolescence" spans the age of roughly nine to seventeen - the second and third thirds of a child's life. And it is a label we cannot treat so lightly for it is probably, potentially the time of the child's greatest confusion and therefore suffering. The psychologists define this time as beginning with puberty and ending with the attainment of physiological or psychological maturity. One might say therefore that many people are in a permanent state of adolescence.

Puberty, in turn is defined as the time when the sex organs become reproductively functional.

Science in this case triumphs through definition, through drawing lines and setting limits. This begins here and ends there. And it is this method of engineering life which can often cause such agony in us all.

We believe, because we have been told by those we think know, that adolescence really does begin and end, that puberty is a fixed period of growth in a fixed time span. And so we wait for it to happen. We put off the day until the last and then say "Oh dear, poor Jennifer has entered puberty" as though the child has somehow walked through a hoop of fire and is burning up. There is little we can do to help her because it's natural, it happens to everyone and we just have to do the best we can. Of course we love the child, care for her well - being, and no doubt most parents will accord as much attention as understanding permits during this span of life, but we look at the whole of adolescence as something of an enigma for we have forgotten it, probably more readily than other parts of childhood, because it may not have been a particularly happy part of our own past.

But what if adolescence began, not at the onset of puberty but much much earlier? And what if puberty took two different forms, one physical and one spiritual/sensual?

Consider this: children, with their inbred sense

of shame and distrust of the adult world are generally not permitted to express sexual or intimate physical feelings openly. This is taught them from the very earliest years. They grow to around the age of eight or nine years with this veil over the senses and much of their life is circumspect in terms of interest in their bodies.

Girls will begin to use make up and talk about boys as early as seven or eight years old. They gather together in small groups and gossip about the whole fascinating romance of the music business, for example; rock and roll concerts are frequented as much by eight year olds as those whom we recognize as being in their adolescence. Pro-

blematic adolescence does not begin at puberty — it begins when the problem of knowledge is created — i.e. when knowledge and healthy understanding is not provided and shame replaces freedom. And puberty occurs first as a spiritual maturing and then after as a physical maturing.

Sexual energy and an awareness of it come from the heart, not the genitals. The medical community will tell you that once a child sprouts pubic or under-arm hair he or she is into puberty. This is the last sign, for the body often picks up the signs after the heart has already encompassed them. But how many children open their hearts to their parents? The parents see the arrival of

puberty in the bathroom, rarely in the heart. And a girl especially is already well into her physical/sensual awareness period long before the advent of her menstrual cycle. Boys approach puberty long before they are capable of ejaculating semen. The expulsions of the body are already a complete maturing for this is the ability to connect through the body with the rest of existence. The heart has been doing it for several years before, secretly.

And ultimately it all goes back to one thing - if we are honest with children from the very beginning all this can be shared and nurtured right through adolescence with the minimum pain and pressure on the child and the adult.

And in a sense, this third third of the child's life is akin to the present age of the whole world, for we are in the Age of Information right now. The advent of the communications revolution, the computer, the telephone, television and all the other advanced systems of linking up the globe into one network extension of mankind and womankind. This could be thought of as the planet's teen-age period. We haven't yet reached our maturity and so should understand most clearly how it is to be a growing child about to enter what is so dearly and apprehensively termed adulthood.

All our failures and flounderings with atomic weapons, pollution, scientific advances in which we put so much store, all these things are perhaps viewable as the stumblings of teen-age boys trying to prove something to mother Earth and this "nature" which we have separated ourselves from. Such are the ways of the growing child.

It must be pointed out here that there is, of course, a negative side to the view that children grow into puberty and sexual awareness at a younger and younger age. In the United States, for example, the subject of the disappearance of childhood has become a major topic. Premature sexuality, as Joseph Pearce pointed out in his editing of this book, is on the increase and causing childhood somehow to be squeezed out. This in turn puts a much greater burden on a child who might, prior to this age of television advertising, pornographic cinema billboard and a general awareness of sex and violence,

have been playing dolls or cowboys and Indians — much simpler and more innocent pursuits.

There is little doubt that media presence, particularly in the form of cable TV in America is bringing a potential sickness to childhood which is already hard to deal with.

But the problem, once again, does not lie with the early growth of sexual awareness in the child. The solution is also not to protect the child or

provide understanding and love. Between these two alternatives we all too often choose, unconsciously the former. But we inevitably fail because we cannot stop our children from mixing with others who have not been censored in this way. The story spreads through school and other social filtration and the child is left feeling excluded because she does not know the whole truth of what is going on. A little knowledge is somehow worse than all of it.

But the suggestion is not that we let the wind blow in all directions — that somehow we leave the pornographic cable TV channel on all day and permit our children to experience these obnoxious and false ideas of life enter into the picture constantly. It is also not suggested that we only provide understanding through constant and perhaps tiresome explanation of what the real truth is in these matters. But that we mix and match.

An intelligent approach must be the best. If a child is aware that certain stimulus is surrounding him, and that he cannot but be open to incoming data because his body is also changing and interested in such things then the parent can be open too. We cannot immediately change society by cutting out the top layer of its influence, we can only change it over a long period by cutting its roots. And the roots lie with the young people who will tomorrow not wish to have anything to do with the unhappy side of life.

If children are encouraged to understand that love and happy sexuality have nothing to do with pornography and violence but that these influences derive from sickness and unhappiness then the child will more naturally search out the goodness that also exists in plentiful form.

Open discussion and playfulness, clarity and lack of conditioned judgment gives the youngest child an awareness of the other side of the coin. A willingness to talk and listen to anything that is troubling a child gives her or him the chance to see that adults are not all patterned in the ways that are depicted on cinema billboards but can also, more often, be broadly based in a natural appreciation of love-sexuality.

somehow subdue the available input in order that the child should remain with her dolls. This is not a root solution, it is an avoidance or repression which will in its inevitable development achieve only unhappiness through pretense. The adult who is faced by a child's early sexual development has two clear choices. She or he can try to stem the stimuli — filter out the incoming data which is believed to accelerate such growth or accept it and

THE BREAK

There is little to be said about the time when a child is ready to leave the adults in his or her life. It is very simple. If the adults try to prevent a child from moving out then the child will wish to leave all the more and separate him or herself from the loved ones all the more. Prevention is the better part of determination.

If there is, once again, an allowance, a freedom for the child to test the possibility of departure from the family then there is also every possibility that the child will not need to run far away. Even if the physical distance between child and parent is great, the hearts involved will still be in touch.

Permit distance. Allow freedom. Let the child go out into the world and provide anything that seems useful for this purpose. The child will not die. If the background to his or her life has been intelligent and loving then the break can be the same.

If the parent or parents have great trouble with the departure of the child then this too may be expressed and the scenario may even be reversed, where the parent shows the leaving child that he or she feels insecure. In this sense the child then becomes the parent and this too can be a game.

CHAPTER ELEVEN
DIFFERENT LANDSCAPES
Multi-Parent Families and the Commune

Few of the readers of this book will consider that they are living or ever likely to live in a commune or that they have any chance or desire even, to share their family with other families.
Yet the facts are that 100% of the readers do live in a commune and already do share some of their family responsibilities with other families. The problem is that we have forgotten our communal state, we are not aware that our local town is a commune, that our country is a giant commune and our planet is one vast whirling communal and shared world. All this got lost somewhere along the way when we decided to separate from one another.

If you were to go, for example, to Switzerland you would find a greater awareness of communal living. Switzerland is divided into "Cantons", rather like States, and each local town has an office called the "Commune" office, which is basically the center of the communal activities.

Swiss towns and rural areas are run on commune lines with re-cycled goods, local referendum for all laws and administration. There is no political side-show system to divert the people of the country from their determination to organize themselves efficiently. This way they can concentrate on having a good time, making money and living comfortably.

But the only real difference between Switzerland and most of the other civilized countries of the world is that the Swiss have not lost sight of their communal life. It cannot, however, be said that the Swiss are particularly less separatist than other peoples.

We all live in communes, it is inescapable. However hard we try to avoid other people by isolating ourselves, we are totally dependent on each other for life itself, in fact we are joined inescapably with one another in our dependence on the same world for our existence and happiness.

The only reason why people don't smile at us or speak to us in the street is because we do not speak to or smile at them. We do not make the contact and they are the same as us — scared to be the first in case we don't respond.

In deliberately set-up communes these human fears are the first things to go. People who determine to join together and make a "family" have a common aim in doing so and therefore their primary motivation must be to work together and solve quickly any of the emotional or personality problems that arise from living in closer circumstances.

Because communes are not bound by the traditional family ties, i.e. marriage, exclusive sexual behavior, discipline and other social mores, they can create a freer environment based on a simpler form of love and mutual concern. Their concern is therefore primarily for one another and the preservation of the commune within a wider social environment. They also, still today, often face some prejudices from the outside, and therefore must create within themselves a loyalty and mutual acceptance in order to withstand any confrontations.

The funny thing about all this special behavior is that it is not in fact very special because it has been going on throughout the world for centuries. In the Middle Ages local villages were bound together against other villages who might come and plunder their resources. Somewhat later, around the beginning of the 19th century and the Industrial Age, national boundaries became more evident and the commune of the country would stand together against other countries who might well, as happened almost continuously from the 1830s until today, come and plunder the resources of your land.

We have not yet taken the jump of looking at our world as a commune for until now there has been no threat from outer space and other species of intelligent creatures. No doubt this will one day happen but for the time being the greatest threat to our global commune are its own inhabitants, or at least a specific portion of them.

For the moment then, perhaps we can look at the alternative measures we can take, for the benefit of the new wonder children in our lives and for our own greater freedom.

MULTI-PARENT FAMILY

The idea is simple. Children fare better if they are not confined to single nuclear family units which are isolated from other people and dependent for their attitudes on a very small and very often, even with the best will in the world, prejudiced view of life.

If you live, day-in and day-out, in one small house or apartment constantly only relating to two or three other people you must necessarily become narrow in your view of the world. Schools are supposed to provide children with other social contact but, as we have seen in the chapter on

285

education, the purpose of most schools today is not to broaden the child's mind but to narrow it still further with fixed and mostly confined ideas. It will be a very long time before education authorities or individual school organizations come to a new understanding of life but in the meantime, those individuals who have other ideas about how life can be, can begin a process of change. This individual changing and discarding of old ideas is what will eventually lead to larger social changes, for society is nothing, after all, but a collection of individuals.

There are some very simple ways in which individual family units can expand their awareness of group and commune activities without having to sell their homes and move en masse to an agricultural commune system! There is no need to drop out.

Many mothers or fathers who have the job of taking children to school each day, arrange a more convenient method of doing so by sharing the school trips with other mothers or fathers. It is not an uncommon sight in American or European schools each morning to see a station wagon draw up outside and off-load up to eight or nine children from one local community area or street. The mothers of each of these families are therefore already familiar with one another, they are friends, so that the initial contact has already been made. The small nuclear family is already opened up to this extent and it is only a matter of widening the opening a few steps at a time.

Next time you get a chance have a party! Invite all the mothers and fathers and children to dinner, all of them together. At first it is probably better to keep the numbers to your most intimate friends which probably will entail up to fifteen people so perhaps best do it in the garden of your home on a Sunday afternoon when there is time and space to be together. It may sound like hard work, but do it anyway and make sure to emphasize that the children are all invited especially. Tell them they must bring something. It doesn't matter what: juices, drinks, cakes, sandwiches, jams, anything that can be consumed at the party. And when everybody is happily settled into the gathering and maybe a bit tipsy with the wine or whatever, stand up and make a speech!

Tell them all that you have a suggestion to make — that you would suggest that you all form a sort of group together and you do something like this every month, to begin with and more frequently after a few months. In fact, if your group is a particularly broad-minded lot, suggest you set up a rota of gatherings — that each week or two weeks one of the families makes dinner for everyone and you all troop around to one of the houses and eat together — fathers and all.

That the "duty" family cooks, serves table, washes up and generally provides for the other families on that day.

What you will also suggest is that those who wish to help on nights other than their own can do so. You might want to make a special dish for someone else's night and bring it round. You might want to get involved in washing dishes, whatever. But the basic idea is that the small group present at this gathering become one big extended family during one part of each day or every few days.

The shopping for these big dinners could also be done by smaller groups of people, in fact, why not suggest that the older children in the groups take on this responsibility, perhaps with a different parent each time. Spread the work across the group as much as possible and encourage discussion and other ideas.

If you are familiar with a group of people who find enthusiasm for such an idea then it will naturally blossom into more and more togetherness and group activity. Probably the husband will

complain for on the whole men are less open to such changes than women, but they can drop out of it if they wish. Once they find that they have to cook their own meals at home that night when everyone else seems to be having a good time next door, they will drop their prejudices.

The additional intimacy that will be created by such a method will cause changes and happiness that you will not anticipate. It will also extend the realm of influence of the children for they will feel part of a greater whole and have access to a wider series of influences.

Such an experiment can, of course, give rise to more permanent communal living and should you find yourself getting together with a group of people to set up a home which includes several families there will be some interesting results which we can touch on briefly here.

Within a normal nuclear family the political realities, the jealousies and emotional responses to living together with only a small number of people can tend to turn inwards and become somewhat claustrophobic. This very often leads to stresses and anxieties, particularly if there is only one power/love source — the parents. Within a larger group of people, however, these problems seem to become somewhat diluted as there are a greater range of responses to all normal human dilemmas. If there is unhappiness within one relationship for some reason, then other relationships can create a better balance because of the lack of exclusivity.

One misconception very often suffered by those who have only second-hand knowledge of commune life, is that within communes there is somehow a lot of non-exclusive sexual relating — that somehow the partner who was "safely" within a monogamous relationship in the nuclear family will suddenly start relating to other partners once within a commune lifestyle. The rule seems to be, however, that if couples are close and loving together outside a commune, they do not change inside one. It is much more that the non-sexual relationships grow to be more open and the sexual bondings become, if anything, more together through the additional presence of greater experience in relating to others.

Communes are rather like individual people in the sense that they have a homeostasis of their own. Early on in a group of people working or living together, there is a shifting and changing takes place in which each individual is testing and searching for the space that is available within the group.

One individual may hate or love another or several others and conflicts or preferences arise which make for confrontations or factions. There is a search for balance between personalities and preferences which continues as the chemical and physical differences are explored between the members of the group. This might be called the "testing" time — like Chinese wrestlers moving around one another, checking out each other to see what the possibilities are.

This seems then to be followed by either a successful harmonizing or a break away of those who cannot sustain the care and open-mindedness needed for a group to be maintained. For a commune to be happy and successful, the right people need to be in the same environment. If there are a greater number of "cells" that rub against one another, then disease occurs and the organism breaks down. If the cells are in harmony they can work together for a greater whole.

And there is no reason whatever why a commune cannot be sent up with separate areas of home for each couple or family. The group comes together perhaps at meal times or in work and retires at night to the haven of exclusivity where intimacy and togetherness is enjoyed all the more because of the lack of it during the day.

Communes create air — they open human understanding and increase the individual's capacity to love. They also, and best of all, give children a wide view of human potential.

MEDITATION AND UNREASON

In a book such as this, where a great many spiritual viewpoints are expressed, where the information supplied and the ideas given have a taste of "The New Age," it might seem a natural follow-up to suggest that meditation is an important part of the process — in short that children should be encouraged to meditate.
Meditation, however, is not so simple as this.
The mechanism that exists within almost all adults today when presented with a problem or a state of affairs that does not seem satisfactory, is to somehow solve the problem or change the state of affairs with some answer, with some expert method which will then improve the matter. Meditation is often used in this fashion — somehow the cure-all of the late 20th century.

Adults *can* find a great deal in meditation. It helps to release a lot of the reasoning and anxiety that lives inside an adult, matters that need the process of not-thinking in order to bring the adult back in touch with a natural process that he or she has forgotten through the over dominance of the ego/mind.

But children are not the same in this sense, in so far as their ego growth process is not completed or matured and the determined or regular use of meditation in childhood can shorten the ego growth process and therefore do damage to the child's growth pattern. There is nothing *per se* wrong with the ego — it is just as natural in its

existence as everything else. There is nothing wrong with having an active mind — the mind is an absolutely essential tool for the individual to live within a social structure. What is sad is that the ego and the mind become obsessively dominant in us and eventually overpower us with anxiety, egotistical habits and therefore shroud other essential states of being from our sight.

It is essentially wrong to suppose that if a child "diligently" meditates and follows yogic or other practices, he or she will therefore get a head start on the rest of the crowd and the proud parents may then have the "ultimate New Age, spiritual child." This is simply following the same breathless passage that parents follow in pushing a child into some demanding profession in order that they may show off the child to their neighbors and friends. It is substituting "the New Age" for the "old Age" and changing nothing.

Meditation practices should be applied only

as games in childhood, for if they become serious they can certainly damage the child's awakening efforts.

To put this in a more familiar frame — if we think of a child as a being who has recently arrived on this planet from, presumably, a higher plane of existence or at least from a position of not understanding what life is all about, then that child must first learn how to come "down-to-earth."

The purpose of spiritual practices such as the stronger and more absorbing forms of meditation, are to help the initiate into "higher" states of understanding — somehow to reach back to the more elevated or etheric realms, *after* the anxiety and pain of the ego has been thoroughly sampled. The adult needs to step up the ladder of spiritual awareness and is eminently equipped to do so because he or she has a good grounding in the ways

of life and the "down-to-earth" aspects of it.

Also adults are on their way up while children are on their way down and to confuse the two at an early age is to do the exact opposite of what is needed. Meditation with children should not be more than a game of communication with each other and with the self. The greater benefit of meditation for a child is to understand the communication of silence. Complex and powerful yogic practices must be reserved for the years after the ego has been established and if there is an understanding of meditation within childhood as a game — as something that is fun, then the grown up child will recognize the method and take it on all the more easily — that is if he needs it. Given enough freedom and love, perhaps the anxieties and pains of social adulthood will not be so great and meditation could be an unnecessary cure.

ANCIENT MAGIC

We have mostly lost the arts of ancient magic. Much of it has been destroyed by the dark side of witchcraft coming to the surface and putting people off. There is as much superstition and uncertainty on the positive side of magic as there ever was on the negative side.

Within the white magic of the past there is much for us to re-sample and the following games are tremendous fun to give children and family as a whole, a fresh appreciation of that wonder-full existence that we have been mentioning so often in the rest of this book.

During the early work on Wonder Child, the author met a genuine witch while visiting Italy and was shown a hand-written book which she had received from her mother who had in turn received it from the previous generation of witches. This particular family had been in the witch business for more than a thousand years and the book which was shown, with great reverence, was said to have

been written in the 13th century!

One's expectation, in such a situation might have been to see a dark and dangerous set of spells and incantations, whereas instead it turned out to be the most sensitive and delicate expression of natural phenomena, involved in fundamental connections which the original writer recommended should be made with nature and the surrounding flora and fauna. In effect the book was about what we now call "oneness", in different words and with an unpretentiousness that would be rare today. The writer, a witch living over two hundred years before the Renaissance, close to a city named Florentia, knew everything there was to know about all the ideas of The New Age, without any need for books or gurus or California! She *was* one with everything around her.

Here is a game she proposes which she offers to mothers who wish to understand how a child sees flowers. The text is here reproduced with some editing to give adults a chance to view the natural world through the eyes of a child.

A CHILD'S FLOWERS AND HOW TO SEE THEM

If you love flowers, if while walking down country lanes you find yourself stopping and staring at those little creatures of light and color, if you have been standing over them in wonder, feeling that there must be more to flowers than just the pleasure they give to your sight and smell — then flower magic is for you.

 Doing magic with flowers is both very easy and extremely difficult since there are no rules to go by. It is no good trying to see the flowers as an adult — as one who wishes to use the flowers because then they will not respond. First you must see the flowers as a child. This is not the case, for example, with herbs, which have an identity of their own and work much in the same way as whoever is using them. Flowers react strongly to outsiders when magic is happening. Flowers act on the emotions, and their magic moves through feelings and only children and witches are truly in touch with feelings without using the thoughts. All other adults use thoughts too much ever to be listened to by a flower. So first begin to look "with" the flower like a child.

It is a precise and delightful task learning to know flowers. It means choosing them, watching them, smelling them, having them close by for a length of time, and noticing the reactions to that flower's closeness. A cornflower will always work for me in a fertility philter, but it might not do so for you. Therefore working with flowers is a very creative exercise, where you will have to get to know the flower and the way you can work with it.

You must first know the plant in your heart, in the way its force works with your force. That working might mean cleanliness to some or devotion to others. So first take the flower in both hands and hold it before the eyes just where the eyes do not become furry. Let the eyes fall upon the flower and not blink the lashes. Remain so that the eyes do not blink until they begin to water and feel some pain. Still do not blink the eyes but keep them close. At the same time allow the smell of the flower to enter the nose. Do not say that the flower has no smell, all flowers have a smell and if you have forgotten it, it is only because you have been so busy smelling stronger and nastier things. Smell the flower as you allow your eyes to receive it.

Then also you must listen to the flower for flowers make noises. At first you will not hear it but listen carefully and for long time and soon the sound will come to you. When you have all this inside you, smile. Be a flower.

Some people feel there is something sad about a cut flower because it has been taken away from its place of birth and it will soon die. They think that the true beauty of a flower can only be seen when it stands free in its home ground. This is true. But it is also true that flowers are made to do magic with those that can feel them. Flowers are not afraid to die like we are, for they know they will soon be back again.

Also it must be remembered though that the spirit of the flower leaves it when it dies. A dry flower carries the memory of what it once was, but not much of the magic, so any flower magic must be made when the flower is still fresh and not dried out.

You need also to use its essence, its perfume. A flower carries much of its magic in its scent. Using that you will be able to find its presence and its magic.

Take one of the flowers that most attracts you, a flower with whom you would wish to have a love affair and keep it alive in your magic place

for at least three days. To become close to the flower during those three days find the time each day to sit silently by her.

Be open to her, breathe in her scent. Look at the flower, noticing all the details, but most of all be receptive to the emotions and feelings that the flower will evoke in you. If you find some memories and old tales surfacing in your mind pay attention to this, as it might be important to the work that the flower will draw for you.

FLOWER MAGIC

Here we shall explain some of the methods which you can use to do magic with your flowers:

BY AIR Write a spell and keep it under the flower's cup, until it has blossomed; or keep the flower by your bedside, and as you fall asleep, ask its spirit to show you an answer to your query, a way out of a situation.

BY FIRE Burn the essence of the flower; or let a candle burn continuously until the blossom you have placed next to it is open.

BY WATER Let the flower's petals steep in a glass of well water, under the full moon, for a whole night. Drink the water while calling the powers.

BY EARTH Plant a seed in a little pot, giving it the desire, or purpose, you want it to accomplish. When the plant is ready the wish is granted.

Children will understand magic and it will do them no harm — they are the magic from which the flower was born.

LAST WORD

Within this book, the author and the expert editors; Dr. Meredith, Joe Pearce, Frederick Leboyer, have provided many ideas, some of which will be very new to the readers. There will perhaps be those who find all this too much but hopefully also, others who want more. So, for the benefit of this latter category, there is one concept which we have read about which can be developed in this last word of the book. It is a concept that somehow brings the whole feeling of the book together into one avenue and it is derived both from the Eastern way of feeling and the Western way of scientific thinking.

We spoke briefly about two members of the scientific community who have found that there is a possibility that we have a DNA, environmental memory within us. This memory, if we remember, takes in experiences and phenomena within a lifetime which are recorded in the genetic make-up of the body, thus surviving death and in the meantime being passed on to the next generation. Our own suggestion was that such a memory, if it is proven to exist, would alter our whole perspective of our evolutionary power. It would mean, in effect, that we make our planet ourselves and not only our present conditions — the environment, the global changes, but also our future. We would no longer be able to pass off the way the world grows for we alone would be responsible for its growth.

We can even take the idea a step further again — because if the cells that contain this experiential memory derived from our lives, die, as inevitably they must, their substance becomes once again the earth — the cells deteriorate into the ground and

reappear as animals, plants, trees — all containing that memory of experiences. The flowers that you see in your garden, therefore, are the past experiences of the people who died.

Alongside this concept it is interesting to note that many of the things we imagine are going to happen to us, do happen. Science fiction is a prime example of this in that many of the stories dreamed up by science fiction writers come to be true — devices of science and technology for example — and we very often today witness the visions of the past coming to fruition in our own time. Perhaps therefore we really are dictating our future by dreaming of it!

So if we consider this philo-scientific idea in relation to our children we have to come to the conclusion that everything we do within the life time of a child not only affects the life of that child but also the life of the child's child and so on into their future. We are, therefore, each of us, creating the realities of life to come — and the key words are *each of us*.

And finally, to take the argument to its extreme — imagine that it is proven that we reincarnate. The Eastern religions and philosophies have long believed it to be so that we do not simply live one life but many. And if we come back to Earth in future lives, bringing the same soul and heart of this life, who are we ultimately going to influence in the future? Who are we creating the evolutionary environment for in the future? None but ourselves again.

Looking into the eyes of a child, who do you see? A child, an adult or a mirror?

MAKING GAMES
Real things to make and do with children.

BREAD

Bread was once the "staple" diet of man, at least until about 20 years after the Second World War. But then Plastic Mush Bread was invented and to get a direct experience of this chemical cotton wool, go to a factory where it is made. There are plenty of them in the United States and Europe (though interestingly none at all in Italy), and you will get the shock of your life when you observe the air being pumped into the "dough"!

This bread recipe was given to me by a 15 year old boy named Rupert Brasier and it makes the best bread I have ever tasted. Rupert is not a baker in any commercial sense, he just has the right way with bread. With luck you may be the same.

This recipe makes two large loaves so you may wish to half it for family use. On the other hand a loaf made this way will stay fresh if wrapped in silver foil, for up to four days.

Ingredients:
4 oz of fresh yeast.
2 lbs of brown wholemeal flour.
1 lb of white plain flour.
3 table spoons of salt.

Mix the two types of flour together with the salt, then add appoximately two mugs of water (hot) and one mug of cold milk. Add two table spoons of oil.

Mix together and crumble the yeast into the liquid. Mix slowly with your clean fingers until the whole mixture is gooey but floury on the outside. Add flour to the outside to achieve this. The inside needs not to be dry at all.

Wrap the whole thing in a clean towel or cloth and leave it for 45 minutes, preferably in the sun.

Split the dough into two parts and shape it to fit your bread baking tins. Grease the tins and turn on the oven to 350 degrees fahrenheit or 200 centigrade. When the oven is up to temperature put the bread in. While you are waiting for the oven, break an egg and paste the slightly whipped egg onto the top of the bread.

Cook for about an hour.

You will know if the bread is ready by tapping the top of it. If it is hard with a kind of shell, it should be OK. Test one of the loaves by cutting and if it is not done you can simply put it back in the oven for longer. The inside will be soft when ready, though not wet.

HAND BOILED EGGS

Many things in our everyday lives change if we consider ourselves as resonating with life. Take eggs for example — those perfectly formed unborn creatures that have the irritating habit of bursting when we put them from the refrigerator into a pan of boiling water for breakfast. Maybe they crack because they get such a terrific shock from the change of temperature. But maybe they also crack because they don't feel they want to give themselves to us for food — perhaps if we treated them with a little more care and respect they would remain whole and taste better too.

So — while water is coming to the boil, take the egg in the palm of your warm hand and hold it gently for the duration. Or hold one egg in each hand if you plan to eat with your family. Do this for each egg to be enjoyed. As the sides that are in contact with your hand warm up, slip the eggs round until the whole surface is warmed by your body heat. Once the eggs are warm all round, slip them gently, using a wooden spoon, into the water. Surprisingly they rarely crack this way. Make love to an egg!

RANDOM CAKE MIX

Cake baking can be an instinctual ceremony. The supermarkets give us packets to make cakes from or we buy them ready made in the stores because they generally look better than those we manage to flop in the oven. Many people will not believe that they can make cakes at all because somehow the recipe books are too complicated and the result never quite turns out the way it should.

But there are some who can somehow make a cake perfect every time. They are the "Mrs Beetons" of the world who take a bowl and almost anything good from the pantry and make an incredible cake like magic. And it is magic, but more of us can do it than we might imagine.

Cake recipes do produce good cakes, but the cake that the recipe writer made in order to test the recipe, would never be the same as the cake you will make from the same recipe, simply because the cake recipe writer and you are two different people. The people make the cakes. Part of the recipe is in your hands, your spoon, your home and your mood at the time.

We have all probably heard the stories of how pancakes or griddle cakes don't work properly on a full moon night. Some say also that a woman during menstruation cannot successfully make good batter or bake bread. Something in the chemistry changes with these powerful forces present. This is not to say that menstruation is a bad time or negative, only that it is sometimes more powerful than the recipe!

So the following cake recipe is made up of something more than just flour and margarine.

INGREDIENTS

1 lb plain flour (white)
Half pound of sugar (brown)
Half pound of margarine or butter (Margarine is less greasy in the result)
Two table spoons of honey (pure)
4 large brown fresh eggs from free range farm.
Small packet of raising agent
1 lb raisins or currents
Half a cup of Brandy
2 bananas
Half pound of ground almonds
One large wooden spoon.

At least three people who will be present to admire and eat the cake (if family is only three altogether, invite friends or neighbors).

A child present to watch, joke with and help stir.

No mind.

A willingness to have the cake fail or succeed, either way!

A sense of fun - at least ten minutes of the cake making process must contain laughter.

Clean hands and a warm heart.

METHOD

Place the sugar, honey and margarine into a large bowl and mix with clean hands until it becomes soft and fluffy. After the warmth of the hands has melted the margarine, use the wooden spoon to complete until the goo is right. "Splash" a small amount of flour over the goo and then add two of the eggs, broken on top. Mix until the mixture is smooth and disolved. Repeat with more flour and the other eggs. Once the mixture is well smoothed and fluffy once again, add the rest of the flour and the raising agent and mix again. You should now have a smooth paste.

Now add the raisins and ground almonds and mix again.

Take the bananas and pulp them in a separate bowl with perhaps a drop of lemon juice (a real lemon) to stop them turning brown. Then add them to the mixture and stir in quite vigorously. Add the brandy and stir again.

Tell jokes and allow the child to stir plus anyone else who is going to eat the cake.

Heat the oven to 350 degrees F (200 c) and grease a cake tin all round. Empty the mixture into the tin and smooth the top.

Put in oven and make a prayer (please cake - don't let me down!). Leave for approx one hour but check by opening the oven very quickly and tapping the top of the cake with a knife. But make sure its quick or the middle might slump from the temperature change. The finished cake should not look floppy on top when you tap it but it should still be slightly wet when you take the cake out and slip the tip of the knife into the centre an inch. This part is practice and may take more than one baking to perfect.

Once cooked take the cake out of its tin by running a knife round the edge after it has cooled for an hour.

SUGGESTED READING

1. Books by Joseph Chilton Pearce:
   Magical Child
   Magical Child Matures
   The Bond of Power
   All published by Bantam Books.

2. Books by Alan Watts:
   Does it Matter? — Pantheon Books/Random House.
   Nature, Man and Woman — Vintage/Random House.

3. Frederick Leboyer:
   Birth Without Violence — Knopf/Random House.

4. **Mind is a Myth** — U.G.Krishnamurti
   (This is a difficult book to get hold of — not yet published in the West. Best thing is to write to: Dinesh Vaghela, Dinesh Publications, Post Betim (Volant), Goa-403 101 INDIA Send currency equivalent of 100 Rupees by money order and with luck you'll get a copy!)

5. **The Spectrum of Consciousness** — Ken Wilber — published by The Theosophical Publishing House, Wheaton, Ill USA.

6. **The Presence of the Past** — Rupert Sheldrake — published by William Collins, London.

7. **The Awakening Earth** — Peter Russell — published by Routledge and Kegan Paul, London.

8. **Unknown man** — In Search of a New Species — Yatri — published by Simon & Schuster Inc.

9. **The Secret Life of Kids** — James W. Peterson — published by The Theosophical Publishing House, Wheaton, Ill.

10. **The Radiant Child** — Thomas Armstrong — published by The Theosophical Publishing House, Wheaton, Ill.

11. **The Natural History of the Mind** — Gordon Rattray Taylor — published by Granada Publishing, London.

12. **The Book of the Hopi** — Frank Waters — published by Penguin Books.

13. **New Life** — Janet Balaskas
    Active Birth Partner's Handbook — Janet Balaskas — published by Sidgwick and Jackson Ltd., UK.

14. **The Quest for the Great Happiness** — Cecil Collins — published by Barrie and Jenkins, London.

15. ***Leboyer's Chanting Tapes*** —
Write to Labyrinth Publishing S.A., Chamerstrasse 50, 6300-Zug, Switzerland for audio and video tapes. The instructions in these tapes are in German but the translation in the "Chanting for Birth" section of this book is sufficient to follow the methods.

16. ***Natural Birth Centers*** —
to find a natural child birth center in your area, call the following places.
Telephone numbers are not given because of possible changes but all these centers can be located through directory assistance —

In the USA —
The International Childbirth Education Association, POBox 20048, Minneapolis, Minnesota 55420.
Telephone — 612 854 8660.

In England —
The Natural Childbirth Trust, Alexandra House, Oldham Terrace, Acton, London W36NH
Telephone 01-992 8637.

ACKNOWLEDGEMENTS

The author would like to thank the following people for their help in giving birth to this child:
Frederick Leboyer for his inspired friendship and deep appreciation of the spiritual nature of birth.
Joseph Chilton Pearce for his thorough and positive help and comments concerning the more recent developments in child-care.
Sidd Murray-Clark for his help with the art games.
Barbara Gess for her editorial eye.
Caroline Herter for her gentle strictness in the production of the book.
Yatri, for his inspired and wonder-full original illustrations.
Padma Morgan for her extraordinary design, illustration and "handwriting"
Ben and Lily for surviving happily the doubtful parenting of their father.
Chris Tomasino for her unbeatable enthusiasm for everything good.
All the staff of Labyrinth Publishing — the creators of this book.
And my wife, Manuela, for her keen eye and soft heart.

I would also like to acknowledge the photographers who have contributed both original and stock pictures to the book, with special thanks to A.J. Sullivan, whose eye for the natural child is in my opinion unsurpassed in the artistic world.

A.J. Sullivan, New Highlands, Massachusetts: *17, 19, 26, 34, 35, 36, 37, 40, 42(right), 43, 46, 62, 63, 64, 65, 71, 75, 76, 78, 90, 96, 100, 111, 118, 120, 121, 124(right), 133, 138, 150, 160, 166, 167, 170, 171, 176, 177, 182, 186, 194, 195, 245, 250, 251, 259, 264, 276, 278, 286, 295, 298, 303.* Hand Colored Photographs: Padma Morgan, Labyrinth Publishing, Switzerland: *17, 64, 65, 76, 100, 109, 112, 133, 161, 264/265.* Bruno Kortenhorst, Labyrinth Publishing, Switzerland: *15, 32, 74(background), 104, 114, 146, 181, 215, 217, 227, 228/229, 260, 279, 282, 285, 289, 294, 296.* Harold Feinstein, Life Magazine c 1988 Time Inc.: *9.* W. Eugene Smith/Black Star, New York: *7.* Wayne Miller/Magnum, Paris: *18.* Valerie Clement/Jerrican, Paris: *20, 153.* Ace Photo Agency/Michael Bluestone: *21.* Mary Evans Picture Library, London: *22.* Mike Hollist/SOLO, London: *23.* Yatri, Tuscany, Italy: *24, 25, 28/29, 89, 93, 95, 124(left), 168/169, 223, 236/237.* Padma Morgan, Labyrinth Publishing, Switzerland: *30, 53, 226, 293.* Morgan/Murray-Clark/Kortenhorst, Labyrinth Publishing, Switzerland: *55, 154.* Colour Library International/I.C.P. Milano: *49.* Ron Oliver/Apple Tree Studio, London: *52.* Michele Salmieri, New York: *54.* Barnaby's Picture Library, London: *56, 57, 58, 73, 79, 84, 91, 92, 108, 109, 136, 137, 218, 220, 300.* Sally & Richard Greenhill, London: *59, 206, 240.* The Photo Source/I.C.P. Milano: *60/61, 77, 159, 211, 269.* Jan Saudek/Courtesy Torch/Art Unlimited, Amsterdam: *68, 69, 162, 179, 196/197, 224, 249, 270, 271, 272, 280.* Beatrice Kunzi, Zurich: *74.* TSW/Speranza, Milano: *80, 82, 83, 247, 268.* Hulton Picture Library, London: *87, 157.* Margaret Turner, London: *97.* Matt Beale-Collins, London: *116, 257.* Frederick Leboyer, London: *122, 190, 239, 243.* Fortean Society, London: *123.* Sidd Murray-Clark, Labyrinth Publishing, Switzerland: *128, 131, 216.* DeLaubier/Scoop, France: *244.* Ken Heyman, New York: *248.* Philip Dunn, Labyrinth Publishing, Switzerland: *139, 277.* Eve Morcrett, Paris: *147, 163.* MGW Picture Library, Norfolk, England: *151.* Bel Ami, Lecco, Italy: *152, 207.* Ton Huijbers, Holland: *158.* Noel Butcher, Bayswater, Australia: *161.* Picturebank Photo Library/I.C.P. Milano: *164.* Martin Adam, St. Moritz: *172, 173, 200/201, 202, 203, 204, 205, 208.* Edouard Boubat/RAPHO, Paris: *189.* Ace Photo Agency/Ian Stokes: *192.* The Bettmann Archive, New York: *213.* Scala, Firenze,: *219, 284.* Elliott Erwitt/Magnum, Paris: *231.* Martine Franck/Magnum, Paris: *258.* Malcolm Murray-Clark, London: *254, 261.* Picturepoint/I.C.P. Milano: *232, 233.* Magda Valine, Tuscany, Italy: *255.* Rene Burri/Magnum, Paris: *256.* Canada Wide, Toranto: *262.* Henri Cartier-Bresson/Magnum, Paris: *263.* Greater London Photograph Library: *266.* Mary Ellen Mark Library, New York: *275.* Ace Photo Agency/Terry Sims, London: *290.* Phoebe Dunn/Pictor International, Munich: *297.*
Song lyrics on page 8 entitled "The Circle Game" by Joni Mitchell C 1966, 1974 Siquomb Publishing Corp. Used by permission of Warner/Chappell Music, Inc. All rights reserved.